Praise for

The Lost Sheep *of* Ancient America

"I stand amazed at the talent and insight of Phyllis Olive to open my mind to think deeper and ponder what I have never thought of before. Her thousands of hours of research and organizing her thoughts and findings into this book astounds me. She is someone to be respected and listened to. Her conclusions and insight blow my mind. You cannot discard them. She is amazing!"

—Ginger Ewell, owner and operator of Latter Day Tours

The LOST SHEEP of ANCIENT AMERICA

The LOST SHEEP of ANCIENT AMERICA

BRINGING THE LANDS
AND PEOPLE OF THE
BOOK OF MORMON TO LIFE.

PHYLLIS CAROL OLIVE

CFI
An imprint of Cedar Fort, Inc.
Springville, Utah

ISBN 13: 978-1-4621-1661-4

Published by CFI, an imprint of Cedar Fort, Inc.
2373 W. 700 S., Springville, UT 84663
Distributed by Cedar Fort, Inc., www.cedarfort.com

LIBRARY OF CONGRESS CATALOGING-IN-PUBLICATION DATA

Olive, Phyllis Carol, author.
The lost sheep of ancient America / Phyllis Carol Olive.
pages cm
Includes bibliographical references.
ISBN 978-1-4621-1661-4 (perfect bound : alk. paper)
1. Book of Mormon--Criticism, interpretation, etc. 2. America--Discovery and exploration. 3. Indians--Origin. I. Title.
BX8627.O445 2015
289.3'22--dc23

2015024976

Cover design by Shawnda T. Craig
Cover design © 2015 Lyle Mortimer
Layout by Jessica B. Ellingson

Printed in the United States of America

10 9 8 7 6 5 4 3 2

Printed on acid-free paper

Contents

Preface

In studying prehistoric America from the time of the flood onward, it becomes increasingly evident that America's prehistory is linked to that of the old world. Though information on the ancient post-flood world is minimal, it is amazing how much has been gleaned from local legends and the documents written by early Bronze Age historians who helped identify many of the families who descended from Shem, Ham, and Japheth. Trying to reconcile the history of the ancient occupants of the New World has been difficult at best, since nothing prior to the sixth century can be documented with any sense of reliability. Moreover, conjecture and supposition came into play as various early writers attempted to make sense of the complicated subject of America's prehistory.

Gratefully, the Book of Mormon has cleared up some of these misconceptions, such as the long-standing notions that no one arrived in America prior to Columbus and the few who did so traveled by foot from Asia across the Bering land bridge into Western America. In addition, it explains why so many Hebrew traditions exist among the Indian tribes of eastern North America, being offshoots of two main colonies who escaped the destruction of Jerusalem: namely the colony of Lehi, a descendant of that Joseph who was sold into Egypt, and Mulek of the royal house of Judah, who together formed a mighty civilization whose influence spread across much of the country.

New findings in DNA and recent archeological discoveries have now brought to light an impressive body of new evidence that a number of other immigrants also made it to America from the royal house of Judah, a line of immigrants through Zarah, the twin brother of Perez, who fathered the Mulekites. The merger of the two royal lines of Judah in America—along with the seed of Joseph, who held the birthright in Israel through his two sons, Ephraim and Manasseh—became some of America's first empire builders, a mound-building empire called Hopewell.

Thus, the prehistory of America is not a simple one. For that reason, this work will start from the beginning, with the arrival of the Jaredites from the Tower of Babel and some of the Celtic tribes of western Europe, some of whom were giants, followed by a historical review of some of the old world kingdoms set up by the royal seed of Zarah-Judah throughout Western Europe, Scandinavia, Mexico, New England, and the ancient Atlantic. At long last, the story of how the people of the Book of Mormon fit into the historic record of ancient North America and Mexico can finally be told. All the missing pieces of the puzzling disposition of some of God's most choice children can now be knit together in a story that flows from Babylon to the Restoration.

1

The Jaredites

When the blossoming nations of Europe first began to realize that the tales they heard of strange new people, animals, and plants never before seen in the Old World actually existed in lands far beyond the western sunset, the subject of the New World suddenly became a matter of much discussion. *How could all this be?* they wondered. How could people and animals exist on a continent cut off from the rest of the world by vast oceans? They could only surmise that the biblical account of the flood of Noah's day must have some validity, with the post-flood populations migrating out in all directions once the ark landed but before the earth was divided in the two or three centuries thereafter. Theories about what families migrated here and there over the years have been the source of continuing speculation, but few Christians dispute the ideology that the distant ancestors of every people and nation on earth stemmed from the common stock of those who descended from Noah once the ark rested and the floodwaters abated.

As the children of Noah began to migrate out into new territory, the children of Ham settled along the east coast of the Mediterranean Sea and Egypt; the children of Japheth settled around the Black and Caspian Seas and the Caucuses; and Shem's descendants were the first to enter Mesopotamia, where they settled chiefly in southern Mesopotamia between the Euphrates and Tigris Rivers. A number of the earliest post-flood populations were born along the Tigris and Euphrates Rivers, where they began to build such great cities as Ur and Babylon, home of the Sumerians and the later Babylonians, whose trading and military skills forged a mighty empire.

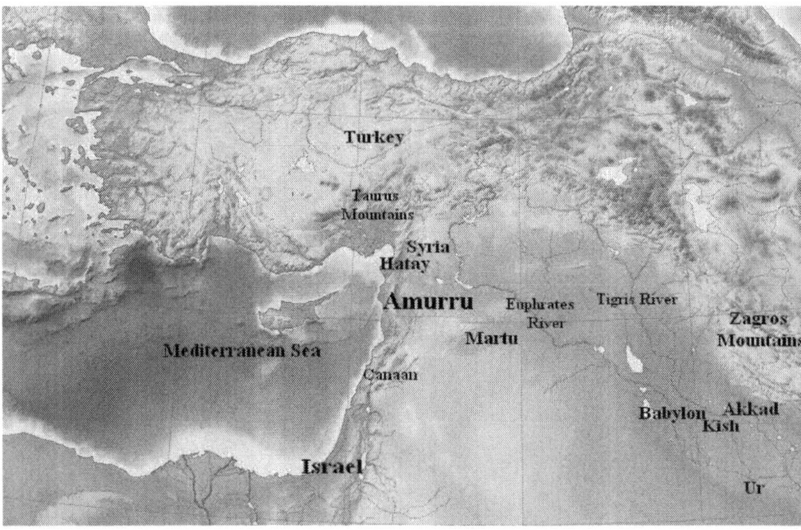

By the mid-third millennium BC, a number of states and cities in Mesopotamia were dominated by the Semitic-speaking people, including the city of Kish, the first city to have kings following the deluge. Kish lay in the Semitic empire of Akkad, just to the east of Babylon. It was one of the most important and impressive cities in the ancient world, a city the Jaredites would have been aware of, for they carried the name Kish into their own genetic line, along with variants such as Akish and Riplakish. The name Kish is also noted among some of the later Semitic tribes of Israel for producing large men. This is recorded in the book of 1 Samuel:

> Now there was a man of Benjamin, whose name was Kish, the son of Abiel, the son of Zeror, the son of Bechorath, the son of Aphiah, a Benjamite, a mighty man of power.
>
> And he had a son, whose name was Saul, a choice young man, and a goodly: and there was not among the children of Israel a

> goodlier person than he: from his shoulders and upward he was higher than any of the people. (1 Samuel 9:1–2)

About 2500 BC, another powerful Amorite kingdom called Amurru, also known for its tall-statured people, embraced a large part of Mesopotamia and Syria. The term *Amorites* in the Bible refers to certain highland mountaineers who inhabited the steppes to the west of the Euphrates River as far as Canaan and Syria. The term *Amorite* in Genesis 10:16 refers to the tall descendants of Canaan, son of Ham, who were described as a people of great stature "like the height of the cedars" (Amos 2:9).

Yet, some of the nomadic children of Shem also lived in Amurru. Even some of Japheth's tall children may have settled the north. Old Egyptian writings noted that the Israelites of old came from *Amurru,* meaning the land of the Amorites, where they were described as being of mixed kinds. Egyptian artists depicted the Amorites as being a blond, blue-eyed, and sometimes red-headed race of men, which led a number of researchers to tie the Amorites to the Indo-European family of Japheth through Gomer, the father of the blond, blue-eyed, sometimes red-haired Cimmerians, who often reached the enormous statures of six, seven, eight, and even nine feet. Other scholars insist that the pictorial representation of the tall men with pointed beards in Egyptian art depict a race of tall Semitic people.

Albert Tobias Clay, author of *Amurru, the Home of the Northern Semites*, noted that the remains of the Semitic people living in Amurru around 2500 BC, who buried their dead by inhumation (a Semitic trait), showed they were a taller, stronger, and larger-boned race than the earlier people of the area.[1] Considering the large and mighty stature of the Jaredites and the predominance of Hebrew names among them, it could very well be that the tall-statured Semitic Amorites were the root stock of the Jaredites, who are described in the scriptures as large and mighty men as to the strength of men—the same physical traits given of the Semites in Amurru, who were taller, stronger, and larger-boned than those who lived in the area before them.

THE FRIENDS OF THE JAREDITES

LDS archaeologist Hugh Nibley noted the possibility and probability that the blood relationship of Jared and his brother was different than that of the twenty-two friends they brought with them to the New World. He felt that had they been related, they would have been numbered among the families of either Jared or his brother. Thus, a merged company may have existed, with Jared and his brother being of Semitic origins and some of their friends perhaps part of Japheth's huge children through his son Gomer.

In a blessing given to Japheth by his father, Noah promised that "God shall enlarge Japheth, and he shall dwell in the tents of Shem" (Genesis 9:27). This is perhaps one way the Lord intended to get the seed of Japheth to the New World as well. The many sons of Japheth founded and laid the foundations of many of the same nations of Western Europe that the ten lost tribes of Israel would one day settle. America should also be included here, for a number of Japhetic tribes also made it across the sea to the New World, the gathering place of the Gentiles from whom many of the lost tribes would be gleaned.

THE KINGDOM OF MARI

Along the west bank of the Euphrates River, there existed an economically prosperous farming and cattle breeding region called Mari. The Jewish Virtual Library explains that the residents of Mari were western Semitics—those ultimately related to the Israelites and the descendants of Abraham. Enough evidence has surfaced to establish that the Mari had dominance over the entire Middle Euphrates River Valley. Known Amorites wrote in a dialect of Akkadian found on tablets at Mari dating from 1800–1750 BC. Since their language shows northwest Semitic forms and constructions, the Amorite language was presumably a northwest Semitic dialect, as opposed to the east Semitic Akkadian language.

Numerous linguistic, cultural, and social data from Mari have helped in the study of ancient Israel and the Bible. Their political and economic ties extended over a wide area, stretching from the Persian Gulf to southern Iraq, to Cappadocia in the north, and to Phoenicia and Palestine in the west. Because of this, their culture was bound more to those in the west, at least in relation to religion, economic, politics and ethnic background. Mari documents show that Israel's patriarchal homeland lay within Mari's horizons, with the later Israelites ethnically and linguistically of the same Semitic stock. In fact, their description of tribalism comprises the most extensive insights in the nomadic and settled phases of the later tribes of Israel.

SEMITIC PROPHETS

A number of Amorites from Mari, including Jared and his brother, settled in Ur and other Babylonian cities to facilitate trade with Ur, the homeland of Abraham. Mari archives show that their tribal leadership was in the hands of family heads, just as it was among the Jaredites, with both people having prophets among them. Bible scholars noted the phenomenon of apostolic prophecy among the Mari, in which individuals delivered messages in the name of God.

From the Book of Ether, we learn that the brother of Jared was also a prophet, and one highly favored of the Lord. During his abridgment of Ether's account, Moroni noted that he was omitting those parts of Ether's record that are found in the Bible and would thus begin his account of the Jaredites where the biblical account left off, which was the time of the confusion of tongues. It doesn't seem reasonable that the Jaredites would have transported an entire set of records all the way to America unless they contained the history and genealogy of their own ancestral line—the line of Shem, through which the later children of Israel would come. The title page of the Book of Mormon affirms that tie. It says in relation to the Jaredite account,

> An abridgment taken from the Book of Ether also, which is a record of the people of Jared, who were scattered at the time the Lord confounded the language of the people, when they were building a tower to get to heaven—which is to show unto the

> remnant of the House of Israel what great things the Lord hath done for their fathers.

THE TOWER OF BABEL

To understand the story of Jared's transition from the Old to the New World, we must begin with the story of the Tower of Babel and the confusion of tongues. This takes us back to the post-flood descendants of Cush, the son of Ham, the son of Noah, who produced one of the greatest superstars of antiquity: Nimrod, who became such a mighty man that the people throughout the land esteemed him greatly. Little more is given about him in the Bible, but the apocryphal book of Jasher adds some interesting insights into that ancient time in history:

> And all the earth was of one tongue and words of union, but Nimrod did not go in the ways of the Lord, and he was more wicked than all the men that were before him, from the days of the flood until those days.
>
> And they made gods of wood and stone, and he bowed down to them, and he rebelled against the Lord, and taught all his subjects and the people of the earth his wicked ways. (Jasher, Chapter VII, verses 46–47)

As various tribes and nations began to spread out across the land, Nimrod's counselors met together and decided to build a great city with a tower high enough to reach into heaven. The tower's lofty top was intended to provide them with a place for sacrifice and worship—not the worship of Jehovah, but the worship of pagan gods, particularly the sun god. We learn from the Pearl of Great Price that

> My fathers . . . turned from their righteousness, and from the holy commandments which the Lord their God had given unto them, unto the worshiping of the gods of the heathen . . . ; For their hearts were set to do evil, and were wholly turned to the god of Elkenah, and the god of Libnah, and the god of Mahmackrah, and the god of Korash, and the god of Pharaoh, king of Egypt; . . .

> and also unto the god of Shagreel, [who] was the sun. (Abraham 1:6-9)

THE CONFUSION OF TONGUES

As the great Tower of Babel grew higher and higher, the Lord became concerned and came down to see the city and the tower that the sons of men had built. He said,

> Behold, the people is one, and they have all one language; and this they begin to do: and now nothing will be restrained from them, which they have imagined to do.
>
> Go to, let us go down, and there confound their language, that they may not understand one another's speech.
>
> So the Lord scattered them abroad from thence upon the face of all the earth: and they left off to build the city.
>
> Therefore is the name of it called Babel; because the Lord did there confound the language of all the earth: and from thence did the Lord scatter them abroad upon the face of all the earth. (Genesis 11:6–9)

It was apparently during such time of turmoil that Jared's brother pled with the Lord to give them direction. The apocryphal work of Jasher maintains that after the confusion of tongues, there were so many misunderstandings among the people, who could no longer understand one another, that some were driven clear out of the land—one of the many ways the Lord set about to scatter the people. Thus, the brother of Jared went to the Lord at the insistence of his brother and asked what their destiny might be.

> And it came to pass that the brother of Jared did cry unto the Lord according to that which had been spoken by the mouth of Jared.
>
> And it came to pass that the Lord did hear the brother of Jared, and had compassion upon him, and said unto him:
>
> Go to and gather together thy flocks, both male and female, of every kind; and also of the seed of the earth of every kind; and thy families; and also Jared thy brother and his family; and also thy friends and their families, and the friends of Jared and their families.
>
> And when thou hast done this thou shalt go at the head of

> them down into the valley which is northward. And there will I meet thee, and I will go before thee into a land which is choice above all the lands of the earth. (Ether 1:39–42)

Once they were all gathered together, the Lord instructed them to go north, likely from the city of Ur, which would have taken them *down* into the lowlands between the Euphrates and Tigris Rivers. The lush lands along the Euphrates River Valley was home to a number of animals including the wild boar, the gray wolf, the golden jackal, the red fox, the leopard, and the lion—any or all of which Nimrod, who was known as a great hunter, may have enjoyed hunting; perhaps this was the reason it was called the Valley of Nimrod. The shallow valley along the lower Tigris/Euphrates River Basin was filled with one of the most extensive wetlands in the country, covering nearly 8,000 square miles. The marshes included an endless variety of birds, fish, plants, reeds, and bulrushes—a perfect place for the Jaredites to catch the fish and snare the birds they are said to have taken with them.

> And they did also lay snares and catch fowls of the air; and they did also prepare a vessel, in which they did carry with them the fish of the waters (Ether 2:2).

The seeds they were to gather could also be found in the region, for the Sumerians gathered much of their food from the nearby marshes and rivers. While the honey bee could have been gathered from the neighboring Zargos Mountains, the Jaredites might already have had access to some; an old text maintains that the Mari brought bees down from the mountains to Ur during the Ur III period (2200 BC), with the text noting that "one shekel of sliver brought only two pounds of honey."[2]

> And they did also carry with them deseret, which, by interpretation, is a honey bee; and thus they did carry with them swarms of bees, and all manner of that which was upon the face of the land, seeds of every kind (Ether 2:3).

Somewhere in the valley of Nimrod the Lord came down in a cloud and spoke to the brother of Jared and gave him further instructions. Ether said,

> And it came to pass that the Lord commanded them that they should go forth into the wilderness, yea, into that quarter where there never had man been. And it came to pass that the Lord did go before them, and did talk with them as he stood in a cloud, and gave directions whither they should travel. (Ether 2:5)

The route the Lord took the Jaredites on cannot be determined with any sense of certainty. But because their initial instructions were to move north, we can suppose they continued in that direction across the wetlands to the Tigris River and beyond into the forested wilderness of the Zargos Mountains, which bordered the Tigris on the east. The Zagros Mountains contain both forests and steppe areas, which would have provided periodic grazing land for their flocks. The rich and complex variety of plant life—such as wheat, barley, lentils, almonds, walnuts, apricots, plums, grapes, and other fruits—all grew wild throughout the mountains and could have sustained the Jaredites along the way.

Moving steadily northward, the Jaredites would have eventually reached the Taurus Mountains of southwestern Turkey and then the Amanus Mountains bordering the eastern shores of the Mediterranean Sea. A mountain pass leading through the Amanus Mountains would have taken them down into what today is the Province of Hatay, a coastal regions squeezed between the pine-covered Taurus Mountains and the Mediterranean Sea, once a part of the ancient Semitic empire of Akkad.

Interestingly, the Cimmerian princes of Japheth were also gathered together in the Amanus and Taurus Mountains following the confusion of tongues. The historian Josephus adds that the territory they were to destined to pass through was totally uninhabited, something the Lord made mention of when instructing the Jaredites on their route: "go into the wilderness, yea, into that quarter where there never had man been" (Ether 2:5). Josephus said of the Cimmerians,

> Japhet, the son of Noah, had seven sons: they inhabited so, that, beginning at the mountains Taurus and Amanus, they proceeded along Asia, as far as the river Tansis [Don], and along Europe to Cadiz; and settling themselves on the lands which they light

> upon, **which none had inhabited before,** they called the nations by their own names.[3]

Perhaps Europe was that quarter of the land the Lord mentioned had not yet been inhabited by man, thus their destined westward course of travel. It is not likely that the Lord would have expected them to walk the entire distance across Europe on foot with their animals and children and other supplies; the distance from Hatay along the east coast of the Mediterranean Sea to the Straits of Gibraltar at the other end is over three thousand miles. Thus the Lord had the Jaredites build ships for them to take the bulk of the way.

> And it came to pass that they did travel in the wilderness, and did build barges, in which they did cross many waters, being directed continually by the hand of the Lord. (Ether 2:6)

In constructing their barges, the Jaredites may have used the cedars of Lebanon, which are native to Lebanon, Syria, and southern Turkey but also grow on the coast of Hatay. The Lord instructed the Jaredites to take the barges across the "sea in the wilderness" (Ether 2:7)—we can suppose this was the Mediterranean Sea—which loomed out to the west of them as far as the eye could see.

2

The Journey Begins

The Mediterranean Sea was an important trade route for merchants in ancient times, for it allowed for trade and cultural exchanges between the emerging peoples of the region. The Mediterranean Sea is considered the center of ancient world history. It was from here that the Jaredites made it halfway around the world to the promised land.

What type of vessels the Jaredites initially built to cross the "many waters" left across Europe after the last Ice Age is unknown. Boats in ancient Sumer, Babylon, and Egypt were initially made of tightly packed reeds. Wooden ships showed up on the Nile around 2950–2700 BC. Ships depicted in rock art and on pottery from the Nubian civilization of Africa around this time were similar to those used by the ancient Egyptians, with their bows and sterns curving upward and pointing vertically. Naval historians believe some of the curved hulls shown on the rock art may have been to keep them buoyant. The character and appearance of these ships have also been reflected in Scandinavian boat-building traditions, particularly their longship—a graceful, long, narrow, light, wooden boat with a shallow-draft hull, which allowed it to navigate in shallow waters and permit beach landings, while its light weight enabled it to be carried over portages. The double-ended symmetrical bow and stern allowed the ship to reverse direction quickly without having to turn around, which allowed the ship to be used in northern latitudes where sea ice posed hazards to navigation. Such ships were also used in warfare to transport troops, with the boats sometimes tied together in battle to form a steady platform for infantry warfare. (The Jaredite barges were also likely tethered together.) Nordic ships, once finished, were waterproofed with animal hair, wool, hemp, or moss drenched in pine tar. They were tarred in the autumn and then left over winter to dry.

Could the Jaredites have used a similar design? We may never know what type ship the Jaredites initially built, but once in the open waters of the Mediterranean, they would have been carried along by the currents in a counter-clockwise direction. This would have taken them to the north shores of the Mediterranean Sea and in and out of the peripheral seas of the Mediterranean such as the Aegean Sea, the Adriatic Sea, and the Tyrrhenian Sea. They "did build barges, in which they did cross many waters, being directed continually by the hand of the Lord" (Ether 2:6).

A distance of over 3,219 miles would have been covered from their starting place at the east end of the Mediterranean Sea to the other side near Gibraltar. That is a long way to travel, even by ship. It would be impossible to say how long such a voyage took the Jaredites, especially if they stopped periodically to rest, graze their animals, and gather fresh supplies and water along the coasts of the Balkan Peninsula, Greece, Crete, the boot of Italy, or the isles of Sicily and Sardinia. The wives of Jared, his brother, and their friends had babies along the way. Thus longer stops may have been needed at times. But eventually they would have found themselves in the Balearic Sea between Spain and Italy, heading toward the Straits of Gibraltar (the Pillars of Hercules) at the west end of the Mediterranean Sea, where they appear to have stopped for a time, for the great unknown lay beyond. The Lord had no intention of letting them remain there forever, for their journey had just begun. Only "the sea in the wilderness" (the Mediterranean) had been crossed, with a journey across an even greater sea (the Atlantic) yet to begin.

And the Lord would not suffer that they should stop beyond the

> sea in the wilderness, but he would that they should come forth even unto the land of promise, which was choice above all other lands, which the Lord God had preserved for a righteous people (Ether 2:7).

No explanation is needed for the last part of that scripture, for the Lord promised the brother of Jared to lead them to a land of promise, the destined site of the New Jerusalem. In detailing the destiny of the promised land, the prophet Ether said,

> And that after the waters had receded from off the face of this land it became a choice land above all other lands, a chosen land of the Lord; wherefore the Lord would have that all men should serve him who dwell upon the face thereof;
>
> And that it was the place of the New Jerusalem, which should come down out of heaven, and the holy sanctuary of the Lord . . . and it should be built unto the house of Israel. (Ether 13:2–5)

As to where that holy city will be built, we read in the Doctrine and Covenants that it will be built "in the western boundaries of the State of Missouri" (D&C 84:3). There can be no doubt that the Jaredites were led to the promised land of America.

After a lengthy explanation about the responsibilities of the inhabitants of the promised land, the prophet Ether picks up the narrative of the Jaredite's long migration by simply saying that the Lord brought "them forth even to that great sea which divideth the lands" (Ether 2:13). Using the word *great* to define the sea in this instance suggests he was referring to the great Atlantic Ocean, which divides the Eastern Hemisphere from that of the Western. Thus we can suppose the Lord gently urged the Jaredites through the narrow Straits of Gibraltar, between modern-day Spain or Portugal and Morocco.

The prophet Ether continues,

> And now I proceed with my record; for behold, it came to pass that the Lord did bring Jared and his brethren forth even to that great sea which divideth the lands. And as they came to the sea they pitched their tents; and they called the name of the place Moriancumer; and they dwelt in tents, and dwelt in tents upon the seashore for the space of four years. (Ether 2:13)

In the minds of the Jaredites, it may have looked like they had reached the end of the world, for nothing but an endless sea loomed out before them. Some may have even been afraid to ask what lay beyond and therefore stopped praying, consoling themselves with the idea that this was as far the Lord wanted them to go. So they began to settle into their new surroundings and rest from their long hard journey.

The breathtakingly beautiful Mamora Forest near the city of Rabat in Morocco would have been a perfect place to unwind and find some measure of peace. Today's brochures speak of it as the perfect location to find peace, quiet, and seclusion from the bustling world outside. Unfortunately, the Jaredites relaxed far too much and for far too long, for over the course of the next four years the brother of Jared neglected to call upon the Lord. The Lord was not too happy about that and let him know in a scolding that lasted for a full three hours. After being pulled up short by the Lord, the brother of Jared dropped to his knees in sorrow, repented of the evil he had done, and pled with the Lord to forgive him, which He did but only after making it clear that he must not sin anymore.

THE JAREDITE BARGES

In preparation for the next leg of their journey, the Lord then instructed them to start on a new set of ships after the manner of those they had previously built. The Lord gave them special instructions, for these barges would be totally covered over and closed in, like the ark of Noah.

When the Lord instructed the Nephites to build the ship that carried them to the promised land, he told them that it would not be made after the manner of men. Nephi said,

> And it came to pass that they did worship the Lord, and did go forth with me; and we did work timbers of curious workmanship. And the Lord did show me from time to time after what manner I should work the timbers of the ship.
>
> Now I, Nephi, did not work the timbers after the manner which was learned by men, neither did I build the ship after the

> manner of men; but I did build it after the manner which the Lord had shown unto me; wherefore, it was not after the manner of men. (1 Nephi 18:1–2)

We do not know what type of ship the Jaredites built. Even the traditional view of what Noah's ark looked like is being challenged after the discovery of a four-thousand-year-old cuneiform tablet in Mesopotamia. The tablet contains detailed instruction for building a huge round coracle ark, with palm-fiber rope and wooden ribs, coated in hot bitumen to make it waterproof. Dr. Irving Finkel, of the British Museum in London, is one of the few people in the world who can read a cuneiform tablet. He claims the coracle was 220 feet in diameter with 20-foot high walls, with two levels and a roof on the top. The craft was divided into sections so that the various animals could be confined to their own sections. Finkel says, "A round boat makes sense. Coracles were widely used as river taxis in ancient Iraq and are perfectly designed to bob along on raging floodwaters. It's a perfect thing. It never sinks, it's light to carry."[1] Other sources say the Babylonians around 1700 BC believed the ark of Noah was a giant version of the coracle they used in their rivers to transport goods, animals, and supplies to trade centers along the length of the Euphrates River.

In searching for the type of wood the Jaredites would have used to build their barges, I was surprised to discover the prevalence of cork oak forests along the western edges of the of the Mediterranean Sea, particularly in Morocco in the northwest corner of Africa. The Maamura Forest near Rabat contains 134 thousand hectares of cork wood trees. A large number of cork oak trees can also be found in Portugal. Oliveira's *Livro da Fabrica das Naus* (1570–80) notes that ship builders in Portugal used the inner oak of the cork oak tree for the skeleton of their skips, since cork oak is hard and does not rot in water. It further notes that the natural curves of its timber made it adaptable to the sides and to the ribs of the ship. The Portuguese considered the corkwood perfect for ship building—it never rotted and could withstand harsh weather conditions.

While we can only speculate about the wood the Jaredites

used, the fact that the barges would be floating along in water for nearly a year, under harsh weather conditions, suggests that the local corkwood tree might have been used in their construction. Could the tree's inner oak have been used for the skeletal weave of the barge, with the tree's outer cork layer perhaps used for its skin? When flattened, the cork can make sheets 10 feet square, which could then be cut into strips of whatever size was needed or even layered. Cork planks are highly sought after today for cork flooring, buoys, and lifeboats. The natives of Africa sailed in cork-wood canoes and floated their heavy cargo down their rivers on rafts made of corkwood and pulled by canoes. Cork is made of water-resistant cells that have unique properties not found in any other naturally existing material. It is lightweight, rot resistant, fire resistant, termite resistant, impermeable to gas and liquid, and soft and buoyant. Interestingly, it has also been used to make beehives.

The cellular structure of the cork repels water due to the suberin that is naturally created by the cork tree. Because of the air trapped in its cells, cork is also a natural cushion, which would have prevented serious damage to the Jaredite barges if one bumped into the other during their long voyage across the sea. (The barges were likely tethered together to keep them from drifting apart.) The cork cell membranes are so flexible that when they are compressed and released, they regain their original form. In light of it all, we cannot help but wonder whether cork was part of the building material the Jaredites used in the constructing of their barges, for they were described as being as light as a fowl upon the water, and when they sank beneath the waves, they popped right back up again, just like a cork would do if it were submerged in water.

Ether records,

> And it came to pass that the brother of Jared did go to work, and also his brethren, and built barges after the manner which they had built, according to the instructions of the Lord. And they were small, and they were light upon the water, even like unto the lightness of a fowl upon the water. (Ether 2:16)

The bark of the cork oak tree is also a great insulator, something else the Lord would be mindful of as they moved out into the cold waters of the Atlantic. The prophet Ether relates what the Lord described would be in store for them.

> For behold, ye shall be as a whale in the midst of the sea; for the mountain waves shall dash upon you. Nevertheless, I will bring you up again out of the depths of the sea; for the winds have gone forth out of my mouth, and also the rains and the floods have I sent forth.
>
> And behold, I prepare you against these things; for ye cannot cross this great deep save I prepare you against the waves of the sea, and the winds which have gone forth, and the floods which shall come. (Ether 2:24–25)

I often wondered what the Lord meant when He said He had to prepare them in some way for the perilous journey ahead. If we factor the corkwood into the construction of their barges, more than one question can be answered about that mysterious voyage. For instance, being confined to a small space for nearly a year, during which time they endured crashing waves and torrents, the Jaredites may have become totally incapacitated with sea sickness. Some may have even died. But not in this instance; the corkwood tree contains a chemical similar to that used for motion sickness and to cause sleepiness. Maybe they even took advantage of the medicinal properties in the corkwood to sleep the day away, thereby letting their near year-long voyage simply slide by. Chewing the leaves of the corkwood tree would have also warded off hunger, pain, and tiredness. In fact, the medical properties of corkwood are used to treat a wide range of conditions today including malaria, sexually transmittable diseases, amoebiasis, cough, liver inflammation, stomachache, colic, measles, and snakebites.

Someday, the Lord will reveal the whole story of the Jaredites long ocean voyage and the mysterious barges they built—a story well worth waiting for. All He has seen fit to reveal thus far is that they were completely closed in both top and bottom, sealed tight like a dish, and as light upon the water as a fowl.

LIGHT FOR THE BARGES

After following the Lord's instructions on how to construct their eight barges, the Jaredites became concerned about the fact that there was no light in them. In response, the brother of Jared went to the Lord in prayer.

> And it came to pass that the brother of Jared cried unto the Lord, saying: O Lord, I have performed the work which thou hast commanded me, and I have made the barges according as thou hast directed me.
>
> And behold, O Lord, in them there is no light; whither shall we steer? (Ether 2:18–19)

After giving it some thought, the brother of Jared decided to have the Lord touch sixteen small stones he fashioned out of a rock so that they might shine forth in the dark and give them light. In Genesis 6:16, the footnote to "window" says, "Some rabbis believed it [the window] was a precious stone that shone in the dark." Perhaps the brother of Jared, in searching for an answer to his problem, turned to the scriptures for his solution. Reading Noah's account of the ark may have inspired the brother of Jared to ask the Lord for the same blessing He had given Noah.

The stones he found may well have come from the Atlas mountains, which rise to an elevation of 13,665 feet in northwest Africa. Here crystals of all types and colors can be found—some totally translucent. The Atlas Mountains may even have been the high mountain on which the brother of Jared saw the finger of the Lord and then His entire premortal body (see Ether chapters 2–3), for it was on such high mountains that the Lord often spoke to his ancient prophets.

> And it came to pass that the brother of Jared, (now the number of the vessels which had been prepared was eight) went forth unto the mount, which they called the mount Shelem, because of its exceeding height, and did molten out of a rock sixteen small stones; and they were white and clear, even as transparent glass; and he did carry them in his hands upon the top of the mount. (Ether 3:1)

After preparing all the things for their journey across the mighty deep, and no doubt offering prayers for their safe journey, the Jaredites made themselves and their animals as comfortable as they could be in the eight barges the Lord instructed them to build and shut the door behind them, waiting for the mighty winds to begin to move them along.

> And it came to pass that the Lord God caused that there should be a furious wind blow upon the face of the waters, towards the promised land; and thus they were tossed upon the waves of the sea before the wind.
>
> And it came to pass that they were many times buried in the depths of the sea, because of the mountain waves which broke upon them, and also the great and terrible tempests which were caused by the fierceness of the wind.
>
> And it came to pass that when they were buried in the deep there was no water that could hurt them, their vessels being tight like unto a dish, and also they were tight like unto the ark of Noah; therefore when they were encompassed about by many waters they did cry unto the Lord, and he did bring them forth again upon the top of the waters. . . .
>
> And thus they were driven forth; and no monster of the sea could break them, neither whale that could mar them; and they did have light continually, whether it was above the water or under the water.
>
> And thus they were driven forth, three hundred and forty and four days upon the water. (Ether 6:5–11)

SURFACE WIND CURRENTS

Modern research has determined that the ocean's surface currents are regulated by the wind, while the deeper "ocean currents" are regulated by other factors, such as the salinity of the water and the ocean's temperature. The Lord could easily have instructed the Jaredites to build a sea-worthy vessel strong enough to withstand the raging waters of the Atlantic, just as he did for the Nephites. But at this point the world was just coming out of the last Ice Age, and the Atlantic had just been infused with a massive amount of fresh water from some of the huge glacial lakes in North America that had previously been held back by glaciers. Once the ice began to melt, fresh water was released through newly opened channels into the North Atlantic, where the fresh water, which is less dense, inhibited the sinking of the water in the north and effectively shut or slowed down the pumping mechanism that creates the ocean's currents. Thus, "the Lord God caused that there should be a furious wind blow upon the face of the waters" (Ether 6:5).

Because of the ocean's relatively flat surface, the winds blowing across it created surface currents that propelled the Jaredite's barges along. The ocean is largely unobstructed by topography, so winds can blow for long distances for prolonged periods of time. Ocean currents move south, from northwest Africa to near the equator, where the swirling currents would have swept the barges west around the Cape Verde Isles and then northward toward Cuba and Florida. From that point, the Gulf Stream would have then carried them north up the Atlantic Coast to the St. Lawrence River. From there, they sailed inland down St. Lawrence, a large arm of the sea at one time, and down into Lake Ontario, with their initial landing perhaps on Point Peninsula Island at the east end of Lake Ontario, where some of their artifacts have been found.

We really cannot tell where the Lord took them or their mileage, but we can estimate. Starting perhaps from Rabat, the capital of Morocco just off the coast of northwest Africa, they may have traveled to the Verde Isles (1,664 miles), then across the Atlantic to Cuba (3,562 miles), then to Florida (485 miles), and then up the Atlantic Coast to the St. Lawrence River (1,739 miles), and down to Lake Ontario (710 miles). This was a journey of approximately 8,160 miles. Their rate of travel can also be only approximated, for the wind currents in the Atlantic flow at different rates in different areas. Thus oceanographers suggest a net of about one mile an hour, for a total of twenty-four miles a day. Dividing 24 into the 8,160-mile-long voyage gives us 340 days as the length of time it took to make their journey, a time period surprisingly close to the 344-day journey the scriptures say it took the Jaredites to reach their promised destination.

Two routes were possible from Florida: the first, already noted up the Atlantic Coast to the St. Lawrence River. The second possible route could have been up the Hudson River to the lower course of the St. Lawrence River. Hermon LeRoy Fairchild said, "If early man was then living in America, as certainly he was in Europe, he could voyage from the open Atlantic up the Hudson-Champlain strait, around through the St. Lawrence and pass into the Ontario Basin."[2]Adding the mileage in the second scenario does not change it appreciably, with the total mileage calculated to be approximately 7,934 miles. Dividing 24 miles a day into the 7,934-mile voyage gives us 330 days as the length of their journey—still surprisingly close to the to the 344-day journey the scriptures say it took them.

ARRIVING AT THE PROMISED LAND

We can only imagine the joy the Jaredites must have felt when they finally arrived on the shores of the promised land after such an arduous journey.

> And they did land upon the shore of the promised land. And when they had set their feet upon the shores of the promised land they bowed themselves down upon the face of the land, and did humble themselves before the Lord, and did shed tears of joy before the Lord, because of the multitude of his tender mercies over them. (Ether 6:12)

The region they were to settle in northwest New York had just come out of the last Ice Age and was void of both animal and fish in many areas. Thus, it becomes evident why the Lord instructed the Jaredites to bring animals and birds with them to the promised land. While some of the animals that had migrated southward would ultimately return, and others endured the icy conditions such as the great mammoth and mastodon, the more domesticated animals the Jaredites brought along provided the root stock of the herds and flocks that would sustain them throughout their long sojourn in the land. Even the rivers, so recently covered with ice, needed reseeding with the fish the Jaredites brought along.

By examining fossil samples and the radiocarbon dates pertinent to this region, it was determined that the northeast experienced a warm, dry climate following the Ice Age that considerably surpassed the present in average warmth. Such conditions accelerated the melting of the great glaciers, which left behind numerous large bodies of water, ponds, rivers, and streams, with their surrounding forests so thick that one author claimed a squirrel could jump from tree to tree from the Atlantic coast clear to the Mississippi. This was truly a land choice above all others, a land the Jaredites would call home for the next millennium and a half.

3

The Jaredites' Early Kingdom

THE FAMILIES OF Jared, his brother, and their twenty-two friends began to settle along the southern shores of Lake Ontario in northern New York as soon as they made landfall. Because an earlier, broad-headed people called the Laurentian had already staked their claim to eastern New York, the Jaredites settled chiefly in northwestern New York across the Niagara River Frontier, along the northern course of the Genesee River, across the Finger Lakes region of central New York, and along the rivers and lakes of southern New York.

The history of the Jaredites spans nearly a millennium and a half, with the archaeological record showing their populations ultimately spread over a wide range along every available river in the territory. Like the civilizations of the ancient world—such as Mesopotamia, Egypt, Syria, Rome, and China—the Jaredites' civilization began around rivers, which were not only essential to life, farming, and industry but also aided in the spread of culture and religion. And like many of their ancestors, the Jaredites were hunters, herdsmen, and farmers, with much of their wealth in cattle. During their life on the Syrian Steppes in the Old World, the ancestors of the Jaredites cultivated all manner of cattle, and many of their people settled in previously mentioned Mari. Cattle and sheep made up much of the Jaredites' wealth once they arrived in the New World as well.

The Jaredites ultimately built up settlements along every creek, stream, and river in the region, just like their predecessors did in the Mesopotamia Valley. The smaller streams were used seasonally while the larger creeks and rivers, which provided an abundance of fish, were used all year round. The shallow ends of lakes and various marshes were also popular places to settle, because migratory birds and small game could be found all around their shores. Thus, the lifestyle of the Jaredites in the New World was not very different than it had been back in the steppes and along the Euphrates River. All too often we tend to look for remnants of grand cities when looking for the Jaredites. However, Hugh Nibley encourages us "not to oversimplify our picture of what life was like in the first civilizations and dream up Cecil B. DeMille ideas about 'primitive' conditions that never existed."[1] He said further that "in all the Book of Mormon we look in vain for anything that promises majestic ruins."

THE ARCHAEOLOGICAL RECORD

A New York State archaeologist noted the arrival of a late archaic people known as the Lamoka culture in New York, which has been firmly radiocarbon-dated to about 2500 BC. They are described as a long-headed race (typical of the Semitic tribes). While five skeletons were of average stature, recent researchers describe the Lamoka to be tall and strong. Interestingly, two divisions are noted among the Late archaic people, the Lamoka and the Meadowood, who show up in the archaeological record around 1000 BC. This timing is remarkably close to the time the Jaredites all but destroyed themselves in civil war, save Omer and his household and thirty souls, who then gave rise to a new kingdom that fits the timeline for the Meadowood Culture, which rose to prominence in western New York around this time in history. The rise of successor kings flourished in the same regions until they succeeded in totally exterminating themselves in another terrible civil war in 600 BC.

Another long-headed people showed up on the scene around 600 BC and flourished as a people until around AD 400, a people who have since been classed as the Point Peninsula culture. Early researches initially thought the Meadowood and Point Peninsula culture were one and the same people since they overlapped in time and had the same skull type. But more recent research has led to the consensus that they were two entirely separate cultures.

THE JAREDITE'S LAND OF FIRST INHERITANCE

The scriptures place the land of the Jaredites' first inheritance, or the land of Moron, to the west of the Hill Ramah or Cumorah. In the modern-day New York setting for the Book of Mormon, this would be the region known as the Niagara Frontier, a region incorporating all the territory within a radius of fifty miles from the present city of Buffalo. This limited territory is the same region the Nephites inhabited, although both civilizations ultimately expanded throughout the northeast. Keeping the record of so large an area would have been impossible during such primitive times. Thus, only the sagas played out in this limited territory was kept and preserved for our day, for it was the heartland of both cultures.

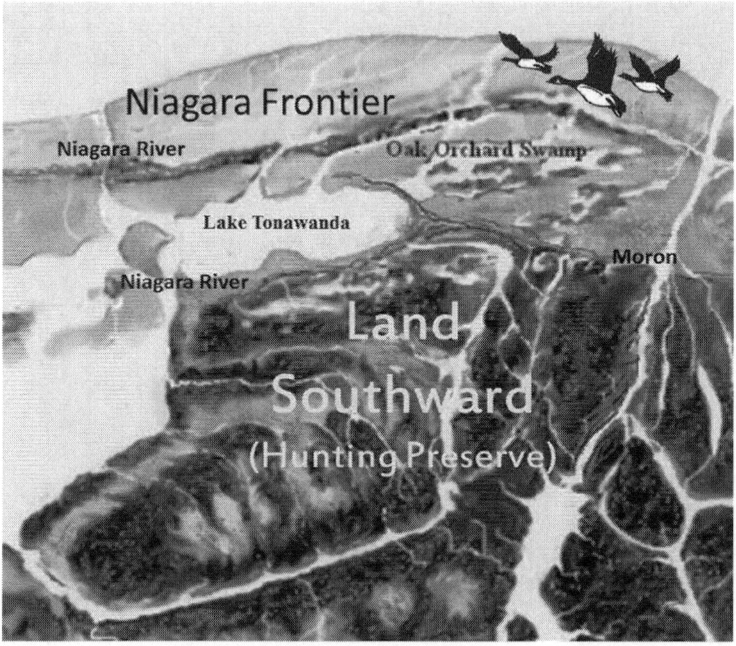

Because extensive forests filled the Allegheny Plateau farther south, the land southward was kept as a hunting preserve, for it was populated with a variety of animals including the bear, wolf, woodchuck, elk, deer, moose, and bison. Herman LeRoy Fairchild noted that three species of elephants also made the region home, particularly along the Genesee River, which is the dividing line between western and central New York.[2]

> And also all manner of cattle, of oxen, and cows, and of sheep, and of swine, and of goats, and also many other kinds of animals which were useful for the food of man.
>
> And they also had horses, and asses, and there were elephants and cureloms and cumoms; all of which were useful unto man, and more especially the elephants and cureloms and cumoms. (Ether 9:18–19)

THE SEA THAT DIVIDES THE LAND

Numerous streams, creeks, ponds, and shallow lakes filled western New York after the last Ice Age. Meadowood settlements have been found all across western New York and also along a glacial lake called Lake Tonawanda on the northern plains between Lake Erie and Lake Ontario, a fifty-eight-mile-long extension of what today is the Niagara River. As to its long existence in the land, radiocarbon samples taken from areas in the vicinity of Niagara Falls (Lake Tonawanda's westernmost spillway) suggests that Lake Tonawanda existed until around one thousand years ago.[3] That would be a full six hundred years after the close of the Nephite era, which can only mean that Lake Tonawanda was a prominent feature of the western New York landscape during both the Nephite and Jaredite eras and was likely the sea the Jaredites described as "the sea [that] divides the land" in Ether 10:20. The historian O. Turner noted that skeletons exhumed in a fort to the south of a dry lake bed, which we can now identify as ancient Lake Tonawanda, were of "giant size, not less than seven to eight feet in length,"[4] and were thus likely of Jaredite origins.

Oak Orchard Swamp, the largest of the three remaining

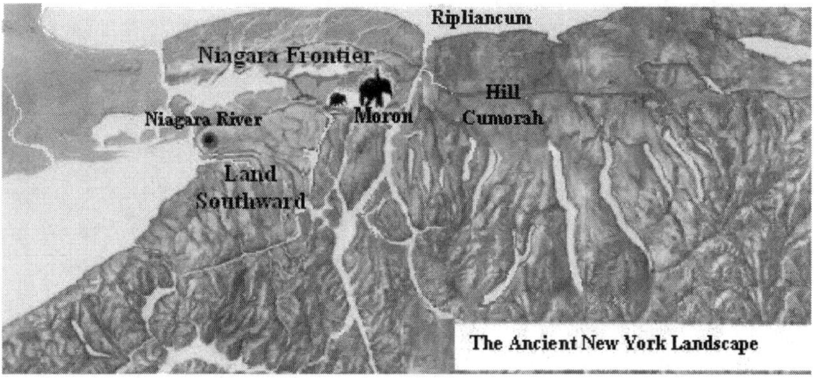

The Ancient New York Landscape

swamps along the lakebed, is simply teeming with life today, including thirty-three different types of mammals, the same type of mammals that likely lived in the swamps during Jaredite time, for Joseph E. Granger assures us that the swamps existed back into archaic times as well. A variety of birds, ducks, and geese can be found there, since the swamps continue to be a regular stopping place for them on their migratory routes across the country. Thus, the Jaredites began life in the New World in an environment much like the one they left behind in Ur along the shores of the Euphrates River, which was also adjacent a major wetland.

The king's capital city of Moron was likely located somewhere along the crest of the Onondaga Escarpment that bordered Lake Tonawanda on the south, because the scriptures refer to going *up* to Moron. The city may well have been located near the modern city of Scottsville, where a Lamoka site was discovered sixty-five feet above the floodplains along the Genesee River that appears to have been occupied longer than some of their other sites. The historian O. Turner noted giant skeletons a little to the west of Scottsville at modern-day LeRoy and Batavia—two other good candidates for the city of Moron, both being up from the flat plains below. The bones were said to average one third larger than those of today. Large skeletons have been found in this very region. Professor O. Turner noted that "the skeletons found at LeRoy, Batavia, and other forts in that area 'averaged one-third larger than at present.'"[5]

THE NARROW NECK OF LAND

The "narrow neck of land" described by the Jaredites in Ether 10:20 shows up on an old survey map created by Frank Leverett in 1902, which reveals a ridge of glacial debris called the Batavia Moraine that extends from Batavia northward down the Onondaga Escarpment and across the lakebed of old Tonawanda. This essentially separated the lake into two basins, one to the east of the narrow neck, and one to the west, with a great city apparently built near the place where it cuts across the sea. "And they built a great city by the narrow neck of land, by the place where the sea divides the land" (Ether 10:20). The Batavia Moraine only rose to a height of 30–50 feet. While it was not very high, it was still high enough rise above the lake's shallow waters, which in the shallow east end of the lake were only 20–30 feet deep. Time and the elements have diminished the moraine until it is barely noticeable today above the surrounding landscape, especially after being graded down over the years for modern roads.

THE LAND OF MANY WATERS

A Meadowood/Jaredite site found on Grand Island in the Niagara River radiocarbon dated to 998 BC—a date that falls in line with the temporal range of the Meadowood. The Meadowood people ultimately spread along the upper Susquehanna River in central New York and its tributaries, especially the Unadilla, Chenango, Chemung, and Cohocton. Culturally related people have also been found on Frost Island in the Seneca River and also

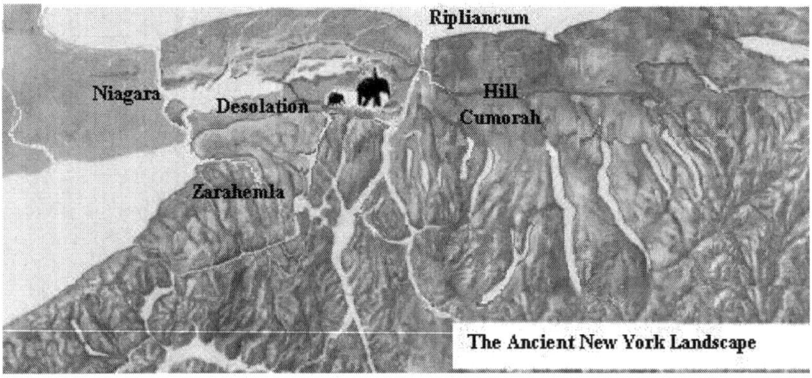

The Ancient New York Landscape

in the neighboring Oneida and Oswego River Valleys further east. When King Limhi sent scouts out to find the way back to Zarahemla, they appear to have bypassed Zarahemla and ended up in central New York, in what the Nephites would later refer to as a land of many waters in Mormon 6:4 and Mosiah 8:8.

From the Book of Mosiah, we read,

> And they were lost in the wilderness for the space of many days, yet they were diligent, and found not the land of Zarahemla but returned to this land, having traveled in a land among many waters, having discovered a land which was covered with bones of men, and of beasts, and was also covered with ruins of buildings of every kind, having discovered a land which had been peopled with a people who were as numerous as the hosts of Israel.
>
> And for a testimony that the things that they had said are true they have brought twenty-four plates which are filled with engravings, and they are of pure gold.
>
> And behold, also, they have brought breastplates, which are large, and they are of brass and of copper, and are perfectly sound. (Mosiah 8:8–10)

Most of the burials of the Meadowood-phase people produced nothing more than dust. Yet fragments of bones from four adults showed they were a long-headed race with narrow noses,[6] with their artifacts proving that they were a larger than average sized people. Ritchie noted the discovery of "enormous carved antler combs ranging up to 14 inches in length, large engraved bone daggers, massive harpoons, and extremely long stone blades, all of which suggest an energetic people imbued with definite and objective ideas."[7]

THE WIDE-SPREAD JAREDITE CIVILIZATION

While Meadowood sites were concentrated chiefly in New York, William A. Ritchie found a significant relationship between the Meadowood people of New York and the Glacial Kame populations living in neighboring Michigan. One of the Glacial Kame sites dated to 1980 BC, plus or minus 120 years,[8] about the time we would imagine the Jaredites first arrived. Because those in

Michigan buried their dead in small mounds of glacial debris called kames, they were given the archaeological name Glacial Kame culture. A skeleton found in a grave in Ohio and assigned to the Glacial Kame people was described by the man who discovered the remains as the largest human bones he had ever seen. While Ritchie could not say that the frame of the skeleton was taller than others in the grave, its vertebrae "seemed as large as those of a horse."[9] Such a description hails back to the comments of Albert Tobias Clay, who noted that the Semitic tribes living in ancient Amurru, tentatively identified as the root-stock of the Jaredites, were taller and larger-boned than the people who preceded them in the land. Such large and powerfully built men fit the description of the Jaredites perfectly, for the scriptures describe them as "large and mighty men as to the strength of men" (Ether 15:26). The discovery of such large-boned people was so commonplace during the early years of European colonization that the reports of such discoveries often simply reported that the aborigines of America were much larger than those of the later Indian tribes.

Any number of reasons precipitated the movement of some of the Jaredites into neighboring regions, not the least of which was rebellion.

> And when Corihor was thirty and two years old he rebelled against his father, and went over and dwelt in the land of Nehor; and he begat sons and daughters, and they became exceedingly fair; wherefore Corihor drew away many people after him. (Ether 7:4)

The many cultural and material similarities between the two regions and people led Ritchie to conclude that the Glacial Kame and Meadowood people must have been intimately related, with the Glacial Kame populations simply overlapping the Meadowood's northern range which was centered in the Niagara Frontier. Related people ultimately spread over a wide range covering parts of Michigan, northwestern Ohio, and eastern Indiana. The Meadowood and Glacial Kame people had sites as far away as Wisconsin among the Old Copper culture. Joseph E. Granger Jr., quoting M. L. Papworth, defined this wide area as the Lake Forest Archaic Cultural Tradition, with New York simply the easternmost extension of what appeared to be the Jaredite's wide spread civilization—at least during the early years in the land. Papworth said,

> We offer here a definition of a shared environment which encompasses the archaeological remains of these culturally related peoples. This environment is called the Lake Forest region by several ecologists . . . The people of the Lake Forest shared common burial practices reflecting widespread beliefs. In addition to these supernatural beliefs these Archaic peoples shared many tool types and materials. . . . New York State contains Point Peninsula (Meadowood) artifacts linking it to the Lake Forest as the easternmost area of common adaption.[10]

We can suppose related sites in Michigan and Wisconsin were set up principally to take advantage of the copper mining going on in those regions during the Bronze Age, because the copper mines around Lake Superior in Wisconsin and Michigan hold the richest copper deposits in the world. Other minerals were also available, such as iron, silver, gold, and nickel. Ash-carbon-dating tests made by the University of Michigan indicate the copper mines were worked most extensively by unknown miners of great skill between 3000–1200 BC, who excavated an estimated 500,000 tons of copper.

J. R. Jochmans said,

> A lost civilization once existed on the North American continent which worked in copper and other metals; possessed art and writing; attired themselves with crowns and other clothing; knew of and perhaps domesticated several animals including the horse; utilized acids for etching in a manner that is still not understood today.[11]

The Lord promised the Jaredites that if they always remembered Him, they would prosper, and so they did.

> And they did work in all manner of ore, and they did make gold, and silver, and iron, and brass, and all manner of metals; and they did dig it out of the earth; wherefore they did cast up mighty heaps of earth to get ore, of gold, and of silver, and of iron, and of copper. And they did work all manner of fine work. (Ether 10:23)

By following the trail of copper artifacts, it is believed copper was transported from Lake Superior along the Trent or Ottawa Rivers to waiting ships in the north end of Lake Ontario just to the north of New York, and from there along the St. Lawrence River to larger ocean-going vessels anchored in the Atlantic for transport across the sea. We can suppose the New York-based Jaredites were heavily involved in the transfer of trade items going on in that region; other than the large population center in western New York, no other area held such a large deposit of ancient relics than the territory at the east of Lake Ontario. Metal relics were found all across New York during the early years of European colonization, some no doubt of Jaredite origins, others of Nephite. Those made of iron disintegrated upon being excavated, leaving nothing but traces of rust behind. But some, found in a mound which dated to Nephite times, survived a little better; one mound investigated by a Mr. Atwater, as recorded by Josiah Priest, contained not only instruments made of stone, but well-manufactured swords and knives of iron and possibly steel. Their antiquity was so apparent that he could only conclude that the primitive people of America either discovered the use of iron themselves, as the

Greeks did, or they carried a knowledge of this ore with them at the time of their dispersion; as received by Noah's family, who brought it from beyond the flood.[12]

WARFARE, PLAGUE, AND DISASTERS

The early Jaredite kingdom experienced a number of wars during their near millennial-long stay in the region, even among the royal family, whose children often sought the throne of their fathers. Battle after battle raged across the region as wickedness and sin escalated. The Lord sent prophets to warn the Jaredites that their despicable behavior was incurring His wrath, but they listened not. Nor did warfare stop until the mighty hand of the Lord came down upon them in the form of famine and pestilence, followed by the collapse of the Bronze Age, which deprived them of much of their wealth, since overseas copper trade stopped for a time. The rise of natural disasters added to their troubles, including a sequence of earthquakes, storms, and droughts. Once things got bad enough, the people finally recognized the hand of the Lord in their troubles and repented. Thus God sent rain down on their thirsty crops, and they began to prosper again.

Unfortunately, it was not long before they introduced the secret works of the devil into the land in their quest for power, which ultimately led to more bloodshed. Once again, the Lord sent prophets to warn them that they were incurring His wrath, but as usual, they heeded them not. Thus, God warned King Omer to flee the land so that he and his righteous family would be spared the great civil war that ultimately erupted in the land and "lasted for the space of many years, yea, unto the destruction of nearly all the people of the kingdom, yea, even all, save it were thirty souls, and they who fled with the house of Omer" (Ether 9:12). Ether 9:3 reads,

> And the Lord warned Omer in a dream that he should depart out of the land; wherefore Omer departed out of the land with his family, and traveled many days, and came over and passed by the hill of Shim, and came over by the place where the Nephites were destroyed, and from thence eastward, and came to a place which

> was called Ablom, by the seashore, and there he pitched his tent, and also his sons and his daughters, and all his household, save it were Jared and his family.

Not surprisingly, directly east of the Hill Cumorah is the great Montezuma Marsh, the swampy northern end of Cayuga Lake, one of the eleven Finger Lakes of central New York—a seashore right where the scriptures place one.

The Glacial Kame culture disappeared around 1000 BC, leaving only the New York-based Meadowood phase of the Jaredites to start again—the few righteous Semitic tribes left of their many friends and relatives. As time passed and they began to spread across the land again, they moved chiefly east this time—far from the carnage of the civil war that wiped out the bulk of their people, though their heartland remained in the Niagara River region of western New York.

4

The Celtic Children of Japheth

According to the most ancient writers of Greece and Rome, the tribes that descended from Japheth, the third son of Noah, are the oldest known family in the world, a huge and powerfully built people often referred to as giants. It is said that after the flood and confusion of tongues, the descendants of the seven sons of Japheth became shepherds and settled in what today is known today as Ukraine and lower Russia. In time, the descendants of Japheth's oldest son Gomer divided, with the nomads among them settling to the north of the Black Sea, while the more civilized moved to the south of the sea and became known as *Sacae,* meaning robbers, for they had robbed their brothers of their land. Gomer's posterity initially settled on the Eurasian Steppes, where they came to be known as Cimmerians, later changed to Celts.

Gomer's Celtic descendants are described as a race of tall, fair-skinned, and golden- or red-haired people with blue eyes. While the average-sized Celt probably stood no more than a foot over the ordinary men of their day, who averaged 5' 4"–5' 6", Steve Quayle, the leading authority on giants, asserts that the Gomarians often reached heights of seven, eight, and nine feet, some even taller, upwards of nine to twelve feet.

While some of the tall Cimmerian children of Gomer in the Near

East spread across a vast area between northern Mesopotamia, east Anatolia, and Canaan, offshoots settled in what today would be Greece, the isle of Crete, North Africa's Mauritania, and Europe's France and Spain, with those who moved into Europe best known as Celts. Not a lot is known about the Celts except that they migrated across Europe and into what have become the Celtic countries of Wales, Scotland, and Ireland, where they ultimately grew to some sixty different tribes.

While most of the posterity of Gomer's Scythian brothers through Magog settled in Asia Minor and from there into India and China, others headed west and made it to the Iberian Peninsula of Spain and Portugal. It is said that once they reached the peninsula, they divided, with one branch moving north into Ireland and the other continuing north into Denmark, Sweden, and Norway. Thus, much of ancient Europe was settled by both Gomer and Magog, especially the islands along the Mediterranean and western Europe.

The link between Japheth's seed and the isles of the sea—namely, Greece, Crete, Sicily, England, Ireland, and Scotland—can be found in Genesis 10:5, where it prophecies that the sons of Japheth would one day fill up the isles of the Gentiles. As an additional blessing, Noah promised that God would enlarge Japheth, which He certainly did (see Genesis 9:27), for Japheth's posterity ultimately spread eastward from Asia Minor to the Pacific and westward clear to the Atlantic. Thus, in time, Japheth enlarged himself until his posterity literally encircled the earth.

Being stopped in their westward migration by the Atlantic Ocean, hoards of Celts ended up in Brittany and the Iberian Peninsula, leaving a trail of megalithic stone monuments behind spreading into Spain, Portugal, Ireland, and Scandinavia. Interestingly, the same type of megalithic monuments also show up in New England during the Bronze Age, which suggests the Celts also made it to America. After the extensive study of the various ancient scripts found scratched on rocks or stone tablets in New England, Barry Fell was able to determine that many of New England's stone monuments were indeed built by European Celts who made it across the sea to procure America's natural resources and to form permanent settlements in the area. Trans-Atlantic migration of such people has recently been suggested to have taken place when the weather was four to six degrees warmer than at present, and with the currents stabilized, sea merchants could sail and row from island to island, island-hopping across the north Atlantic to Labrador.

Vilhjalmur Stefansson said,

> A statement of the new Archaeologist position was made by A.W. Brogger, director of the National Museum of Norway in his Presidential address to an International Congress of Archaeologists at Oslo in 1936. There he treated as an established fact the idea of a Golden Age of Navigation, which was at its height surely 1500 years before Christ, and that it may have been on a high level for as much as a thousand years or even two thousand years before. During this golden age, man is pictured as having swarmed over the Atlantic, discovering all the islands and plying between the continents that lie east and west of the ocean.[1]

The Celts of Ireland, Gaul, and Spain apparently developed a vast maritime trade network that included Scandinavia as well. Thus Iberia became a major port responsible for the import of copper that was coming in from the New World to various Bronze Age nations in the Old World. Tin was readily available nearby, but little quality copper, which was needed to make bronze, was available in the Old World. Apparently many of the New England settlements began to rise as merchants from the tin mines of Britain crossed the Atlantic to procure Lake Superior copper.

While copper was being mined in a variety of places in Britain and Europe around this time, the best bronze of this early period was being made in Ireland, with trade going on between England and Ireland regularly. England was one of the areas in Europe where prosperity was producing wealth that was being concentrated in the hands of an aristocracy. They could therefore afford to acquire some of the things that contemporary aristocrats in other parts of Europe were able to possess, with some of that wealth apparently coming from the vast copper mines around Lake Superior. Copper from an estimated five thousand mines around Lake Superior was either transported down the Mississippi to waiting ships in the

Gulf of Mexico or out through the St. Lawrence River to ships anchored along the New England Coast, and from there across the north Atlantic to fuel the European Bronze Age.

A great stone astronomical calendar that dated to about 1600 BC was found in New England and was similar to those built by the European Celts of the same period in Brittany and Iberia, with Brittany being one of the six Celtic nations. Mounds, dolmans, stone circles, and standing stones were all represented in Ireland, Brittany, and Scotland. At least two hundred stone chambers have now also found across New England, many of them oriented in such a way so as to show they were used in sun worship and to regulate their calendars, with outdoor altars found in both regions dedicated to the Celtic god Bel.

A particularly interesting megalithic find in New England was noted by Roger Jewell. Because a city contained an entire complex of bath houses, it was referred to as the City of Baths, with the time of its construction thought to be around 1500 BC. Within a radius of four miles, three other lost cities of stone were found, dating to roughly the same time period. One included a 50-acre ceremonial center with a 70-acre mortuary acropolis. Both were set high on a mountainside with a residential neighborhood consisting of eighteen round, 16 foot-diameter pit dwellings identical to Neolithic residential sites in Britain. In searching for similar monuments around the world, you might be continually drawn to Western Europe, particularly Scandinavia, the Iberia Peninsula, and the British Isles, with the inscribed stones found in the area showing an influx of European Celts and Druids.

Along with the Iberian Celts, New England was also visited and colonized by Phoenician traders from Spain, who spoke the Punic tongue but wrote it in the peculiar style of lettering known as Iberian script. The Punic, or Phoenician-Punic language, is an extinct Semitic Canaanite language formerly spoken in the Mediterranean region of North Africa and several Mediterranean islands by the Phoenicians and the Canaanite Berbers who lived largely in the ports of Sidon and Tyre. Fell noted that the various writers of the scripts in New England spoke languages as diverse as Phoenician, Punic-Celtiberian, Celtic, Greek-Roman,

Coptic, Semitic, and Arabic. Many of these are Semitic-based languages—especially Phoenician, which has many affinities to Hebrew—that were spoken among the twelve tribes of Israel, some of which had joined the Phoenician fleets in search of treasures for King Solomon's temple in 1000 BC. The ships of Tarshish created the Golden Age of Phoenicia, with the Hebrew tribes of Dan, Asher, and Naphtali as participants in their maritime enterprises and thus likely among those who had settlements in New England and beyond.

5

The Jaredites' Second Rise and Fall (1000–600 BC)

The fall of the initial Jaredite kingdom was complete and final, with only the household of King Omer remaining in the wetlands to the east of the Hill Cumorah. No record of the Glacial Kame populations exists beyond 1000 BC. The people living on Frost Island in the Seneca River of central New York also disappeared around this time, with William A Ritchie noting that

> The Frost Island phase seems to have expired without clear survivals . . . Vignette 1 pottery, . . . increased in frequencies in the succeeding Early woodland state, represented in the same area by the Meadowood culture. . . . there may have occurred a slight overlapping of these two culture, with the final submergence of the Frost Island phase in central New York taking place at about this time.[1]

Once the war was over and the Lord told Omer that it was safe to return, they retraced their footsteps westward to the land of Moron to begin again, with every hope that they would get it right this time and not fall victim to so much sin. Back they went to the Niagara Frontier, where they began to spread all around Lake Tonawanda again, for archaeologist Joseph Granger maintains that the physiographic province of the Niagara Frontier was the most heavily occupied by the Meadowood culture[2] between 1000–600 BC, the very time the second phase of the Jaredites rose to power after the people in their initial kingdom all but destroyed themselves. While their numbers remained rather scant in New York, archaeologists acknowledged that the Meadowood had greater stability than in earlier times, with their settlement patterns approaching a semi-sedentary character, which spread throughout the Ontario/Erie and St. Lawrence lowlands. Ritchie, quoting Witthoft, states, "During the Transitional Period, we can see a number of cultural subareas which make up one big culture area, included within the drainage basins of the Potomac, the Susquehanna, and the Hudson-Mohawk," with Ritchie adding, that "he could have extended this range to include Long Island and the Finger Lakes-Seneca River region of Central New York."[3]

To date, over 240 Meadowood sites have been documented in northeastern North America over an area extending from Virginia and North Carolina in the south, to the boreal forest of Ontario and Quebec in the north, and from the prairie grasslands in the west to the Atlantic Ocean in the east. With the Bronze Age now over, the Jaredites' new rise in power appears to be chiefly east this time, from their heartland in the Niagara Frontier to the Atlantic Coast. While movement has been noted on both sides of Lake Ontario in both New York and Canada, Canadian archaeologists are quick to point out that the heartland of the Meadowood culture remained in the Niagara area. One of the reasons the Niagara region was of such importance was because of the high grade Onondaga chert found along the Onondaga Escarpment, which was used to make arrowheads and other weapons which have been found throughout New York. In fact, the importance of Onondaga chert found on both the Onondaga and Niagara Escarpments may be why the Jaredites built a great city by the narrow neck that lay between the escarpments.

TRADE BEGAN

As the rising generations of Omer's posterity began to grow and spread across the land, they developed a widespread trade network, called by archaeologists the Meadowood Interactive Sphere. This network took them west to procure copper from the numerous copper mines around Lake Superior and east up the St. Lawrence River to the Atlantic Ocean to collect shells and other trade items. A particularly important group settled in New York's Long Island, where they came to be known as the Orient Phase, which radiocarbon dated to between 1043–763 BC. Sites related to this phase have been found on Staten Island, in the Hudson Valley north at least to the Catskills, and in Connecticut and Rhode Island. Burial sites with strong ties to Orient Phase traits have also been found in Massachusetts, with lesser ties found in sites found in Pennsylvania and eastern New York.

While the Jaredites continued to mine copper from the cooper mines in Michigan and Wisconsin, the Bronze Age was over and there was less demand for copper from the Old World. Thus their interest was drawn more toward the acquisition of shells from the Atlantic and other commodities foreign traders were still bringing into the New England ports. It was likely there in New England that the Jaredites met and traded with the Celtic tribes who appear to have passed along some of the magic and pagan rituals relative to the burial of their dead. While the Orient Phase shared many of the same burial customs of their more inland brothers, others were picked up from the New England Celts and their Druid priests.

THE TERMINAL PHASE OF THE JAREDITES

Various Jaredite kings came and went in the succeeding years. Some were good kings, some were not, with those who were wicked once again spreading the works of darkness across the land in their efforts to acquire more power and riches. Thus began the terminal phase of the Jaredites, for they would never know peace again, since the Lord had withdrawn His Spirit from this stiff-necked people. No matter how much He blessed them, they continually retuned to sin. It was during this time of decline that Ether mentions the arrival of robbers in the land, perhaps some of the Gomarians who settled in New England, who were known across Asia Minor and Europe for their robbing and plundering ways. To make matters worse, the robbers adopted the secret works of the devil that the Jaredites introduced into the land sometime earlier and began to spread their demonic covenants far and wide. Thus fear and havoc spread throughout the kingdom, with few willing to do anything about it, for far too many of the people themselves had embraced the works of darkness and knew that death awaited any who broke its code of silence. Because of this, no one could successfully stop them. Nor was the Lord inclined to help them, for the people had forsaken Him. The Lord sent prophets to warn them that they were bringing a curse upon the land, but as usual, they listened not. Therefore, the Lord preached His own sermon to these corrupt people through His servants the prophets and caused a great destruction to come upon them, with famine and pestilence wiping out huge numbers of their populations again (see Ether 11:6–7).

No matter how many disasters the Lord sent upon the unrepentant, they continued to slip right back into their old ways. In fact, the robbers were no more wicked than some of the Jaredites. Thus, the Lord had the prophet Ether warn them that if they did not repent, He would not just send disease and famines upon them this time but would totally wipe them off the face of the earth. He had simply had enough! Ether tried to explain to the people that this was a land choice above all others, and the place where the Lord would rule the nations from the New Jerusalem for a thousand years of peace, but they refused to listen. The wickedness of the people was so deeply ingrained in them by this time that they ignored the prophetic warnings of Ether. So he began to record the history of his people, knowing that it would also be their legacy. It was not an easy task, for warfare was raging all across the land by now, and Ether had been cast out from among them and forced to hide in the cavity of a rock—likely one of the limestone caves along the Onondaga Escarpment—to do his recording and view the awful scenes of destruction around him.

The scriptures explain that the Jaredites' final battles took them eastward from the land of their first inheritance, for "it came to pass that Shiz did pursue Coriantumr *eastward*" (Ether 14:26; emphasis added). Continuing east and north would have led them to the great waters of Ripliancum, no doubt Lake Ontario, for the scriptures explain that Ripliancum means "large or to exceed all" (Ether 15:8). From Ripliancum, they then moved south to the Hill Ramah or Cumorah, the only known landmark we have of that ancient time in history.

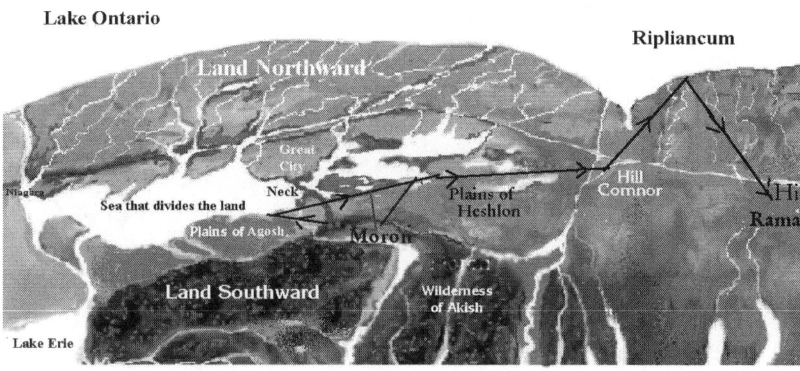

THE BATTLE SCENE AT RAMAH

In speaking of the Hill Cumorah, the Hill Ramah, and Ripliancum, Joseph Fielding Smith said,

> It is known that the *Hill Cumorah* where the Nephites were destroyed is the hill where the Jaredites were also destroyed. This hill was known to the Jaredites as *Ramah.* It was approximately near the waters of Ripliancum, which the Book of Ether says, "by interpretation is large, or to exceed all." Mormon adds: "and it came to pass that we did march forth to the land of Cumorah, and we did pitch our tents round about the hill Cumorah; and it was in a land of many waters, rivers, and fountains; and here we had hope to gain advantage over the Lamanites." . . . It must be conceded that this description fits perfectly the land of Cumorah in New York, as it has been known since the visitation of Moroni to the Prophet Joseph Smith, for the hill is in the proximity of the Great Lakes and also in the land of many rivers and fountains. Moreover, the Prophet Joseph Smith himself is on record, definitely declaring the present hill called Cumorah to be the exact hill spoken of the Book of Mormon.[4]

As was the custom of the times, a period of four years was

agreed upon so Shiz and Coriantumr could gather together their people from all the outlying regions for one final showdown, for with the winning side went the crown and the kingdom. When the time allotted had passed and the Jaredites had gathered together their people in two bodies, all—even their women and little children—armed with breastplates and headplates and all manner of weapons of war, they marched forth to battle. Nothing can adequately describe the horror of the scene when the battle ended. Let the scriptures speak for themselves.

> And it came to pass that when they were all gathered together, everyone to the army which he would, with their wives and their children—both men women and children being armed with weapons of war, having shields, and breastplates, and head-plates, and being clothed after the manner of war—they did march forth one against another to battle; and they fought all that day, and conquered not.
>
> And it came to pass that when it was night they were weary, and retired to their camps; and after they had retired to their camps they took up a howling and a lamentation for the loss of the slain of their people; and so great were their cries, their howlings and lamentations, that they did rend the air exceedingly.
>
> And it came to pass that on the morrow they did go again to battle, and great and terrible was that day; nevertheless, they conquered not, and when the night came again they did rend the air with their cries, and their howlings, and their mournings, for the loss of the slain of their people. (Ether 15:15–17)

In spite of such terrible loses, the battle raged on the next day, and then the next, and on and on until only Shiz and Coriantumr remained alive out of all their people—all save Ether, who was hiding away and recording the horror of the war and the final extermination of his people. In a long protracted struggle between the two men, Coriantumr came out the victor, only to roam the land as a lone and broken man until he was discovered by the Mulekites sometime later.

A LATTER-DAY VIEW OF EVENTS

In contemplating the events of that terrible time in history, Oliver Cowdery, who stood gazing upon the Hill Cumorah where the final battle between the Jaredites took place, recites his own version of that tragic affair. He said,

> This hill, by the Jaredites, was called Ramah: by it, or around it pitched the famous army of Coriantumr their tents. Coriantumr was the last king of the Jaredites. The opposing army were to the west, and in this same valley, and near by, from day to day, did that mighty race spill their blood, in wrath, contending, as it were, brother against brother, and father, against son.[5]

In spite of the bounties the Lord offered the Jaredites in this lush, fertile region, they forgot Him and His everlasting decree: only those nations that worshipped Him would prosper in the promised land, all others would be wiped away once they became ripe in iniquity. Without question, the wickedness of the Jaredites was full to overflowing, and the Lord's decree stood firm.

> For behold, this is a land which is choice above all other lands; wherefore he that doth possess it shall serve God or shall be swept off; for it is the everlasting decree of God. And it is not until the fullness of iniquity among the children of the land, that they are swept off. (Ether 2:10)

THE END OF THE LARGE & MIGHTY JAREDITES

In Josiah Priest's book, *Wonders of the World*, "he expressed the opinion that about 1000 B.C., a nation of giants waged a bloody war south of the West Lakes, among the hills along the southern shores of Lake Ontario and in the rich forest land which concealed so many small lakes and fountains. About 600 B.C., a great 'giant rose on the Susquehanna River, who waged war with the surrounding nations. . . . Cultivated regions, populated cities, and towns were reduced to a wilderness.'"[6] Priest's conclusions sound remarkably like the final battles of the Jaredites, the first one in 1000 BC when the Jaredites' initial civilization was reduced to just thirty souls, and the last and final battle in 600 BC around the Hill Ramah or Cumorah. It also sounds like the great giant that rose up on the Susquehanna was Lib, a man described in the scriptures as being taller than any of the other Jaredites.

The history of Cayuga County, New York, a little to the east of the Hill Ramah or Cumorah, is "filled with accounts of the people who built the forts whose remains are found in that area."[7] McGavin and Bean relate the following from that history:

> Cayuga County yielded a rich harvest of giant skeletons among the ancient ruins, of which we read that "entire skeletons have been found of people of giant proportions, the skulls and jawbones of which could cover the head and face of the most fleshy person of our day." We are told of a tradition which asserts that a destructive war was waged "in this very section of the country, "and with such fury and determination on each side that practically all of the warriors were slaughtered."[8]

The Jaredites were denied continued existence in the land because of their unrelenting use of the secret works of darkness, which the Lord strictly forbade, and because of their unrelenting wickedness. Thus, by 600 BC, the entire region was shattered, nations were fractured, and the entire Jaredite population was completely wiped out as the Lord began the terrible task of cleansing the vineyard in preparation for the arrival of still another people. In His continuing efforts to raise up a righteous people in the promised land, He would this time lead Hebrews, the Nephites and the Mulekites, to the promised land. The world of the Jaredites would now become the world of the Nephites, with many of the same pagan tribes ultimately tempting the Nephites into forbidden paths, just as they had the Jaredites.

6

The Migration of Prince Zarah (of the Royal House of Judah)

Expansion and colonization of the descending tribes of Shem, Ham, and Japheth continued unstopped by many of the post-flood populations until the close of the Bronze Age, when a period of terrible upheavals in both sky and earth plagued the ancient world. The end of the Bronze Age was sudden, violent, and culturally destructive, and, according to some reports, marked the beginning of the Greek Dark Ages. One possible cause of its collapse was the advancing technologies in iron production between 1300–1200 BC, which lessened the need for copper. Only one ore was needed now to make strong weapons, whereas tin was needed to make bronze and rarely found in the same place as iron. Consequently, long distance trade was no longer needed, nor were powerful leaders inclined to maintain friendly relations with neighboring regions to facilitate trade. Thus long distance trade stopped, especially to places as far away as the copper mines of Lake Superior. The effect of all this was unparalleled aggression and warfare. In a short period of time, nearly every city between Troy and Gaza was violently destroyed or abandoned by their people as they fled famine, enslavement, and plague. Sea pirates were on the rampage as well and caused the collapse of seaports all along the Mediterranean Sea. The collapse of the Bronze Age is thought to be one of the worst disaster in ancient history. In fact, many consider this time in history a lost golden age, followed by a breakdown of central authority, a general depopulation, loss of literacy, disappearance of long-distance trade, and an increase in vicious struggles for power among the elite. Various Jewish and Christian scholars note that these calamities seem to coincide with the story of Moses and the exodus of Israel, followed by a migration of Semitic people—meaning the twelve tribes of Israel—from Egypt into Canaan. Yet some of the earliest of the tribes to move out and away from Egypt were the tribes of Dan and some of the sons of Zarah, one of the twin sons of Judah who held the scepter, the right to rule in Israel.

THE SON OF THE SCARLET THREAD

The story of the birth of Judah's twin boys is well known, with the first being named Zarah, known as the son of the scarlet thread, for it was his little hand that emerged from the womb first. A scarlet thread was attached to his wrist to show his birthright as the first born of Judah. However, in the process of birth, Zarah pulled his hand back in, and Perez emerged first, not Zarah. Thus a breach had taken place in the royal line, and Perez was declared the rightful heir of what would later come to be the Royal House of David. From the King James Bible, we read,

> And it came to pass in the time of her travail, that, behold, twins were in her womb.
>
> And it came to pass, when she travailed, that the one put out his hand: and the midwife took and bound upon his hand a scarlet thread, saying, This came out first.
>
> And it came to pass, as he drew back his hand, that, behold, his brother came out: and she said, How hast thou broken forth? this breach be upon thee: therefore his name was called Pharez.
>
> And afterward came out his brother, that had the scarlet thread upon his hand: and his name was called Zarah. (Genesis 38:27–30)

Now, the Lord promised Judah that the scepter would not depart from his line until Shiloh, or the Savior, came. While

Perez's line had claim to the royal scepter, perhaps the twins were to rule jointly.

While the Bible follows the lineal descent of the Perez line onward, the line of Zarah stopped after the third generation, which suggested to many that they were no longer with the main body of Israel. While there is scriptural evidence that some of the Zarahites remained with Israel, others appear to have left the main congregation and founded and ruled the cities of Athens, Troy, and Miletus.

DARDANUS AND THE HOUSE OF TROY

While the indigenous populations of Greece and Troy were made up of a number of races, those of Hebrew stock must also be included, particularly those of the tribe of Dan and Judah. A fair amount of Danites left the congregation of Israel even before the exodus. When Egypt was having troubles with Israel, the Egyptians expelled all the aliens that had gathered together in Egypt. Among the deposed were a large number of Danites who had taken to the sea as merchants to trade with outlying regions. Various Jewish historians follow the Danites from Egypt to Carthage in North Africa, where both Phoenicians and Danite sea merchants already had trading partners, and from there across the sea to ancient Greece. From Greece some also made it to Ireland where the Tuatha de Danaan came to light as the god race of Ireland.

Some from the royal house of Judah also left Egypt before the exodus, chiefly those of Zarah, the twin brother of Perez of the house of Judah, who was destined to rule over the House of David, the line through which the Savior would come. Yet the Zarah line was also destined to spawn a kingly line, one from outside the house of Israel, one of the first being the royal house of Troy. The progenitor of the Trojans is listed as King De Dardania Dardanus, son of Zara (of Judah and Tamar) and Electra, who was born in Goshen, Egypt, where their descendants remained until the Egyptians revolted against foreign rulers. It was at that point that certain groups of the Zarah-Judah line left Egypt, where one group led by Calcol and his brother Darda (or Dara), the sons of Zarah, initially settled in Greece. Ancient Greek traditions and legends have Darda, or Dardanus (the Greek form of Darda), ultimately sailing from Greece to a neighboring island called Samothrace. He subsequently fled Samothrace during a flood over to the northwestern part of Asia Minor adjacent the Aegean Sea, where he named the first city he founded Dardania, after himself. Four miles inland from the Aegean Sea, another city rose up named Troy after Dardanus's grandson Tros, whose people were thereafter known as Trojans.

Dardanus was greeted warmly by the ruler of Phrygia when he first arrived, a descendant of Togarmah, the third son of Gomer, the son of Japheth, who had a kingdom of his own nearby. King Priam, a fifth generation descendant of Dardanus, ultimately married the Phrygian Princess Hecabe and maintained a close alliance with the Phrygians, who repaid him by fighting valiantly alongside them in the Trojan War. The descending princes of Dardanus ruled ancient Troy for several hundred years until the city was destroyed in the famous Siege of Troy. During that war, symbols were painted on the shields of those going into battle to represent the clans involved in the conflict. The leaders of the Greek army carried shields with both eagles and lions painted on them, symbols of both Dan and Judah respectively, although Dan was also represented by the serpent. All the historical evidence indicates that the Greek protagonists were made up of both Dan and Judah, while the defending Trojans were chiefly of Judah, with the symbol of the lion shown on their shields—the traditional symbol of Judah. We read in Genesis 49:9, "Judah is a lion's whelp: from the prey, my son, thou art gone up: he stooped down, he couched as a lion, and as an old lion; who shall rouse him up?"

ZARAH-JUDAH IN ITALY AND ILLYRIA

The Roman poet Virgil tells us that some of the Trojans displaced after the First Trojan War sailed west with Aeneas, a relative of King Priam, who took his father, son, and the idol gods of his ancestors and settled in Italy, where he became the legendary founder of what would become ancient Rome. Others, under the leadership of Hellenes, a prophet warrior and son of Priam, migrated to Thracian Chersonese, the narrow peninsula that extended south from Thrace into the Aegean Sea, where he settled with twelve hundred followers. Encouraged by their expanding trade with the Illyrians in the western Balkans, they went on to establish another new colony in Illyria on the banks of the Vjosa River, just to the northeast of Greece.

THE ZARAH KINGS IN ENGLAND

While Aeneas was taking his followers west to Italy, another colony made its way to England under the leadership of Brutus, the grandson of Aeneas, and thus also a Zarah-Judahite. He became the known in medieval British legends as the eponymous founder and first king of Britain, which he soon filled up with descendants. As the story of Brutus unfolds, we discover from various ancient works that after accidently killing his father with an arrow and being banished for the deed, he traveled to Greece, where he discovered a group of Trojans that had been enslaved and became their leader. After a series of battles that he finally won, he was given the king's daughter in marriage, and ships and provisions, and set sail. These Trojan refugees ultimately landed on a deserted island and discovered an abandoned temple to the goddess Diane. After performing the appropriate ritual, Brutus fell asleep and had a vision of the land he was destined to settle, an island in the western ocean inhabited only by a few of the Gomarian giants, an island which proved to be the isle of England, where he gave the name New Troy to the place now called London.

THE ZARAH KINGS OF GERMANY AND DENMARK

While some of the Trojan refugees fled west, others fled north, where Herodotus also found a link to the Teutons and Scandinavians living in the Danish islands and the Peninsula of Jutland, that large western part of Denmark that borders Germany. The sea-faring Danites had already settled much of that region during the second millennium BC, which became a chief area of trade and commerce, particularly Denmark, or Dans-mark, named after the Danites who settled the region. In the centuries that followed, the Danites there in the north called for a royal descendant of the house of Judah to rule over them. As the story goes, Odin, a descendant of the royal house of Troy, answered the call. The story of Odin goes on to explains that he had the gift of prophecy, which by means of the magic arts, told him his fame would lie in the north. Thus he and his wife set out from Thrace, a region just to the north of Troy, and moved steadily northwestward. One of Odin's sons ultimately founded the ruling houses of the Franks, a Germanic tribe living on the east bank of the lower Rhine River in present-day northern France, Belgium, and western Germany. From Germany, Odin moved on to Jutland, where another son became the king of the Danes.

Everywhere Odin went the land blossomed, and thus his people esteemed him a god. He is described as a red-bearded, middle-aged man of enormous strength who was a force to be reckoned with when going up against his enemies but kind and benevolent to mankind. His character is distinguished most by his wisdom, with reference often made of his skill in poetry and magic.

THE ZARAH KINGS OF SWEDEN AND NORWAY

From Denmark, Odin went on to Sweden where he founded a Trojan colony. Later, still another son became king of Sweden. Finally, Odin went to Norway, where another of his many sons became king. Thus it becomes clear that God meant it when he said the scepter would not depart from Judah until He comes, with a line of ruling kings stemming from both Perez and Zarah, one continuing on in Jerusalem, while the other carried the royal blood of Judah into various other lands the house of Israel was destined to settle after the scattering of Israel.

THE ZARAH KINGS OF THE ATLANTIC AND MEXICO

Language similarities have been found among the inhabitants of the Canary Islands off the coast of Spain in the Atlantic. Scandinavian literature is replete with accounts of Odin's distant journeys, which took him away from his homeland for many months or years, with one trip apparently taking him as far away as Mexico. Humboldt makes Odin the same as the Wodan or Votan of Mexico, a self-proclaimed serpent. While a number of historic pictures of Grecian warriors are denoted by the emblem of the sun, the Trojans were shown with the mystic serpent, perhaps due to their blood ties to the Phrygians, who were unquestionably serpent worshippers. When Priam, the king of Troy, married a Phrygian princess, she no doubt brought their serpent-worshipping religion with her into the house of Troy. As late as the Apostle Philip's mission to Phrygia, a living serpent of great size was kept and worshipped before their conversion to Christianity.

From L. Taylor Hansen's *The Ancient Atlantic*, we learn that Tyre, a son of Odin, had seaports based in the Tyrrhenian Sea, an arm of the Mediterranean, while his father Odin—or Wodan or Votan, depending on who relates the story—was the emperor of a great sea power in the Atlantic.[1] Humboldt makes Odin the Votan of Mexico, with various historians theorizing that Votan III arrived in Mexico from one of the many isles in the Atlantic. Ordenez has Votan arriving on the mainland from Cuba. Brasseur de Bourbourg mentions the Caribbean. Cabrera theorizes that he passed by the thirteen islands in the Canary group and the island of Santo Domingo. Perhaps these islands were part of the fabled Fortunate Isles so often alluded to in legend, also called the Isles of the Blessed, the place the souls of heroes and other favored mortals in Greek and Celtic mythology were received by the gods into a winterless blissful paradise called the Elysian Fields.

While Elysion, or the Isles of the Blessed, would continue to last in the hearts and minds of those sending their loved ones off to a land of bliss, Votan's island paradise was not destined to continue indefinitely. It is said to have been destroyed in a series of natural catastrophes, Joseph Antonio Constantine maintaining that Prince Votan III was the last of the Caribbean sea kings. As large chunks of the islands in the area disappeared, legends say the refugees took to the sea, with one of Votan's sons, Votan III, sailing along the Gulf Coast toward Mexico. After making landfall, he founded Nachan, the City of Serpents. Votan is thus considered a civilizer, a law-giver, and the introducer of the Mayan culture. Though a great civilizer, Votan was also described as a sorcerer who was well versed in all forms of magic. Good or bad, Odin's interaction with the people of both northern Europe and Mexico make Odin, or Votan, one of the first great civilizers of the ancient world. In time, the worship of Odin eventually pervaded the whole continent, with the name Odin, or Wodan, found throughout Mexico and South America, where the tops of the great pyramids in those regions were used as altars for human sacrifice. The last Votan of record is Lord Pacal Votan, who ruled Maya territory from AD 603–683.

Interestingly, Togarmah, the father of the Phrygians who intermarried with the Zarahites in Troy, is credited with being the ancestor of the Mayans, Incas, and Aztecs. Thus the physical type of the Maya was apparently highly influenced by the Phrygians, for the Maya have the same brachycephalic skull type and have the same Q haplogroup noted for Togarmah, the only grandson of Japheth to carry that genetic marker.

From the Jewish Encyclopedia, we read,

> The most important problem suggested by a study of craniometrical results concerning Jews is the relation of the type head of the modern Jews to that of the ancient Hebrews and to the modern Semitic skulls. The pure Semitic skull is dolichocephalic, as may be seen from a study of the heads of modern Arabs, Abyssinians, Syrians, etc. The cephalic index of these races is from 73 to 77. As is at present accepted by nearly all anthropologists, the shape of the head is the most stable characteristic of a given race. It is little if at all influenced by climate, environment, nutrition, or sexual and social selection. The only way the type of the head may change is by intermixture with other races. . . . As has been seen, all the results of craniometry prove that the Jews are brachycephalic, and that the dolichocephalic form is only found among them in less than two per cent of cases.[2]

7

ZARAH-JUDAH *in* NEW ENGLAND

WHILE THE DESCENDANTS of the Zarah-Judah line of kings have been traced from Troy to lands as far away as Scandinavia and Mexico, the descendants of Zarah's son Calcol, who ruled as king of Greece, also spawned a line of Zarah-kings. Historical records reveal that Calcol's descendants migrated out from Greece and set up trading posts all along the Mediterranean Sea, including on the large island of Sardinia and in the Iberian Peninsula, which today is Spain and Portugal. One post came to be known as Zaragoza, meaning "the stronghold of Zarah." From Iberia, some of the Zarah-Judahites also settled in Ireland and Scotland. One of the ancient names for Ireland is *Ibheriu,* or *Iberiu,* a name suggestive of their ancient homeland of Iberia.

The high kings of Ireland all sprang from Calcol through a descendant called Milesius. According to notes on Professor Rendall's *Cradle of the Aryans*, the Milesian invaders of Ireland were tall, fair, and brachycephalic. Regardless of the confusion mix of genealogies for the Milesians, biblical scholars feel confident that the Milesian invaders of Ireland were Israelites of the royal line of Zarah-Judah who created still another branch of royal line of Judah along the fringe of the then-known world.

Paul H. Andree, III said,

> We are beginning to realize the extensive distribution of the

> descendants of Zarah through the various cultures they established over the years. Their effect upon world history has been dramatic. Early in their history, they were not defeated and assimilated by various groups, rather, they were victorious and thus influenced and assimilated those they conquered. Their bloodline continued down through the ages, influenced cultures and set the course of history beginning about 1500 years B.C. [1]

Once the Milesians conquered Ireland, they absorbed all the Celts and Scythians still living in the land, including remnants of the Tuatha de Danaan whom they deposed. While the Milesians were not Celts, once they merged with the Celts and absorbed much of their culture and religion, they essentially became Celts themselves. While the Druid priests of the de Danaan who chose to remain in Ireland continued to preach their form of moral exactness and offer sacrifice to the pagan god Baal, various biblical scholars believe the Milesians kept the law of Moses, for they kept the Saturday Sabbath, paid tithing, offered first fruits and other offerings, and kept dietary restrictions. Some scholars suggest the Irish Churchmen even considered themselves the priests and Levites as defined under Old Testament Law, with great walled precincts built to house their priestly/monastic families, with the general populations protected in great hill-forts built atop long flat hilltops.

According to biblical scholars, Milesius, a descendant of Zarah, the son of Judah, is the father of the Goidelic-speaking people, with the Gaelic language used by a number of Gaels living in England, Wales, Scotland, and Ireland. Gaelic histories assert that the ancestors of the Gaels came to Ireland from Iberia, with DNA findings now successfully linking the populations of northern Spain to the indigenous peoples of Ireland and also Britain. Thus, the Celtic language family is divided into "Goidelic" Irish, Scots, and Manx Gaelic, as well as a "Brythonic" branch: Welsh, Breton, and Cornish. In other words, Gaelic is a part of a larger Celtic language, which modern linguist now say also has an affinity to Hebrew. Such language ties show that many of the Celts also made it to America, where three royal bloodlines were destined to merge: (1) the descendants of Joseph (the Nephites) who carried the birthright in Israel, (2) the royal line of Mulek, a descendant of Perez who carried the scepter in Israel, and (3) the Zarahites who fathered the kings and royal lines of many nations.

The Milesians, and therewith the Gaels, are Israelites and thus can be considered one of the lost tribes of Israel. While such an assumption is correct as far as identifying them, they certainly aren't lost, with one group now having been identified on the New England coast, where a complex of stone-slab buildings have been discovered. They are thought to have been built by the Goidelic Celts of Iberia, Ireland, or perhaps some of the Celts who were related to the Gaels who later settled in Britain and Ireland.[2]

Barry Fell, a Harvard scholar with an avocation for ancient writings, claims to have stumbled onto an ancient alphabet in Dublin, Ireland, written by Irish scribes that helped him decipher some of the Gaelic alphabets found in America, Scandinavia, and Iberia. Certain bilingual manuscripts led not only to Spain and Portugal but also to Libya, the Canary Islands, and ultimately to a remote land which was given the name Iargalon, "Land Beyond the Sunset." Similar Ogam-inscribed stones and dry-stone walls like those found in Ireland, Scotland, and Wales have also now been found in New England, suggesting a tie between the two regions. Barry Fell said,

> About three thousand years ago bands of roving Celtic mariners crossed the North Atlantic to discover, and then colonize, North America. They came from Spain and Portugal [Iberia] by way of the Canary Islands, sailing the trade winds as Columbus also was to do long afterward. The advantage of this route is that the winds favor a crossing from east to west, but for Celts accustomed to a temperate climate it had the one drawback that it led them to the tropical West Indies, no place for northerners. So although their landfall lay in the Caribbean, it was on the rocky coasts and mountainous hinderlands of New England that most of these wanderers finally landed, there to establish a new European kingdom which they called *Iargalon,* "Land Beyond the Sunset." They built villages and temples, raised Druids' circles and buried their dead in marked graves.[3]

The Megalithic stone monuments found in New England, such as dolmans, stone circles, and solstice stones, are of the type that began to rise in England, Iberia, and Ireland during the Bronze Age. Some are thought to represent astronomical events, while some of the outdoor altars are dedicated to the sun-god Bel, who was worshiped throughout pagan Europe, England, and Ireland. Fell claims that the independent origin of the Ogam letters found in Maine and Ireland are incontestably linked. Moreover, he claims the chances of the "17-letter Ogham alphabet of Maine . . . and Ireland . . . [being] of independent origin in these two places are less than one in 300,000,000,000,000"—or in other words, zero![4]

Following the trail of stone monuments and inscriptions, Fell follows the Irish immigrants up the Connecticut River and then northward to Vermont and eastward to the Green Mountains. He said that it was there in these secluded valleys and on the hilltops that priests erected temples and circles of standing stones required by their religious beliefs. Once settled, the newcomers built villages and temples and raised sacred circles, where their Druid priests instructed them in the worship of the sun, the moon, and the stars, and how these heavenly bodies influenced their lives, agricultural pursuits, and prospects for their futures.

The inscriptions left on various stone monuments in New England make it clear that Druids were also present in New

England and raised stone slab buildings for calendar regulation and for religious exercises connected with the worship of the sun-god and other Celtic deities. In fact, the Druid presence in Celtic New England is overwhelming. Mathew Arnold claims the Druidic Order is the oldest religion and educational system in Europe. The Druids are said to have collected the wisdom of the ages and systematically recorded it in prose and poetry for future generations in what is called the Welsh Triads. Natural philosophy, astronomy, mathematics, geometry, medicine, jurisprudence, poetry, and oratory were all proposed and taught. The men who helped initiate the work divided the order into three classes: (1) the Bards, who were responsible for music and poetry; (2) the Vates, who were responsible for carrying out their various sacrifices to the gods; and (3) the Druids, who studied natural science and philosophy, all of which constituted the formal religion of England before the advent of Christianity. Rowlands believed the Druids of Britain were so near the fountain of true religion and worship that they had to have been sired by one of Noah's sons or their descendants through Shem or Japheth. Many suggest that their religion was still untainted in both Ireland and England at this early date, although it would not remain so, for it would eventually become as corrupt as any other pagan religion throughout the world.

Much has been written about the Druidic Order, both for it and against it, the latter objections claiming its philosophies were created by the devil, with their priests considered wizards who perpetuated the dark world of magic. However, it was an order based on wisdom, science, and other worldly philosophies, where men of high learning could hold positions of power and act as their priests and instructors in all the arts of civilized living.

In points of learning, the Druid priests have been compared with the Chaldeans of Assyria, the Magi of Persia, and the Parses of India. Their open-air earthen circles were used by the ancients not only as places to worship the Most High but also as courts of justice and as observatories. Thus Druidism embraced a high standard of religion, justice, and patriotism. It is said that its secular side resembled in some ways feudalism, while its religious side is said to resemble in many ways the Medieval Catholic Church. In the Book of Mormon, we find an order resembling in many ways the Druidic Order religion and order known as the order of Nehor.

8

The Royal Line of Joseph (The Nephites)

While branches of the Zarah-Judah line were colonizing various parts of the western world, the descendants of his twin brother Perez continued on with the rest of ancient Israel, who remained a united kingdom until the death of King Solomon, when the ten northern tribes refused to accept King Solomon's son Rehoboam as their king. Thus Judah, who remained true to the royal line of David, became a separate kingdom from the northern tribes. In time, the tribe of Benjamin joined Judah, along with a smattering of Ephraim, with the northern kingdom thereafter including only the remaining ten tribes. The northern kingdom remained an important power until falling to the Assyrian Empire in seventh century BC, all because Israel began to worship foreign gods and lost the favor of God. Rather than look to God as the Creator, they began to worship the sun-god Baal, a god who demanded child sacrifice. Thus the Lord was constantly stirred up to anger against Israel.

The northern kingdom's ultimate fall from grace reached the point of no return around the close of the eighth century BC. Not only were they constantly provoking the Lord to anger, but they were constantly instigating plots with neighboring kingdoms against Assyria, incurring their wrath as well. Thus the Assyrian king led his armies against Israel's northern kingdom, with thousands subsequently killed and others taken captive. The princes of Israel not taken in battle fled with their followers to the Caucasus Mountains between the Black and Caspian seas. Others fled to a number of Gentile cities. The city of Tyre provided those fleeing the Assyrians sanctuary for a time. But once Alexander the Great began to invade the territory, they were once again on the run, many fleeing in ships, for the Tyrians were master seamen. Many sailed westward to North Africa's Carthage. Others sailed to Italy and Spain, and still others settled regions along the seacoasts of both the Atlantic and Mediterranean. Only the southern kingdom of Judah remained, which enjoyed a short period of prosperity before a revolt against the Babylonian Empire led to their destruction as well, a destruction due largely to the fact that Judah was now also worshipping foreign gods.

The prophet Lehi, of the royal house of Joseph, tried to warn his countrymen that they were calling down the wrath of God upon them, but they listened not. Faithful Lehi petitioned his people over and over again to set aside their pagan ways and return to the Lord. In fact, his pillow must have been bathed in tears at night as he contemplated the terrible end that awaited them if they did not repent. During one such night, he had a dream of the actual destruction of Jerusalem and was overcome with grief and more determined than ever to call his people to repentance. Rather than listen, however, they mocked him, cast stones at him, and even sought to take away his life. Because of this, the Lord led him away from Jerusalem and set him on a course that would end with his arrival in a land with a divine destiny called by the Lord "the land of promise" (1 Nephi 10:13).

LEHI LEADS HIS FAMILY AWAY

Due to his visions and dreams of America, Lehi knew the part Israel would play in the formation of the Lord's latter-day kingdom. In response, he gathered up his and Ishmael's families—Ishmael's daughters ultimately marrying Lehi's sons—and headed out into the wilderness. After several years of trials and hardships, including the building of a ship, they set out into the boundless sea toward the promised land. Various scriptural references to their movement from Jerusalem have them moving south to the Indian Ocean where, after building a boat sturdy enough to withstand the mighty deep, they were carried around the tip of Africa, which is likely where they encountered the terrible storm the scriptures tell us they went through. They then traveled north along various natural currents that ultimately swept them northwestward to the Atlantic seaboard of North America.

Two routes inland from the Atlantic would have been available to the Nephites: one up the Mississippi and one up Chesapeake Bay. Entrance into the land of promise by way of the Mississippi River initially seemed the most reasonable, since a detour east along the Ohio and then north along the Allegheny led directly to southwestern New York in the proposed western New York setting for the Book of Mormon. Yet as research continued and more and more pieces of the puzzle fell into place, it seems the more likely route was inland through Chesapeake Bay and west along the Susquehanna River, the oldest or second oldest river in the world, predating even the Atlantic Ocean. It was along the Susquehanna River that Joseph Smith Jr. and Oliver Cowdery were given the power to baptize from the resurrected John the Baptist, given the Aaronic Priesthood, and later received the Melchizedek Priesthood from Peter, James, and John during the early years of the Restoration. If indeed it was also along the fertile banks of the Susquehanna that Lehi's family first settled, its historical importance is even greater.

The Susquehanna River has two forks, one of which extends north and south and the other east and west through most of Pennsylvania. Today, boats of all sizes and shapes sail the Susquehanna, from canoes to fishing boats to steam driven double-decker paddleboats used to take tourists along the river. Those who sailed the river during colonial days used it as a connecting link to the Ohio River, with a short portage overland at Cherry Tree to Blacklick Creek. How far the Nephites would have sailed inland before they stopped and settled in is unknown, but perhaps they settled somewhere near the beautiful Susquehannock State

Forest, which is filled with a great variety of wildlife. We read in 1 Nephi 18:25,

> And it came to pass that we did find upon the land of promise, as we journeyed in the wilderness, that there were beasts in the forest of every kind. . . . And we did find all manner of ore, both of gold, and of silver, and of copper.

Once they began to explore the region, they found it rich in natural resources, particularly along the lowlands bordering the Allegheny Mountains, which stretch from north to south all across eastern Pennsylvania. Thousands of ounces of gold have been found in the mountains of southeastern Pennsylvania. Silver has also been found, as have rich deposits of copper and iron. Iron ore could also be found further west along the Venango River or French Creek, which is nearer Lake Erie. The whole region thereafter was considered their land of first inheritance.

RELIGIOUS INSTRUCTION CONTINUES

Not by chance, the Lord directed Lehi's people to an area where ore could be found in the nearby hills and along various creeks, for they would need the ore to create new records. While the brass plates held the history of the Lord's people back in the Old World (including much of the Old Testament), Lehi's people had to keep a new record of the proceedings of his people in the New World, including their prophesying and their genealogy, which were to be handed down from generation to generation, lest they lose sight of their status as children of Israel and the Lord's design for His people. Because of the tender mercies of the Lord in leading them to the promised land, Nephi was determined to continue their schooling in the ways of the Lord once they arrived. Thus, over the course of the next eighteen years or so, Nephi read to the family regularly from the four books of Moses. He also read to them out of Isaiah, for this young company was the root stock of what was to become a mighty civilization, and it was imperative they knew who they were, who gave them life, and what the Lord expected of them.

Lehi had been just as dutiful in tutoring his children. In gratitude for the Lord's tender mercy in leading them from sure destruction in Jerusalem to this favored land of destiny, he gathered his people about him and rehearsed to them the promises and curses due the inhabitants of the promised land in direct relation to their behavior. One can almost see him sitting on a rock on a hillside with his grey hair whipping about in the wind as his posterity sits down around him and listens to their aging patriarch, knowing full well that he would likely not be with them much longer. After greeting them each one by one and acknowledging their special place in his heart, he gave a recital of things yet to transpire in the promised land, including what would happen to the latter-day Gentiles if they set at naught the God of the land, who is Jesus Christ. Some of his final recorded words were,

> Awake! and arise from the dust, and hear the words of a trembling parent, whose limbs ye must soon lay down in the cold and silent grave, from whence no traveler can return; a few more days and I go the way of all the earth. (2 Nephi 1:14)

After blessing his children and grandchildren one by one and saying his good-byes to each, Lehi passed peacefully from this life into the next and was buried by his children. We can assume that their mother Sariah had also passed on, for nothing more is heard of her.

THE FLIGHT OF NEPHI

With unrest growing among Nephi's brothers Laman and Lemuel and also the sons of Ishmael, all of whom had become so hardened and impenitent that they began to threaten Nephi's life, the Lord warned Nephi to take his family and all those who would go with him and flee into the wilderness (see 2 Nephi 5:5). It must have been hard for Nephi to contemplate leaving the lush region after eighteen years, with its rich hunting grounds and navigable waters. A small village had no doubt already been built and crops grown in well-kept fields. And to make things worse, his mother and father were buried there. His heart must have been heavy and filled with a mixture of emotions as he laid out his plans for their flight and rehearsed the plan to his righteous family. It is not likely that they announced their departure; utmost secrecy must have been employed as they gathered up their tents and provisions and snuck out into the wilderness to seek a new place to live as far away as possible from the constant threats of the Lamanites. What path the Nephites actually took to escape their brothers is not known. All the scriptures say is that they headed into the wilderness. The Susquehannock State Forest just to the north of them would have offered their best hope of escaping detection by their brothers, who surely would have been in hot pursuit of them as soon as they discovered they were gone. Continuing on a northwestward course would have taken them through the forest and ultimately to the upper loop of the Allegheny River into southwestern New York. Looming out before them was the beautiful Lake Chautauqua, all too obvious a location for those who wanted a place to hide. Thus they likely continued up the valley to a more secure location.

As to where they may have ultimately settled, Arthur C. Parker, former New York State archaeologist, claimed that "perhaps the greatest variety, most abundant and most interesting evidences of aboriginal occupation in the county have been found at the head and along the borders of the valley of the Cassadaga which has its sources in a number of little lakes not far away from the shore of Lake Erie, although more than 700 feet above the lake."[1] The valley of the Cassadaga is a picturesque country of green and gently sloping hills so rich in ancient works that we cannot help but wonder if this little valley was the location of much of what transpired in the land of Nephi during Book of Mormon times. The fertile fields, lakes, and ponds in the area must have seemed like a paradise to the Nephites. Not only was it nearly 125 miles from their wicked brothers, but the area was filled with a number of small lakes, and Cassadaga Creek was filled with an abundance of fish.

Adding to the favorability of the region was the fact that the fertile fields along Lake Erie and the western plateau were of just the right kind to plant and harvest grapes. Wine was essential to the religious worship of the Nephites, who followed the law of Moses religiously, and thus it was important that they live in a region where grapes could grow. While the entire region is fertile and produced an abundance of crops well into modern times, the lowest elevations were especially suited to the growth of grapes. Westfield, for instance, home of the Welch Grape Juice company today, moved to the region in 1897 to take advantage of the ideal climate for the cultivation of grapes. Ultimately, vineyards from various companies stretched all along southwestern New York and northern Pennsylvania. While the tropics have a more genial climate than northeastern North America, the Lord knew the Nephites needed to settle a region that had four distinct seasons so that they could comply with all of the ordinances relative to the law of Moses, which included the planting and harvesting of the various fruits and grains they needed for their religious ceremonies.

The entire Cassadaga Creek Valley was once filled with a huge glacial ancient lake. All that remains of the huge lake are the three connected bodies of spring-fed water called the upper, middle, and lower Cassadaga Lakes. Even today, it is a beautiful and lush region.

Image taken from Google Earth

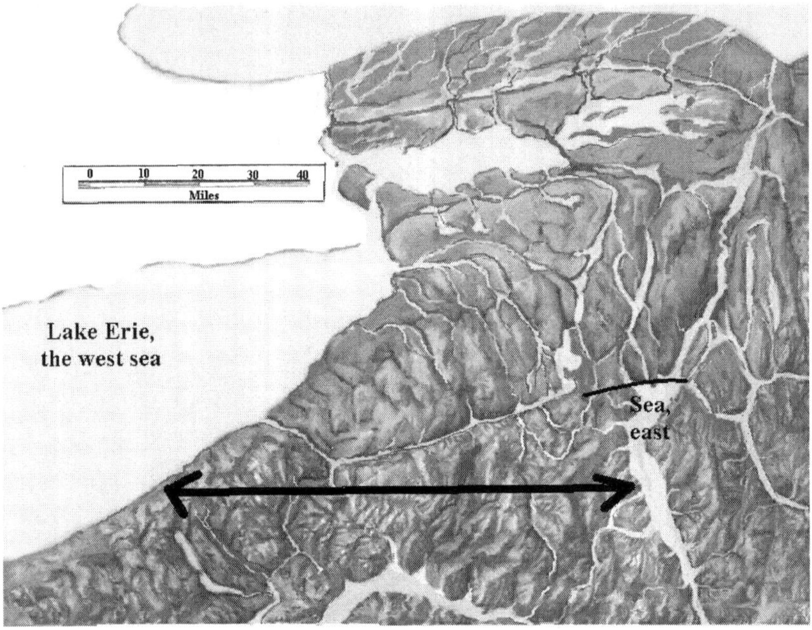

As the Nephites grew and prospered, they settled all along all the various creeks in southwestern New York, where they are known in the archaeological record as the Point Peninsula culture, a culture that emerged in western New York in 600 BC—the time the Nephites set sail for the promised land, with the Mulekites not far behind. The land they initially settled, or the land of Nephi, took in the entire region sandwiched between Lake Erie on the west and an ancient glacial lake that once filled the southern course of the Genesee River on the east. Frank Leverette notes that the lake in the southern course of the Genesee existed in the area for a considerable length of time, for it had first had to cut through 75 feet of drift and then 125 feet of portage shale before it could drain further northward and out to Lake Ontario.

The fact that seas flanked their east and west borders is noted in Alma, which says,

> And it came to pass that the king sent a proclamation throughout all the land, amongst all his people who were in all his land, who were in all the regions round about, which was bordering even to the sea, on the east and on the west. (Alma 22:27)

DISCOVERY BY THE LAMANITES

The Nephites lived in the land of Nephi for thirty years in relative peace before the Lamanites found them. Yet by the time forty years had passed away, they were already having regular wars with the Lamanites, some of whom settled throughout the Susquehannock Forest, where they came to be known as the Susquehannock branch of the Iroquois, with those found in the forests bordering Lake Erie known as the Erie.

> Now, the more idle part of the Lamanites lived in the wilderness, and dwelt in tents; and they were spread through the wilderness on the west, in the land of Nephi; yea, and also on the west of the land of Zarahemla, in the borders by the seashore, and on the west in the land of Nephi, in the place of their fathers' first inheritance, and thus bordering along by the seashore. (Alma 22:28)

But because of the continuing attacks of the Lamanites, some appear to have struck out to find safer territory, and chiefly

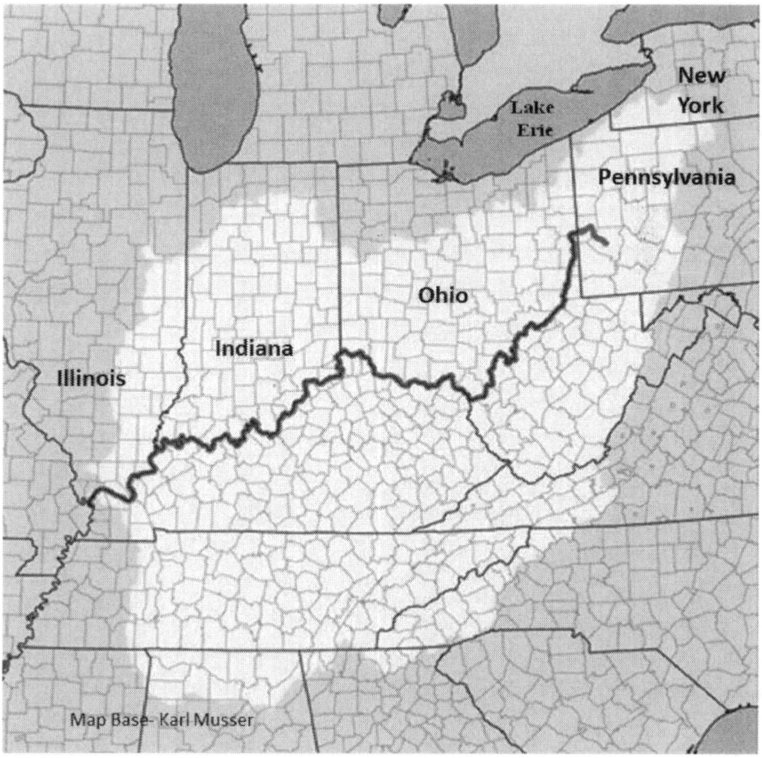

west, for Don Dragoo noted that the basic theme of the Point Peninsula burial customs were remarkably similar among several different groups scattered from New York to Illinois. By following the course of the Cassadaga lakes, the Cassadaga Creek, the Conewango Creek, the Allegheny and Ohio Rivers, and ultimately the Mississippi, groups of Nephites settled various regions all along the way. The pottery types shared by these widely separate cultures were so strikingly similar that both Don Dragoo and William Ritchie maintained that a "direct genetic relationship seems to have existed."[2] Thus, it appears that a number of the Nephites moved west once their struggles with the Lamanites became too intense where they established new cultures, with those in Illinois referred to as the Central Basin Culture.

In speaking of the ties between the two regions, Don Dragoo said,

> In western New York and adjacent areas, the Lenid [long-headed] peoples of the Point Peninsula Culture during the early phases of their development shared many of the basic traits of their western Central Basin relatives. At this level there seems to have been a generalized Point Peninsula–Central basin-like culture scattered throughout the areas around and just below the Great Lakes.[3]

Although the Point Peninsula populations were spread over a wide area, the Book of Mormon follows the line of Nephite kings, who moved north from the land of Nephi into the land of Zarahemla among the Mulekites, where their merged populations left an abundance of archeological evidence.

9

The Royal Line of Judah (The Mulekites)

When Jacob, the grandson of Abraham and father of the twelve tribe of Israel, gave his twelve sons a final blessing before his death, he associated each of his sons with some animal, which was to act as an emblem for their tribe. The lion was chosen as the emblem of Jacob's fourth son, Judah, who carried the scepter in Israel and thus the right to rule. Later, the addition of a crown became the emblem of the royal House of Judah. Of Judah's twin sons, the Pharez line continued on in biblical history through all the kings of Israel until the days of King Zedekiah. Following the siege of Jerusalem in 597 BC, King Nebuchadnezzar of Babylon installed Zedekiah as tributary king of Judah at the age of just twenty-one. However, Zedekiah revolted against Babylon and entered into an alliance with Egypt. Thus Nebuchadnezzar invaded Jerusalem in another siege that lasted thirty months. Around 587 BC, the powerful army of Nebuchadnezzar finally broke through the walls of Jerusalem, conquered the city, and destroyed everything they came across, including the Temple of Solomon. King Zedekiah and his followers attempted to escape but were captured on the plains of Jericho and taken to Riblah. After being forced to watch as each of his sons were killed, Zedekiah was blinded, bound with chains, and taken captive to Babylon, where he remained a prisoner until his death.

The Book of Mormon tells us that one of the sons of King Zedekiah managed to escape detection, a son named Mulek, who was secretly carried away to the promised land. Thus it must have been during the king's attempted escape that the young prince was whisked away in a different direction to a place of safety. Considering King Zedekiah was only twenty-one when he was placed on the throne and his reign only lasted eleven years, we would have to assume that Mulek was still a small child or baby—perhaps still in the womb—when his brothers were all killed and his father taken captive. In either case, some of the king's family managed to see the child to safety, perhaps one of his uncle Zarah's kinsfolk, whose long-time affiliation with the seafaring Danites may have put him a position to secure a place for himself and the young prince on one of their ships destined for the New World. The name Zarah was thereafter perpetuated among the descending tribes of Mulek.

With the death of King Zedekiah's sons (all but Mulek), the world at large believes the royal line of David was permanently severed, except for his daughters, who are said to have escaped to Egypt in the care of the prophet Jeremiah. But the Lord in His wisdom preserved the line of David by bringing Mulek across the waters to America, where in time they merged with the Nephites—one line from Joseph and the other from Judah. Remember that there were two leadership roles in Israel, one represented by Judah, who held the scepter in Israel, or the right to rule, and the other by Joseph, to whom Jacob ultimately gave the birthright blessing through his two sons, Ephraim and Manasseh. Thus, with Joseph's line destined to arrive in the promised land with the colony of Lehi, it was apparently important for Judah's line to be there too, that the purposes of the Lord could be fulfilled on both sides of the ocean, with both ruling families finally uniting in Zarahemla. It was actually the Nephites who revealed that the seed of King Zedekiah had been spared and brought to the promised land.

> And now will you dispute that Jerusalem was destroyed? Will ye say that the sons of Zedekiah were not slain, all except it were Mulek? Yea, and do ye not behold that the seed of Zedekiah are with us, and they were driven out of the land of Jerusalem? (Helaman 8:21)

The Book of Mormon does not provide the route the Mulekites took to the New World. Yet the fact that they came across the bones of the fallen Jaredite nation as soon as they disembarked suggests that they arrived in the Niagara Frontier in northwestern New York. The initial landing of the Mulekites must have been quite an experience. After leaving one scene of carnage back in Jerusalem, they came across another scene of devastation clear across the world; it is no wonder they dubbed the land Desolation. New York's fertile northern frontier would have normally been a favorable place to settle, and indeed it was for the Jaredites, especially around old Lake Tonawanda, which was left between the plains between Lake Erie and Lake Ontario after the last Ice Age. Yet there was no way the people of Mulek could live amid the rotting bones and burned out villages of that once-thriving civilization, whose bones now lay scattered across the northern plains. Thus they moved further south into the more pristine territory the Jaredites kept as a hunting preserve and settled along the fertile river valleys of what came to be known as Zarahemla. The fact that the name Zarahemla, a form of the word Zarah, was given the land they settled strongly suggests the presence of Zarahites in the land. The name Zarahemla appears to have been was passed along through the royal line of Mulek, whose uncle Zarah may have had descendants carrying the same name among those who brought the young prince to the promised land. A later descendant of Mulek named Zarahemla was the first to greet the Nephites when they arrived in the land of Zarahemla. Onni said,

> And they discovered a people, who were called the people of Zarahemla. Now, there was great rejoicing among the people of Zarahemla; and also Zarahemla did rejoice exceedingly, because the Lord had sent the people of Mosiah with the plates of brass which contained the record of the Jews.
>
> Behold, it came to pass that Mosiah discovered that the

> people of Zarahemla came out from Jerusalem at the time that Zedekiah, king of Judah, was carried away captive into Babylon.
>
> And they journeyed in the wilderness, and were brought by the hand of the Lord across the great waters, into the land where Mosiah discovered them; and they had dwelt there from that time forth. (Omni 1:14–16)

Naming the chief waterway in Zarahemla the River Sidon also shows strong ties to the Old World and the port from which they likely came. The Phoenician sea ports of Tyre and Sidon are located on the east coast of the Mediterranean Sea, with Sidon just 124 miles north of Jerusalem. Moving steadily northward from Jerusalem would have brought the people who rescued prince Mulek through the wilderness straight to Sidon, where they could have secured passage on a friendly Danite ship heading for the New World. The Danites forcibly colonized a portion of Sidon when they found their own neighboring territory too small for their growing numbers; the Danites thereafter became part of the Phoenician fleets and were likely those who brought the people of Mulek to the promised land.

MULEKITE ARRIVAL IN AMERICA

The archaeological record places the Point Peninsula people—those the Book of Mormon identifies as the Mulekites—living to the north of the Nephites in northwestern New York and lower Ontario. Yet those who chose to live in lower Ontario came to be known as the Saugeen culture, after the Saugeen River. The joint populations of the Saugeen and Point Peninsula are thought to have been responsible for the emergence of the Proto-Algonquin language in the area around 500 BC. In 1967, Frank Siebert determined, through the reconstruction of terms for natural features, plants, and animals, that the Proto-Algonquin language could be traced to the Saugeen and Point Peninsula people living in southern Ontario between Georgian Bay and Lake Ontario as far south as Niagara Falls.[1] While the two people were much alike, the archaeological record suggests the Saugeen may have had a slightly different ancestry. Some of the differences between the two people show up in the skeletal remains of the Great Lakes' Algonquins, whose head-forms are almost brachycephalic, according to "Access Genealogy," yet show considerable variation. The Nephites with whom they merged were a pure doliocephalic race like all the other Semitic tribes, with no brachycephalic physical types among them. Thus, the variation in the skull type of the Algonquins is likely due to the mixture of the two, with most archaeologists now preferring to class the Algonquins as moderately dolichocephalic, with occasional extreme forms—the extreme form no doubt being the Nephites with whom they merged, or even some of the Danites among them, who were also a tall doliocephalic race.

THE DANITE/PHOENICIAN SEA-FARING TRADERS AND COLONIZERS

The Red Ochre culture living on Manitoulin Island in Lake Huron, just to the west of the Saugeen populations living in lower Ontario, may well have ties to the ancient Phoenicians, for they are believed to have been long-distance mariners and spoke an ancestral form of the Proto-Algonquin language. William A. Ritchie believes a site found in Iowa, which dates to around 470 B.C, give or take 250 years, was a joint Point Peninsula/Red Ochre site.[2] We can assume the two were affiliated with each other in one way or another. The Red Ochre culture was not made up of a large population but widely separate cultural complexes, found particularly around the copper mines and along both sides of the Mississippi and in Iowa and along the Illinois and Ohio Rivers, and on Manitoulin Island in Lake Huron. The oldest radiocarbon date for a Red Ochre site in Saginaw, Michigan, is 1210 BC, give or take 300 years, a date that falls in line with the timeline of the Danite/Phoenicians who came in search of copper for King Solomon's Temple in 1000 BC. Barry Fell believes Phoenician ships used the trading ports along the Mississippi to buy ore that was transported down the river from Lake Superior and Michigan's Isle Royale and then across the sea to the Old World. Perhaps it was on one such trip that a Phoenician ship was hired to carry young

Prince Mulek back to the New World. Danite mariners may well have been aware of the terrible civil war that wiped out the Jaredite civilization and thus knew just where to bring the young prince, for the land was now free for the taking. Knowing that these lands were now free for the taking, they may have brought the Mulekites right to northwestern New York, where they could start in a brand new land, far from neighboring kings who may have challenged their claim to the area. Who knows, but maybe the Danites stayed among the people of Zarahemla and helped colonize the region to assure the survival of the company and the success of the young prince, for the Danites have been described as "the pioneers of Israel" who set up colonies on many shores, including in New England.

Over the course of years, the pottery technology shared by the Saugeen and early Point Peninsula people ultimately extended northward into Canada, where a new culture emerged called the Laurel culture. The Laurel culture was distributed from the border of Quebec, across northern Ontario, throughout much of Manitoba, and into east-central Saskatchewan and lands as far south as northern Michigan, Minnesota, and Wisconsin, in what has come to be known as the Late Western Shield Culture. Pottery in this region, which most agree arrived by diffusion from the Point Peninsula and Saugeen populations, date to around 300 BC. It is commonly agreed that they were contemporary with the northern Algonquin people. Thus, while the Nephites were filling up much of the lands southward, the company who arrived with Mulek was filling up much of the lands to the north—with Canada making up the bulk of the land of Mulek.

> Now the land south was called Lehi and the land north was called Mulek, which was after the son of Zedekiah; for the Lord did bring Mulek into the land north, and Lehi into the land south. (Helaman 6:10)

KING ZEDEKIAH'S DAUGHTERS

Mulek may not have been the only descendant of Zedekiah to

arrive in the promised land. Some of the descendants of his two daughters may also have arrived over the course of time. Historical records reveal that following the captivity of King Zedekiah, the king's daughters were given over to the care of their great-grandfather, the prophet Jeremiah, who initially took them to Egypt and then to Ireland, where he arrived with at least one of the girls and his faithful scribe. The fact that some researchers believe King Zedekiah's daughters were rescued by the tribe of Zarah-Judah and the tribe of Dan, who then took at least one of the girls to Ireland, strengthens the idea that the merged Zarahites and Danites also carried Prince Mulek to his destination in America.

Susan Alfson said,

> There are several Irish and Scottish stories stating that the royal line came to Ireland. One of these from an ancient Irish record makes reference a King's daughter, a prophet, and his companion Baruch. They all arrived in Ireland at approximately the same time, 584 BC. This is the same time that the kingdom of Jerusalem fell. . . . They apparently arrived in Ireland via a sea route; escorted and helped by the tribe of Dan who were seafaring travelers. During the time of Nebuchadnezzar, the remnant, which included Jeremiah, Baruch, and the King's daughters, had to flee Egypt. Apparently, some of the tribe of Zarah, Judah and the tribe of Dan rescued them from the wrath of Nebuchadnezzar and brought them into a secluded Irish kingdom. They came by sea into Scotland then into Ireland.[3]

In time, one of the reputed daughters of King Zedekiah was given in marriage to Heremon, king of Ireland, whose genealogy follows the Zarah-Judah line. According to Irish traditions, still a second group crossed from the port at Sidon to Spain, where a second daughter of King Zedekiah was ultimately married to Spanish royalty. Now considering Spain was a central hive of long distance sea merchants, many of which appear to have made it all the way to America, one cannot help but wonder if some of the descendants of one or both of the daughters of King Zedekiah also made it to America, where they would have merged once again with the descendants of Mulek's bloodline. The prophet Lehi made it clear in the following scripture that the Lord fully intended to bring others to the New World besides his own colony. His reference to those the Lord *shall* bring out of the land of Jerusalem makes it clear that he was speaking of others besides himself who were yet to come, no doubt the Mulekites, but possibly others as well.

> Wherefore, I, Lehi, have obtained a promise, that inasmuch as those whom the Lord God *shall bring out of the land of Jerusalem* shall keep his commandments, they shall prosper upon the face of this land; and they shall be kept from all other nations, that they may possess this land unto themselves. And if it so be that they shall keep his commandments they shall be blessed upon the face of this land, and there shall be none to molest them, nor to take away the land of their inheritance; and they shall dwell safely forever. (2 Nephi 1:9; emphasis added)

In uniting one of the princesses of King Zedekiah (who carried the bloodline of Perez-Judah) to King Heremon of Ireland (whose bloodline followed the Zarah-Judah line), a number of biblical scholars believe the breach that occurred in Judah when his twin sons were born was finally healed. Because the world generally does not know that the Lord preserved one of King Zedekiah's sons and carried him safely to the New World, they could only assume the royal right to the scepter must have been perpetuated by his two daughters who survived and founded royal lines in Ireland and Spain. However, since the Lord preserved one of the sons of King Zedekiah, whose right to rule in Israel was never severed, such a reconciliation of the two lines was never necessary, for the seed or rootstock of the vine was still alive and thriving. Yet, it may well be that the descendants of one of his daughters would also ultimately make it to America, for it has now been determined that around 800–300 BC, Irish and Iberian sea merchants also made it to America. Once there, they set up trading ports and settlements in southern New England and moved from there west across Pennsylvania, Tennessee, and Kentucky clear to the Mississippi.

THE TENDER TWIG RIDDLE

The Lord's riddle of the tender twig, found in Ezekiel 16–17, may shed some light on the disposition of King Zedekiah's children. In giving Ezekiel the information he needed to make up the riddle, the Lord compared the royal family of Judah to a cedar tree in Lebanon, a symbolic name for Jerusalem. The parable has two parts: one that depicts the past and the other the future of the Davidic line, the line through which the Savior would come. The sea-faring people of Dan may even figure into the Lord's riddle, which supposedly reveals the secret disposition of the young twigs (children) of the highest branch of the cedar, which is generally thought to mean the ruling house of Israel, or Judah—in this case, King Zedekiah.

The tender twig riddle mentions Lebanon, which in the context of the riddle appears to represent the cedars of Lebanon, which were used during the construction of the holy temple. The temple of Solomon was embellished with not only precious metals but also with the finest cedar that could be found, most of which came from Lebanon. Archaeologists have dated the wood used in the temple as far back as the first temple periods and thus appear to be among the celebrated cedars of Lebanon, which were shipped on floats from the seaports of Zebulon at Tyre by the Laish Danites to the Danites seaports at Joppa in the south.

The Lord's riddle about a tender twig of Israel being planted by great waters may suggest the early arrival of King Zedekiah's son in the Great Lakes region and maybe even the descendants of one of his daughters who may have settled nearby. From Ezekiel, we read,

> And the word of the Lord came unto me, saying,
>
> Son of man, put forth a riddle, and speak a parable unto the house of Israel;
>
> And say, Thus saith the Lord God; A great eagle with great wings, longwinged, full of feathers, which had divers colours, came unto Lebanon, and took the highest branch of the cedar:
>
> He cropped off the top of his young twigs, and carried it into a land of traffick; he set it in a city of merchants.

> He took also of the seed of the land, and planted it in a fruitful field; he placed it by great waters, and set it as a willow tree.
>
> And it grew, and became a spreading vine of low stature, whose branches turned toward him, and the roots thereof were under him: so it became a vine, and brought forth branches, and shot forth sprigs.
>
> There was also another great eagle with great wings and many feathers: and, behold, this vine did bend her roots toward him, and shot forth her branches toward him, that he might water it by the furrows of her plantation.
>
> It was planted in a good soil by great waters, that it might bring forth branches, and that it might bear fruit, that it might be a goodly vine. (Ezekiel 17:1–8)

Some Christian writers see the fulfillment of this riddle in the story of King Zedekiah's daughters. A number of researchers say that both sisters were ultimately taken to Spain, which is a land of traffic and merchants (Tarshish), with one ultimately making it to Ireland. The great eagle with great wings is seen as the ships of Dan, for the eagle is one of the symbols of Dan, whose many merchant ships sailed beneath great sails. With the added information provided in the Book of Mormon, which speaks of Mulek's transfer to the promised land, still more of the riddle comes to light. Read the scripture again with that in mind.

> He cropped off the top of his young twigs, [*this would have to be King Zedekiah's daughter, for all his sons were killed—all but Mulek, who may have still been an infant*] and carried it into a land of traffick; (*Spain*) he set it in a city of merchants [*Tarshish*].
>
> He took also of the seed of the land [*which would be Mulek*], and planted it in a fruitful field [*promised land*]; he placed it by great waters [*the Great Lakes?*] and set it as a willow tree.
>
> And it grew, and became a spreading vine of low stature, [*under that of the Nephites who took the role of kingship when the two merged*] whose branches turned toward him and the roots thereof were under him: so it became a vine, and brought forth branches, and shot forth sprigs [*many tribes*].
>
> There was also another great eagle with great wings and many feathers [*ships of Tarshish/Dan*]: and, behold, this vine did bend her [*female—one of the daughters*] roots toward him, and shot forth

> her [*female*] branches toward him, that he might water it by the furrows of her plantation.
>
> It was planted in a good soil by great waters [*Great Lakes or New England*], that it might bring forth branches [*tribes*], and that it might bear fruit, that it might be a goodly vine. (Ezekiel 17:4–8)

The "seed of the land" represents the son of the king, not his daughters, for it is through the king's male heir that the line continues. While provisions are made for a daughter to perpetuate the line if no male heir is available and if married to an appropriate candidate, the Lord in his great wisdom preserved the unbroken royal line of Judah by persevering his male heir and bringing him to the promised land of America. He planted that male heir by great waters—the Great Lakes—with some of the descendants of King Zedekiah's daughter perhaps planted in New England and along its coast with the incoming Iberian Celts or Phoenicians merchant princes.

THE SHIPS OF TARSHISH

A script found on a harbor in Rhode Island was deciphered by Barry Fell to read, "Mariners from Tarshish, this rock proclaims."[4] An enormous amount of data implies that the islands off the New England coast were shipping ports, including Monhegan Island, where Ogam inscriptions were written in the old Goidelic tongue of Zarah-Judah. The following comments by James P. Whittall are most informative: He said,

> From previous work by Dr. Fell . . . we now know that ogam was used by the Celts in the Iberian Peninsula at a time when they would have had contact with the Phoenicians. This message implies that both Punic [Phoenician] seafarers and Celtic explorers had been at Monhegan. From research work we would suggest a time frame of about 400 BCE. . . . They dealt in any commodity that would return a profit. . . . In this case, the fishermen were probably Iberian-Celts who left their cargo for Phoenician traders at Monhegan. It is possible that they also included furs, which were in high demand in Europe, at the cargo platform. The message near a high point on Manana would be spotted by mariners

> visiting the island and they would know that they had a trade contact.[5]

Phoenician ships were thought to have even been superior to those of the Celts, who were master seamen, although the two people often combined their forces. According to Julius Caesar, they were bigger, faster, and more maneuverable than even Roman ships. Thus, they were perfectly capable of braving the north Atlantic and making their way to America.

A number of theories have arisen over the disposition of the King Zedekiah's daughters. Unfortunately, only time and much more information will finally solve the Lord's riddle of the tender twig completely.

10

ZARAH-JUDAH *in* TENNESSEE

DURING GROUND EXPLORATION of the area around the Lackawaxen and Delaware rivers in southern New England, inscribed rocks and various inscribed pebbles were found along with a number of conical stone piles which marked the sacred places of a community. Further up the river, more stones were found, one inscribed with grooves and scratches in such a manner that sun worship was implied. Stones with similar grooves and scratches were found all along the Delaware River Valley, with one inscribed stone identified as Iberic script written in the Andalusian language of southwest Spain, one of the strongholds of the Zarah-Judah line where Milesius once ruled as king. Barry Fell believes some of the inscribed stones were primarily burial slabs of the members of an Iberian colony on the upper Susquehanna River, dating to around 800–600 BC. Their Iberian or Irish origin is evident not only from the script they left behind but also similar stonework and hilltop forts. The Milesians followed an old Iberian tradition of building hill forts once they arrived in Ireland, where thousands of hill forts dot the landscape, a few of which have also been found in America. The use of the word *fort* does not seem to fit, however, for most are now thought to be ceremonial enters and the abode of their kings and priests.

Salvatore Trento said,

> We do know that elsewhere in the world various ancient people who worked in stone, like the Celts and Iberians, kept track of the seasons by marking out the solstices. An annual calendar was imperative for seasonal economy of agriculture. But marking out celestial events requires a great deal of time and a system of record keeping. A priestly caste emerged whose function it was to keep records to regulate the routine of planting and harvesting. The association of prayer with different celestial events inevitably led to a wealthy and powerful caste who seemingly communed with sky gods through stone temples on hilltops.[1]

In the late 1890s Cyrus Thomas reported seeing a number of ancient stone walls and hilltop centers across miles of eastern America. Some of the stone walls were eight feet high and wide, with stone-lined pits, stone circles, and conical cairns always situated near their entranceways. A common tie seems to run through them all, leading to the conclusion that the Iberian Celts who settled in Pennsylvania ultimately made it through the mountains and into the fertile Tennessee-Cumberland Valley and along the Ohio River clear to the Mississippi. Passage through the mountains would have taken those in the east to lush, fertile regions further west. An agricultural region, called the Great Valley, lay beside these highlands, with a winding path cut out many centuries ago by a river that created a natural passageway into the Great Valley and beyond. Trento noted strange earthworks atop the pass that consist of gigantic elliptical mounds, circular stone piles, and an assortment of stone walls in a massive complex that covers about two hundred acres. Various investigations gave rise to theories that the massive complex facilitated some type astronomical observation, with the adjacent stone-lined highways suggestive of important paths leading to the ceremonial center. As to who built them, Trento believes the inscribed stones, perched rocks, and various stones aligned to the sun and moon found in the area suggested ties to ancient Iberia. He said,

> When we look to the fifth-century B.C. Celtic Hill forts of Britain and Iberia with their guard chambers, defensive earth mounds with walls 12–14 feet thick and 14 feet high, with their segmented bastions and associated cairns, we are struck by the

curious resemblances to the stone enclosures of eastern North America.[2]

As these overseas colonists began to migrate west across Pennsylvania into West Virginia, Tennessee, and the Ohio Valley, concentric circles carved in stone also began to show up, as did stone cist burials similar to those found in Ireland, sometimes with rings of standing stones surrounded them, and often with a ditch around it. A number of similar inscriptions, and circles thought to be sacred enclosures, have been found in the Kanawha Valley of West Virginia, with a number of stone grave cists found nearby and throughout Tennessee. An inscription found on a tablet in the Grave Creek Mound in Moundsville, West Virginia, radio-carbon dated to around 200 BC. It was deciphered by Barry Fell, who determined that the language on the tablet is Punic (Phoenician), written in a form of Celtic Iberian used by the Celts in Spain around 1000 BC.

Another engraved tablet found in a stream in West Virginia was inscribed in the same Iberian script and employed the same Punic language as the tablet found at Moundsville, which led Fell to believe it was clearly related to the Iberian culture of Moundsville. Portions of a bone imprint stamp for pottery bearing letters of the Celt-Iberian alphabet found in Tennessee radiocarbon dated to the third century BC, which gives a firm date for the presence of these foreigners in the area. Celt-Iberian inscription baffled Spanish scholars for centuries, yet Barry Fell was able to determine that they were simply Iberian versions of what would later become known as Goidelic Celtic. This was the language of the Celtic people of Ireland and the Scottish Highland, and Zarah, son of Judah, was said to be the father of the Goidelic-speaking people of England, Wales, Scotland, and Ireland. The most unique traits of the people living in Tennessee, Kentucky, and West Virginia, however, were their stone box graves, or cist burials, and their impressive artistic ceramicware. A trail of the stone box graves has been found from the Delaware River west along the Susquehanna to the Ohio River and from there along the Tennessee River to the Mississippi, forming a chain of related people and customs from the Atlantic to the Mississippi. No one who has examined the stone cists has failed to notice their ties to the stone builders of northwestern Europe. In fact, the Irish and Scottish citizens of the area during colonial days felt strongly that they were simply settling lands once settled by their ancient ancestors. In speaking of the stone graves, Dr. Joseph Jones said,

> In looking at the rude, stone coffins of Tennessee, I have again and gain been impressed with the idea that in former ages this ancient race [the builders of America's mysterious earthworks] must have come in contact with Europeans and derived this mode of burial from them.[3]

S. D. Peet notes that the civilization of the stone-grave people of Tennessee and neighboring regions were far different than the wilder tribes to the north of them, both in culture and physical type. The majority of the skulls found in the Tennessee/Cumberland areas to the south of the Ohio River were of the round, or brachycephalic, skull type so typical of the Jewish populations, while those to the north of the Ohio River were doliocephalic, a skull type prominent among all the other Semitic tribes. Peet is also of the opinion that brachycephalic people were much more civilized than the doliocephalic tribes to the north, meaning the northern Indian tribes such as the Algonquins, Iroquois, and Sioux.

The faces depicted on the terra cotta figurines found in the mounds of the stone-grave people led S. D. Peet to say,

> The southern mound builders, whoever they were, seem to belong to a different trace from the ordinary Indians. We would take one face to be the face of a Briton [meaning the Celtic inhabitants of Great Britain], and not a North American Indian, and the question arises whether some of those southern tribes may not yet be traced back to early Briton, or Basque.[4]

The same type of stone graves found in Pennsylvania were also found in southern Illinois at the mouth of the Cumberland River and are consigned to the same people. Not only was the character of the graves the same but also the way they were constructed and the relics found within. Even the form and size of the mound was similar, along with the presence of hut rings in both places. Altars made of cubical piles of stones found in eastern Iowa also resemble those found in Tennessee. It is interesting to note that the famous serpent mounds found in Massachusetts, Kentucky, Ohio, Indiana, Illinois, and Iowa also have counterparts in Scotland, Ireland, and England—all places the Gaels are said to have settled.

Not surprisingly, striking similarities have been discovered between the pronunciation and the meaning of some of the words in both Algonquin and Gaelic/Celtic, which has led some to consider this as evidence of not only ancient trans-Atlantic contact but also that a common rootstock exists between the Irish and Native Americans. The fact that they were both from the house of Israel had not even occurred to them. Moreover, if some of the newcomers to the area carried the bloodline of one of King Zedekiah's daughters living in Iberia or Ireland, the similarities would be even more striking, for the Nephites and Mulekites and King Zedekiah's daughters all initially lived in Jerusalem before it was destroyed and its people scattered.

ZARAH-JUDAH IN SOUTHEASTERN AMERICA AND MEXICO

Unsurprisingly, S. D. Peet also noted some kind of connection between the stone grave people of Tennessee and the ancient pyramid builders of Mexico, meaning the Nahuas. They too appear to have come from the same rootstock of Zarah-Judah—likely through Calcol, who ruled as king in Greece. The Nahuatl language has affinities with Finno-Urgic language spoken in ancient Troy, the Etruscan language spoken by the inhabitants of Italy who arrived from Troy, and the Guanche language spoken on the Canary Islands. But it also shows affinities to the Basque or Euskara language of Iberia, where ancient ties have been found linking some of the ancient Iberians and Irish to the descendants of Calcol, the brother of Dardanus, both of whom spawned lines of Zarah-kings. While Dardanus became the founder and king of Troy, his brother Calcol settled in Greece and founded and ruled as king of Athens. An excavated site in Mycenae just to the southwest of Athens covers a wide tract of land where a palace sits right at the base of Mount Zara. Thus the question has been posed about whether Mycenaean royalty also descended from Judah's son—Zarah—"the son of the scarlet thread."

Historical records reveal that Calcol's descendants migrated out from Greece and set up trading posts all along the Mediterranean Sea, including the large island of Sardinia, and in Iberia, which today is Spain and Portugal, where so many of the Phoenician Danites had ports. The tribes of Dan and Judah were often found together, as they were in Illyria, just north of Greece, where some of the Zarahites from Troy established a kingdom along the Thracian-Illyrian contact zone, with their descendants thereafter known as the Dardani (or Dardnaoi or Daradanians), after Dardanus. When Troy fell around 1200–1100 BC, another group of Trojans arrived in the same area, (led by Helenus, son of Priam, king of Troy) who, after fleeing their beloved Troy in ships, came upon the coast of Epirus to the northwest of Greece where they mingled with the native Illyrians. Thus, a number of Danites and Zarah-Judahites were living and mixing together in the Balkan Peninsula. Both may even have been present at the building of the nearby Bosnian temples of the sun and moon. Could they also have been present at the building of the temples of the sun and the moon in Teotihuacan, whose builders were known as Nahuas in the New World? Considering how far and wide the merged Danites and Zarahites traveled, and how many places they colonized, it would not be at all surprising; there are many affinities between the Illyrians and Dardani living in the Balkans and the Nahuas living in Mexico, including physical type, DNA, and language. The Q haplogroup found among the Nahuas is found in Anatolia, the location of ancient Troy where the Trojans mixed with the descendants of people tied back to Togarmah, the only grandson of Japheth to carry the Q haplogroup. Because the Q haplogroup is found in such a large percentage of Mexico's native populations, Togarmah is now also considered the father of both the Maya and the Nahuas.

THE DIVINE RIGHT OF KINGS

Zarah, the son of the scarlet thread, has a true and unbroken bloodline of Judah who carried the divine right of kings. The term *divine right of kings* stemmed from the former awareness of prophecy about Judah and David, whose descendants were literally given a divine right to rule by God. God covenanted with Abraham and said in two separate places that that "kings shall come out of thee."

> And I will make thee exceeding fruitful, and I will make nations of thee, and kings shall come out of thee. (Genesis 17:6)

> And God said unto him, I am God Almighty: be fruitful and multiply; a nation and a company of nations shall be of thee, and kings shall come out of thy loins. (Genesis 35:11)

A company of nations would certainly describe the far-reaching kingly lines of Zarah-Judah. While Perez (the twin son of Zarah) was to father the Davidic line through which the Savior would come, Dardanus (the son of Zarah) went on to father the kings of the Trojans, Franks, Scandinavians, part of the British Isles, the Atlantic Isles, and Mexico. Meanwhile, his brother Calco went on to father the Milesians, whose ties include the Iberians, Irish, and Scottish kings. Other branches of Calco were likely those that made it into regions all along the Atlantic coast of North America and ultimately into Mexico. Zimri, a third son of Zarah, settled around the Black Sea, and his people became the Scythian/Scots, Saxon, and Serbians Slavs who went into Europe, a people who understood the same and different variants of the Gaelic language with its basic roots in Hebrew.

While the line of Zarah-Judah living in Iberia or Ireland has also been traced to New England and westward through Tennessee to the Mississippi, America's southeastern tribes also appear to carry the blood of that illustrious line. After his own extensive study of such matters, the distinguished French architect M. Viollet-le-Duc concluded,

> The whole continent was peopled with wild tribes of yellow blood

> from Asia via the north-west at a very remote period. About 1000 B.C., the Colhuas, a mixed race of black and white blood appeared from the east and introduced agriculture and a slight degree of civilization. Soon after the Culhuas, the Nahuas appear, a white race coming from the north of Europe via the Mississippi Valley, Florida, and West Indies, in successive migrations.[5]

Their place of origin was still unresolved at that point except to note that their customs and language led to northern Europe, with some of their Zarah-Judah cousins also noted among those who settled in Mississippi Valley and the West Indies. The Nahuas themselves appear to tie back to the Deptford culture of Georgia, which culture showed on the scene around 800–700 BC. Their appearance was marked by elaborate ceremonial complexes, mound burials, a noted political complexity, and agriculture. From north-west Georgia, they spread as far north as North Carolina and as far south as the Gulf States. By 500 BC, the Deptford culture was firmly established in the Florida panhandle, southeast Alabama, and southwest Georgia. Around 200 BC, they evolved into the Swift Creek and Santa Rosa cultures, which continued on until around AD 700, when they evolved into the historic Apalachee and Tocobaga tribes.

Hubert Howe Bancroft summarized the historian Sahagun's (and Acosta's) findings this way:

> The Apalches living east of the Mississippi extended their expeditions and colonies far into Mexico and were proud to show the first conquerors of their country the great highways on which they traveled. Acosta affirms that the Mexicans called these Apalaches Tlatuices, or mountaineers. Sahagun, speaking of them, says "they are Nahoas, and speak the Mexican language."[6]

The Apalachees were part of an expansive trade network that extended from the Gulf Coast to the Great Lakes. Evidence indicates that they were an agricultural people, which enabled them to settle in larger groups, increase their trading for raw materials and finished goods, and specialize in production of artisan goods—all traits that show up among the Mexican Nahuas. They are believed to be the most advanced of the indigenous population of Florida with a relatively dense population and a highly complex society and regional chiefdom.

The reports the early Spanish gave of the inhabitants of Florida said they were a huge people, describing the Apalachee as such gigantic people that the bows they carried were as thick as a man's arm. Such reports explain the existence of giants in the land, no doubt the descending tribes of Japheth's son Gomer, whose tall children spread through much of western Europe, Greece, Ireland, Iberia, and along the Atlantic coast of America from New England to Florida.

Brasseur de Bourbourg suggests the Nahuas first appeared in Mexico in 279 BC, the same date given in the Book of Mormon for the destruction of the more wicked part of the Nephites. Could a civil war have been going on in the land southward that precipitated the movement of some of the Nahuas southward into Mexico? Who can say, for that same date is given for a war that sent many of the Greeks away from their homeland and into the sea, likely on Danite ships, with fresh waves of Zarah kings and Danites perhaps making it into Mexico in the two or three centuries before Christ. But that story will come later.

11

Back *to the* Land *of* Nephi

Before the Nephites merged with the Mulekites in Zarahemla, several kings ruled the land of Nephi with the plates kept by the descending sons of Jacob, including Omni, Amaron, Chemish, Abinadom, and Amaleki. It was Amaleki who first spoke of Mosiah, who led the more righteous Nephites from the land of Nephi across a narrow strip of wilderness growing along Cattaraugus Creek; this wilderness formed the border between the land of Nephi and Zarahemla, where they met and merged with the Mulekites. Although the Nephites left Jerusalem slightly before the Mulekites, the Mulekites occupied upper western New York long before the Nephites joined them sometime around 130 BC. We might remember that the move from the land of Nephi to Zarahemla was initiated by the Lord, who warned King Mosiah to flee out of the land of Nehpi (see Omni 1:12). Thus the more righteous Nephites followed King Mosiah into the wilderness

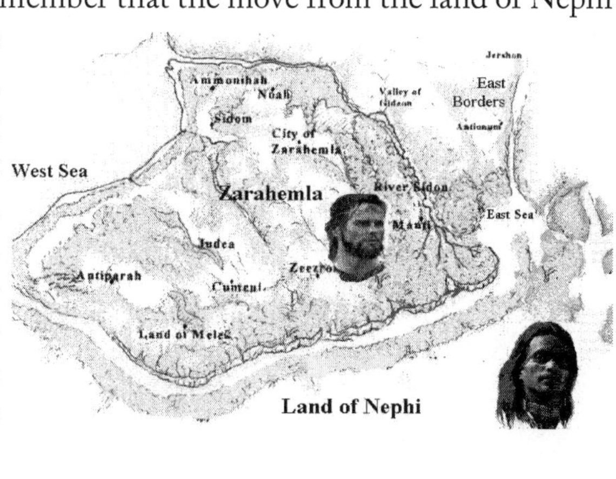

and headed north toward Zarahemla, trusting that the Lord would ultimately lead them to safety, which He did. The merger of the Nephites and Mulekites was a happy one, like brother meeting brother after a long absence. The Mulekites were especially happy to discover that the Nephites had the foresight to bring their records with them, for in their haste to flee the royal palace during the siege of Jerusalem, they neglected to gather up their records. They had lost not only the history and genealogy of their fathers but the teachings of their prophets as well. Over time, they had even lost their language, for without their records to learn and study from, their language had become corrupted. The most tragic thing of all, however, was that without their records they ultimately forgot the God of their ancient Israelite fathers and became a spiritually fallen people. With the addition of the Nephites, the Mulekites' understanding of God was restored, and the blessings of heaven were once again felt in the land.

While the Nephites lived in the land of Nephi for several centuries before they moved north into Zarahemla, the early scribes of the Book of Mormon describe little to nothing of their former homeland. Most of what we know about the land of Nephi comes to us from the records of those who moved back to the land of Nephi to inherit the lands of their fathers, or by way of the missionary excursions of men such as Alma the Elder and the four sons of Mosiah. Other information is gleaned from the topography and geology of the land itself, such as the fact that vineyards thrive in southwestern New York, with the scriptural reference to King Noah being a "wine bibber" (Mosiah 11:15), helping to tie the two sources of information together. In fact, some of the vineyards thriving in the area may well have been planted by wicked King Noah himself, the son of Zeniff. Not long after the Nephites moved north into Zarahemla, Zeniff arrived in the land of Nephi in hopes of rebuilding and settling some of the old cities of their fathers, such as the city of Lehi-Nephi and Shilom, which were spoken of as though they were in close proximity to one another.

THE EMERGENCE OF ALMA

During the days of King Noah, we first learn of Alma, who, after hearing the stirring words of the prophet Abinadi, went about preaching the words of Abinadi to his fellow Nephites, whose numbers had grown considerably since Zeniff's company first arrived. Unfortunately, Zeniff's son and successor, King Noah, was a wicked king who became angry with Abinadi and his prophetic warnings about their sure destruction if they did not repent. In fact, he was so incensed by it all that he had Abinadi put to death and then called for the death of Alma as well. Thus Alma fled the scene and hid himself somewhere in the borders of the land in a place called Mormon, a name given to the region by the king of the Lamanites. Wherever the place of Mormon was, it was apparently not so far away that he could not venture out to teach the Nephites in the privacy of their homes, with those thus converted to the gospel of Christ thereafter following him back to Mormon to be baptized.

Alma 5:3 notes that the land of Mormon was somewhere along the borders of Nephi, which we can take to be the local land of Lehi-Nephi, since the king of the Lamanites did not give Zeniff access to the entire land of Nephi, which the king alone controlled. The modern-day Leolyn Woods are adjacent to a narrow lake along the western borders of Lily Dale, which suggests that the woods may have been the forests of Mormon, and perhaps the waters of Mormon were one of the springs that issued forth in the area from the aquifer below the creek bed. So many small ponds and lakes exist in the region that were fed by the pure spring water that any one of them could have been the waters of Mormon. An especially good candidate would be the beautiful Shumla Falls, or fountain, not more than two and a half miles northwest of Lily Dale. It would have been close enough for Alma and his followers to visit yet far enough away from the spies of King Noah to be safe. The owner of one hidden fall near Shumla claims the stream from which it flows is spring-fed, and thus "pure water," a description found in Mosiah 18:5. Other secret falls along tributary streams in the area might also qualify.

Shumla Falls can't be identified as the waters of Mormon, but it represents the falls that can be found in the area.

> Now, there was in Mormon a fountain of pure water, and Alma resorted thither, there being near the water a thicket of small trees, where he did hide himself in the daytime from the searches of the king. (Mosiah 18:5)

Those subsequently baptized in the waters of Mormon were taught to bear one another's burdens and to meet one day a week, when they could be further instructed in the ways of the Lord. These meetings were apparently held in the forests adjacent the waters of Mormon, perhaps somewhere along Canadaway Creek, another prominent creek which carries its waters from just a few rods of Lily Dale westward down the western slopes of the Allegheny Plataea and out to Lake Erie. Concealed beneath the heavy foliage of the trees in this region are several fine cascades, with others still hidden from the public by landowners who fear tourism will destroy their peaceful settings. So secluded are some of the falls that the earliest pioneers in the area did not know they even existed. Thus it could have been easy for Alma to conceal himself from the spies of King Noah and simple, for those given directions, to make it to the falls and back again by day's end.

THE HILL NORTH OF SHILOM

In the Cassadaga Creek Valley alone, so many possible candidates for so many of the landmarks mentioned in the Book of Mormon exist. Even the hill on which king Noah built a tower to look out over the lands around can be reconciled in this area, for just to the north of Cassadaga Lake, a hill rises to an elevation 1,657 feet above Lake Erie. The modern town of Arkwright is located on the hill, just to the north of the modern village of Cassadaga, which in this setting is the proposed city of Shilom. Canadaway Creek runs across Arkwright from east to west, with Arkwright Falls, a picturesque and secluded waterfall along Canadaway Creek, attracting many a sightseer to its deep gorge and 22-foot waterfall. It is said that no scenery in the country is as picturesque and beautiful as that around Arkwright Falls, which, as it turns out, is a popular place of resort for the people of Cassadaga, and thus no doubt for the children of Nephi living in the area during Book of Mormon days as well.

> And it came to pass that he caused many buildings to be built in the land Shilom; and he caused a great tower to be built on the hill north of the land Shilom, which had been a resort for the children of Nephi at the time they fled out of the land; and thus he did do with the riches which he obtained by the taxation of his people. (Mosiah 11:13)

Another area of Arkwright is high enough to view the land for miles in every direction, and it was perhaps the place King Noah built his second tower. From the history of Arkwright we learn that the Erie Railroad did some grading in Arkwright about 1834–35 and built a stone culvert near the upper end of Walnut Creek Road. The report continues,

> At one time, at a point with an elevation of 2,100 feet, the lights of the City of Buffalo could be seen, until the smoky Lackawanna City hid them from view. At another point on the Arkwright Center Road, Newton Memorial Hospital can be seen perched on the Stockton Hills. In the evening, its lights look like a small town.[1]

How close such a description comes to one written many centuries ago by an ancient people who also once lived in the land. In speaking of King Noah's building projects, we learn,

> And it came to pass that he built a tower near the temple; yea, a very high tower, even so high that he could stand upon the top thereof and overlook the land of Shilom, and also the land of Shemlon, which was possessed by the Lamanites; and he could even look over all the land round about. (Mosiah 11:12)

The Canadaway Wildlife Area along the east branch of Canadaway Creek also seems to factor into the scriptures and Alma's place of Mormon.

> And it came to pass that as many as did believe him did go forth to a place which was called Mormon, having received its name from the king, being in the borders of the land having been infested, by times or at seasons, by wild beasts. (Mosiah 18:4)

THE CITY OF JERUSALEM

The place called Mormon is mentioned again in relation to a Lamanite city called the city of Jerusalem.

> Now when Ammon and his brethren separated themselves in the borders of the land of the Lamanites, behold Aaron took his journey towards the land which was called by the Lamanites, Jerusalem, calling it after the land of their fathers' nativity; *and it was away joining the borders of Mormon* (Alma 21:1; emphasis added).

The reference to Jerusalem being located on the borders of Mormon suggests that the land and city of Jerusalem may have been built along Canadaway Creek, which the archaeologic record shows has always been in the possession of the Iroquois (or Lamanites). The first non-Native American site built along the banks of Canadaway Creek occurred in 1812 and was initially called Canadaway. It later became known as Fredonia. In 3 Nephi, we learn that the city of Jerusalem (possibly in the region of modern day Fredonia) was ultimately destroyed because of wickedness in the terrible destruction that hit the area at the time of the Savior's death.

> Yea, and the city of Onihah and the inhabitants thereof, and the city of Mocum and the inhabitants thereof, and the city of Jerusalem and the inhabitants thereof; *and waters have I caused to come up in the stead thereof*, to hide their wickedness and abominations from before my face, that the blood of the prophets and the saints shall not come up any more unto me against them. (3 Nephi 9:7; emphasis added)

THE DESTRUCTION OF THE CITY OF JERUSALEM

A likely scenario for the reference to the waters coming up "in the stead thereof" may refer to a catastrophic flood similar to an event that took place in western New York in the late night hours of August 9, 2009. Two storm systems intersected over western New York and produced such torrential rains that nearly six inches of rain fell in the area. Such a storm is predicted only every 500 years. Over 240 high-water marks were surveyed by the US Geological Survey in 2009, with the estimated damage to the area estimated to be upwards of 90 million dollars..

The severe weather also produced extensive wind damage across several counties, including a tornado in western Allegheny County. During the evening hours, a second round of severe thunderstorms fell across western New York from southern Ontario that produced damaging winds and near continuous lightning. Over the course of just a couple of hours, some of the highest short-term rainfall totals every recorded hit western New York. A square marked on the map where the greatest destruction took place included Fredonia, which was no doubt devastated by the rising waters of Canadaway Creek. The peak flow occurred in Silver Creek, just to the north of Fredonia, with the flow estimated to be 19,500 cubic feet per second in 2009. With the water rising in each of the small lakes in the area and the land becoming soggy, perhaps the city Jerusalem simply sank down into one of the many small lakes to the west of Lily Dale and drowned all the inhabitants. Floodwaters alone would have destroyed their flimsy wooden structures; if not the flood, then the tempest that was greater than the one recorded in 2009, particularly one accompanied by an earthquake. Moreover, such a terrible storm as recorded in 2009 adds validity to the Book of Mormon's account of a similar tempest in the area at the time of the Savior's death.

THE FLIGHT OF ALMA AND HIS PEOPLE

While King Noah was particularly worried about the invasion of Lamanites, Alma and his people had to constantly be on guard against King Noah. Yet the Lord had no intentions of letting this little band of Christians fall into the hands of wicked King Noah. Being warned of the Lord, Alma and his people (about 450) ultimately departed the land and headed into the wilderness in hopes of finding safer territory.

> Now Alma, having been warned of the Lord that the armies of king Noah would come upon them, and having made it known to his people, therefore they gathered together their flocks, and took of their grain, and departed into the wilderness before the armies of king Noah.
>
> And the Lord did strengthen them, that the people of king Noah could not overtake them to destroy them.
>
> And they fled eight days' journey into the wilderness.
>
> And they came to a land, yea, even a very beautiful and pleasant land, a land of pure water.
>
> And they pitched their tents, and began to till the ground, and began to build buildings; yea, they were industrious, and did labor exceedingly. (Mosiah 23:1–5)

Because the heavily forested highlands further east were somewhat forbidding, Alma and his followers likely opted to stay in the west, in spite of the constant threat of detection by the Lamanites living along the Lake Erie lowlands. This would have been slow traveling, however, for flocks of sheep can only travel about six or seven miles a day. Yet the Lord strengthened his little group who, after eight days, made it to a little spot they thought was safe enough to settle.

With so many ancient lakes already gone from the present scene, it would be impossible to come to a conclusion about where the people of Alma actually came to settle, but a possible candidate would be Canadohta Lake in Pennsylvania, just over the New York State line, 59 miles from Cassadaga, having traveled a little over seven miles a day—fast for those with sheep. Canadohta Lake is considered one of Pennsylvania's best-kept secrets and one of its most beautiful little lakes, known for its clean, clear, pristine spring-fed waters. Unfortunately, the people of Alma were still too close to the Lamanites for comfort, and they ultimately found themselves in bondage to the Lamanites. Bondage was made more difficult because the Lamanites gave the Amulonites control over the little band of converts. This was an unhappy condition for Alma and his people, for the Amulonites were anything but sympathetic to the Christians.

THE SAFE RETURN OF ALMA'S PEOPLE TO ZARAHEMLA

One of the most beloved of all the Book of Mormon stories is surely the story of Alma's conversion and his subsequent success in bringing so many people to an understanding of Christ, notwithstanding the trials they had along the way, including their bondage to the Lamanites. But, true to the mercies of the Lord, the time came for their liberation and safe return to Zarahemla. Once again it was the Lord who saved them. So great was the faith of the people of Alma that the Lord said to them, "Be of good comfort, for on the morrow I will deliver you out of bondage" (Mosiah 24:16). Alma was then instructed to gather his people and their flocks together and be prepared to make their escape at the appointed hour, which came in the morning. The Lord had caused a deep sleep to come upon their taskmasters and the Lamanites, which allowed Alma and his people to depart into the wilderness totally undetected. Backtracking up the Lake Erie lowlands, likely through the forests bordering the slopes of the lower plateau, away from the view of the Lamanites settled along the shores of Lake Erie, they could have made it north to the mouth of Cattaraugus Creek. There the waters were shallow enough to cross into Zarahemla, or east through the wilderness to the head of Cattaraugus Creek, which was also near Buffalo Creek, or the River Sidon, which led directly to the city of Zarahemla. Whichever route they chose, the scriptures tell us that after a twelve-day journey, they made it to Zarahemla: "And after they had been in the wilderness twelve days they arrived in the land of Zarahemla; and king Mosiah did . . . receive them with joy" (Mosiah 24:25).

THE ESCAPE OF KING LIMHI AND HIS PEOPLE

King Noah's successor was King Limhi, whose people also desired to escape their terrible confinement and bondage to the Lamanites, a desire that was finally gratified once Ammon, a descendant of Zarahemla, arrived in the land and helped lay plans for their escape. At a gathering of all the people who were counseling together as to how to deliver themselves from bondage, a man named Gideon came up with the idea of giving the Lamanites a tribute of wine, which caused the Lamanites to become so drunk that the people of Limhi were able to escape.

> And king Limhi caused that his people should gather their flocks together; and he sent the tribute of wine to the Lamanites; and he also sent more wine, as a present unto them; and they did drink freely of the wine which king Limhi did send unto them.
>
> And it came to pass that the people of king Limhi did depart by night into the wilderness with their flocks and their herds, and they went round about the land of Shilom in the wilderness, and bent their course towards the land of Zarahemla, being led by Ammon and his brethren. . . .
>
> And after being many days in the wilderness they arrived in the land of Zarahemla, and joined Mosiah's people, and became his subject. (Mosiah 22:10–13)

Their movements from the back pass and around the land of Shilom suggest that they left from the northwestern corner of modern-day Lily Dale (Lehi-Nephi), moved quietly around the village of Cassadaga (Shilom), and up into the Arkwright hills, driving their flocks ahead of them into the deep forests that covered so much of that region. Moving down the other side would have led them directly to the narrow strip of wilderness that borders Cattaraugus Creek and divided the land of Nephi from the land of Zarahemla. With Lamanite villages all up and down the 68-mile creek, they had to find an isolated place to cross but ultimately also made it safely into Zarahemla, where they joined the people of God.

12

Life in the Land of Zarahemla

The reunion of the people of Alma and those of King Limhi with the Nephites living in Zarahemla must have been heartwarming as they swapped stories and embraced long-lost relatives. The younger generations were just becoming acquainted with their relatives and the Mulekites for the first time. Prayers of thanksgiving were no doubt heard throughout the land in their homes, on hilltops, and in their various places of worship.

The Nephites were just as happy to be in Zarahemla as the Mulekites were to have them, for not only were they among a friendly people but Zarahemla was a beautiful land of gently rolling hills and valleys, where numerous creeks and waterways provided an abundance of fish and waterfowl. While the landscape was generally level, particularly in the north, the central part adjacent the River Sidon, or the Buffalo River, was rolling and hilly. Buffalo River is a well-traveled canoe trial today, although the larger port at the mouth of Buffalo River has become a major shipping port for northeastern Lake Erie. James Sullivan maintains that Buffalo harbor that was once called the mightiest storehouse of grain on earth. In 1850, nearly three and a quarter million bushels of wheat were received from the area, with barley and corn exported in vast amounts as well—grains all noted in the Book of Mormon. Timber

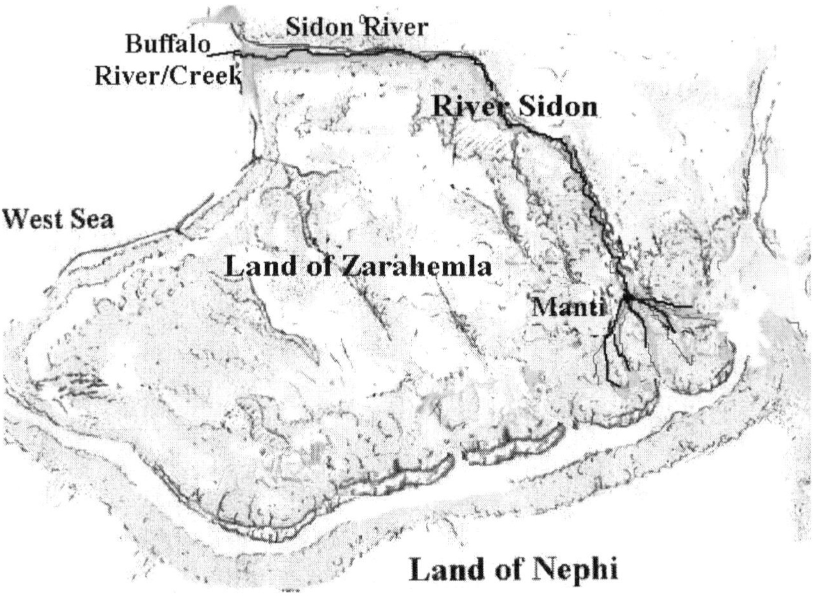

was also an important export item during both colonial days and Nephite times.

> And it came to pass as timber was exceedingly scarce in the land northward, they did send forth much by the way of shipping. (Helaman 3:10)

While western New York has numerous waterways, the Buffalo River matches the Book of Mormon's description of the River Sidon perfectly: both rivers have their heads in the southeast corner of the land and flow northward, an uncommon occurrence.

Remnants of the old forts of the Nephites were found all along the southern course of the Buffalo River or Buffalo Creek. A large site found near East Aurora is about eight hundred feet in circumference with three gateways. Even Little Buffalo Creek, which follows the landscape a little further north, is rich in ancient earthworks. Each of these fortified enclosures, or forts, was built after the manner of the Nephites, with ditches dug around the outside of the fort and the earth taken from the ditch was then cast up against the walls and were then topped with pickets, just as described in Alma 50:1–5.

East Aurora, the proposed site of the city of Zarahemla, shows evidence of being occupied by three different civilizations: (1) the Meadowood phase of the Jaredites, (2) the Point Peninsula (the Nephite/Mulekite populations), and (3) the Iroquois.

Alma was high priest over the Church in Zarahemla, and while the Church flourished under his watchful eye, the time ultimately came when the wicked out-numbered the righteous. To make matters worse, both Alma and Mosiah had sons who went astray until an angel of the Lord brought them to their senses. Alma the Younger ultimately proved his father proud, joined him in the ministry, and took over his position at the head of the Church after he died. The four sons of Mosiah followed a different but just as noble path. Being filled with the Spirit of the Lord after their encounter with the angel, they pled with their father to allow them to go to the land of Nephi as missionaries in hopes of turning the Lamanites toward Christ and perhaps stopping the feuding between their two peoples. Their petition was granted. Off to the land of Nephi the four sons of Mosiah went, with nothing but the assurance that God was at the helm and would lead them to the pure in heart. After separating, each one going his separate way, and each one experiencing much intrigue in the land, they ultimately converted a large number of the Lamanites to the gospel of Jesus Christ and His great plan of happiness.

> Now, these are they who were converted unto the Lord:
>
> The people of the Lamanites who were in the land of Ishmael;
>
> And also of the people of the Lamanites who were in the land of Middoni;
>
> And also of the people of the Lamanites who were in the city of Nephi;
>
> And also of the people of the Lamanites who were in the land of Shilom, and who were in the land of Shemlon, and in the city of Lemuel, and in the city of Shimnilom.
>
> And these are the names of the cities of the Lamanites which were converted unto the Lord; and these are they that laid down the weapons of their rebellion, yea, all their weapons of war; and they were all Lamanites. (Alma 23:8–13)

Once again, people living in the cities of Shilom and Lehi-Nephi were filled with the Spirit of God, but this time it was the

Lamanites who desired to move north into Zarahemla, where the Church of Christ was flourishing. Once they arrived along the borders of Zarahemla, Ammon inquired of the Nephites where he should settle this growing body of converts, and the word came back: give them the land of Jershon.

> And it came to pass that it did cause great joy among them. And they went down into the land of Jershon, and took possession of the land of Jershon; and they were called by the Nephites the people of Ammon; therefore they were distinguished by that name ever after. (Alma 27:26)

The scriptures place Jershon on the east borders of Nephite territory, which in the proposed western New York setting for the Book of Mormon would be the north/south trending waters of Tonawanda Creek. The creek was wider and deeper in ancient times; as late as the 1800s it was referred to as the River Tonawanda. From its headwaters near the head of the River Sidon, or Buffalo Creek, it flows north all the way to modern-day Batavia,

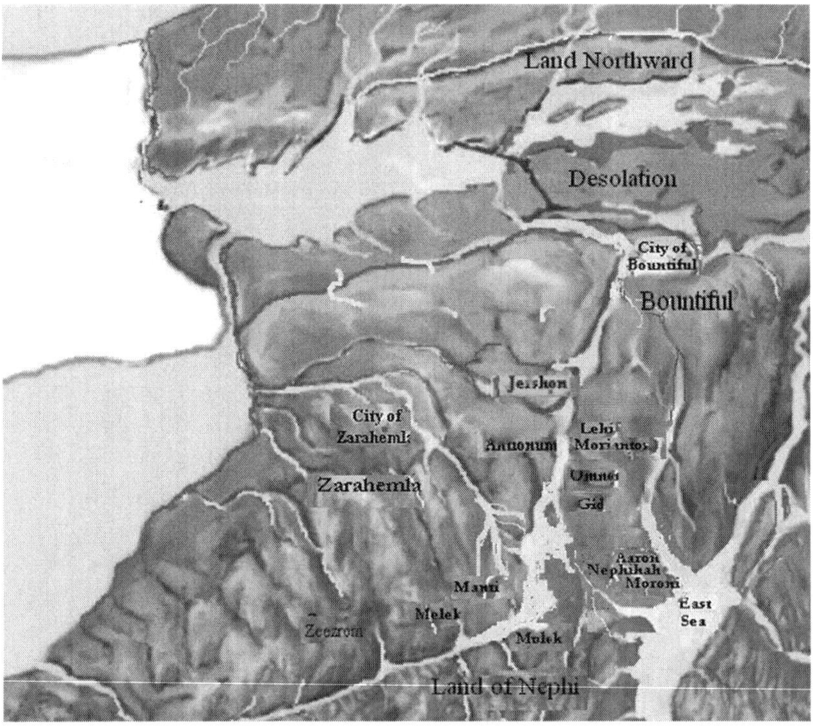

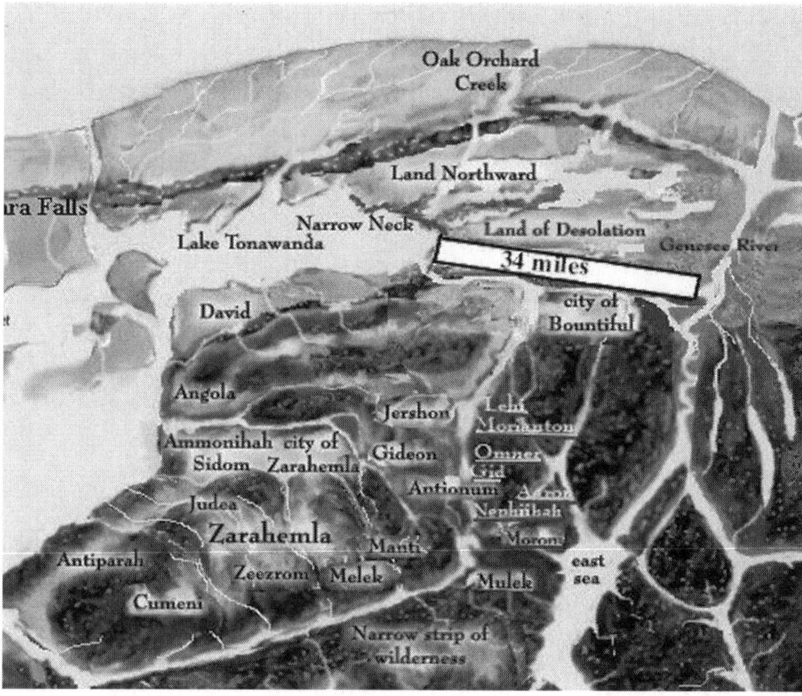

where it abruptly turns west and then north over the Onondaga Escarpment and down its heavily forested slopes and onto the narrow Tonawanda plains between the Onondaga and Niagara Escarpments, which was covered with ancient Lake Tonawanda during Nephite times. The Onondaga Escarpment created a third step up in the landscape from Lake Ontario, thus separating the southern highlands from the lowlands below in what the Nephites referred to as their land northward.

In Alma 22, we learn that Bountiful is the northernmost land in the Nephite's land southward and borders Desolation on the north. The line noted between the two lands may well be the Onondaga Escarpment, which in the New York setting separates the southern highlands from the flat plains below. The distance from the Genesee River bordering Bountiful on the east to the west sea, or Lake Tonawanda's western basin, is a distance of thirty-four miles, or the distance a Nephite could walk in a day and a half. In my earlier work *The Lost Lands of the Book of Mormon*, I proposed the stretch of land from Batavia westward to

Lake Erie, since it too was about thirty-five miles, or a day and a half's journey wide. But a more careful look at the overall picture makes it clear that they were trying to protect access into the land northward across the narrow neck of land that lay just to the north of Batavia, for Lake Tonawanda's western basin barred access into the land northward westward all the way to the Niagara River.

> And it came to pass that the Nephites had inhabited the land Bountiful, even from the east unto the west sea, and thus the Nephites in their wisdom, with their guards and their armies, had hemmed in the Lamanites on the south, that thereby they should have no more possession on the north, that they might not overrun the land northward. (Alma 22: 33)

Bountiful was the northernmost territory in the Nephite's land southward. The lower plains to the north of Bountiful, which take in the Tonawanda Plains northward all the way to Lake Ontario and beyond, was the territory the Nephites referred to as their land northward. The smaller lakes around Lake Ontario were especially appealing, however, for fishing in the deep waters of Ontario was not always easy. The eleven Finger Lakes that border the lake in central New York and Lake Tonawanda, which lay along the Tonawanda plains in northwestern New York, were much more desirable, for the shallow waters around the peripheries of the lakes produced a number of swamps that were teeming

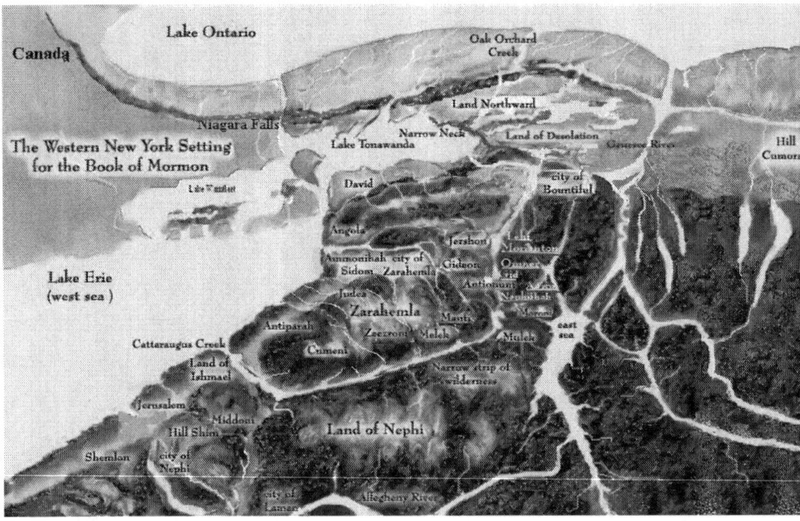

with fish and small wildlife. Thus the lands to the north were beginning to look more and more appealing to the people in Zarahemla, who wanted desperately to be out of the reach of the Lamanites, who held all the lands to the south in their control. Zarahemla included such a diverse group of people by this time that more and more conflicts were rising up among the people. To make matters worse, men came among them, likely from among the Zarahites living in West Virginia or Tennessee, who espoused what came to be known as the order of Nehor, an order similar to the Druidic Order, with one man so popular that the people even wanted to make him king.

> And it came to pass in the commencement of the fifth year of their reign there began to be a contention among the people; for a certain man, being called Amlici, he being a very cunning man, yea, a wise man as to the wisdom of the world, he being after the order of the man that slew Gideon by the sword, who was executed according to the law—
>
> Now this Amlici had, by his cunning, drawn away much people after him; even so much that they began to be very powerful; and they began to endeavor to establish Amlici to be a king over the people.
>
> Now this was alarming to the people of the church, and also to all those who had not been drawn away after the persuasions of Amlici; for they knew that according to their law that such things must be established by the voice of the people.
>
> Therefore, if it were possible that Amlici should gain the voice of the people, he, being a wicked man, would deprive them of their rights and privileges of the church; for it was his intent to destroy the church of God. (Alma 2:1–4)

The events that followed can be found in the book of Alma, a story of warfare between the righteous followers of Christ and the Amlicites, who teamed up with the Lamanites until their numbers were like the sands of the sea, with many Nephites dead when the battles finally ended. As bloody as the battles were, the Amlicites were ultimately defeated, and the Church of God was saved from an unholy end by an unholy people.

Sadly, nothing remained stable in Zarahemla for long. Peace

would fill the land for a time, and then war would break out again, another life-or-death situation filling the hearts of the people with dread. One such episode involved a group of nobles of high birth called king-men who wanted to change the laws of the land and do away with the judges the people put in place after the death of King Mosiah and put a king back on the throne. This was another terrible time in the history of the Nephites, for these king-men wanted to destroy the liberty of the people, a gift of the Almighty to those who lived in this favored land of America in righteousness. Thus war broke out again, which the Nephites once again won, under the capable command of Captain Moroni. But wars did not cease between the Nephites and Lamanites and dissenters among them. Around 55 BC, after the death of Captain Moroni, a company of 5400 men with their wives and children, conceivably well over 20,000 people, left for the lands which were northward, perhaps out of fear that their lives would not be safe anymore without Moroni's expert command.

> And it came to pass that in the thirty and seventh year of the reign of the judges, there was a large company of men, even to the amount of five thousand and four hundred men, with their wives and their children, departed out of the land of Zarahemla into the land which was northward. (Alma 63:4)

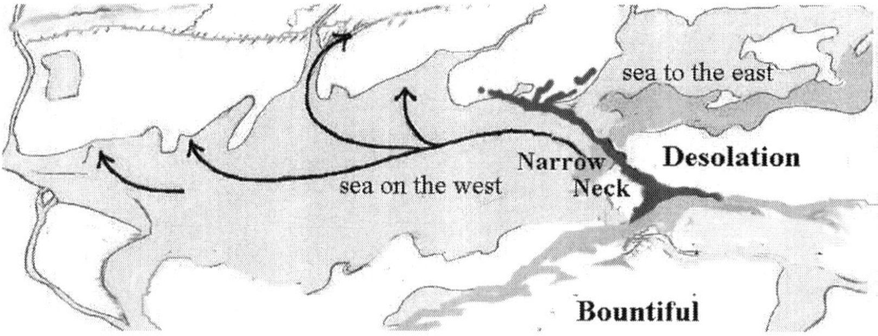

A man named Hagoth is said to have built a large ship to carry both provisions and people into the land northward. With the know-how of the people of Zarahemla among them, many of whom were likely Danites and known for their ship-building skills, a ship of considerable size was built to cross the shallow waters of the old lake and carry people to the other side. The scriptures tell us that Hagoth built his ship on the border of Bountiful, near Desolation, and launched it by the narrow neck into the west sea (the western basin of Lake Tonawanda), heading north across the six-mile-lake, where they would be out of the immediate reach of their enemies (see Alma 63:5).

Once on the other side, the lands around Lake Ontario opened up to them. They likely utilized the portage over the Niagara Escarpment into the lower course of the Niagara River, or Oak Orchard Creek, which carried the discharge from Lake Tonawanda out to Lake Ontario. They also could have used a deep channel that once carried the waters of Lake Tonawanda west to the Mohawk River to carry passengers east into New York's Finger Lakes region and beyond, a channel that was used in our modern day for the creation of the Erie Canal.

During the years of war, Moroni had Teancum fortify the narrow neck, sometimes called a pass or passageway, lest the Lamanites gain control of that "point" and have power to harass the Nephites on every side. The operative word here is *point*, which makes it clear that the narrow neck of land was not too wide to be fortified by a troop of solders straddling the narrow pass, the water barring the way to either side. Thousands upon thousands would have been needed to fortify a larger neck of land.

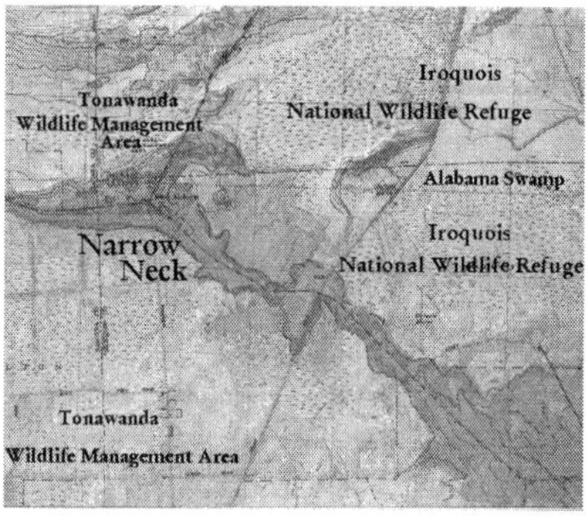

> And he also sent orders unto him [Teancum] that he should fortify the land Bountiful, and secure the narrow pass which led into the land northward, lest the Lamanites should obtain that point and should have power to harass them on every side. (Alma 52:9)

A chain of no less than twenty forts have been found extended from the "Lake Ridge" to the north of Lake Tonawanda, to both the east and west of the narrow neck of land, southward all the way to Buffalo Creek (the River Sidon), a distance of fifty miles. This chain of forts was no doubt used to protect and facilitate trade and people moving back and forth from Zarahemla and Bountiful to the various villages along the north side of the lake. One of the most prominent cities built along the old lake was the city of Desolation, which the scriptures place near the narrow neck. The city of Teancum, a neighbor of the city of Desolation, was also built by the seashore (see Mormon 4:3). The cities of Boaz and Jordan were also built nearby, proving that many of those who moved into the lands northward had no intentions of settling any further than the shores around Lake Tonawanda, where they still had close communication with their families and friends back in Zarahemla. Yet others still sought after lands even farther north.

13

The Land Northward

As tensions continued to rise in Zarahemla, more and more Nephites opted to move north in hopes of finding new lands to settle far from the Lamanites to the south of them and the dissenters in Zarahemla.

> And now it came to pass in the forty and third year of the reign of the judges, there was no contention among the people of Nephi save it were a little pride which was in the church, which did cause some little dissensions among the people, which affairs were settled in the ending of the forty and third year. . . .
>
> And it came to pass in the forty and sixth, yea, there was much contention and many dissensions; in the which there were an exceedingly great many who departed out of the land of Zarahemla, and went forth unto the land northward to inherit the land.
>
> And they did travel to an exceedingly great distance, insomuch that they came to large bodies of water and many rivers. (Helaman 3:1–4)

Some of those who moved north had no intentions of moving any farther north than the shores around Lake Tonawanda, yet others began to migrate east into the land of many waters, where they settled around the northern ends of the eleven Finger Lakes (large bodies of water) in north central New York—a distance of 135 miles, which was an exceedingly great distance for those on foot from their heartland in Zarahemla. The large bodies of water mentioned is a confusing issue, for it seems natural to look to the Great Lakes as the large bodies of water noted in Helaman, a mistake I made at one time. However, with Ripliancum, a lake lying to the north of Cumorah, which the Jaredites described as exceeding in size all the other bodies of water in the area, we can assume the large bodies of water the Nephites mentioned in Helaman 3:1–4 were referring to the elven Finger Lakes and Oneida Lake to the south of Ripliancumin in north-central New York. Lake Ontario is the smallest of the five Great Lakes and therefore could not be described as exceeding in size all others.

Those who continued on from northern New York into Ontario migrated up the Trent River system along the north side of Lake Ontario to Georgian Bay and Lake Huron, and up the Ottawa River, where gold, copper, and silver mines could be found. While silver is found in association with copper around Lake Superior around 2,000 years ago the silver mines form the Cobalt area in northern Ontario were opened up, which is about the very time we hear of the Nephites moving north. It may even have been the Nephites who opened the cobalt silver mines and other ores along the Ottawa River. The Cobalt silver mines near Lake Temiskaming produced 460 million ounces of silver in the last century alone. One vein was so large—containing as much as 10,000 tons of processed silver—that it is considered the largest single find in the world and is referred to as the "silver sidewalk." Some veins had pieces of silver as big as stove lids and cannon balls. A little to the north were gold mines, with gold fever likely bringing still more of their people northward. Ritchie suggests that they located their settlements along various rivers and lakes such as Rice Lake and the Bay of Quinte to facilitate trade such as copper, silver, and perishable goods with the populations to the south of them.

Helaman notes that both the Nephites and Lamanites became exceedingly rich. He said,

> And it came to pass that they became exceedingly rich, both the Lamanites and the Nephites; and they did have an exceeding

> plenty of gold, and of silver, and of all manner of precious metals, both in the land south and in the land north. (Helaman 6:9)

As Helaman's recital of the Nephites northward migration continues, we learn the Nephites settled chiefly in those regions that had not been left desolate by the Jaredites.

> Yea, and even they did spread forth into all parts of the land, into whatever parts it had not been rendered desolate and without timber, because of the many inhabitants who had before inherited the land.
>
> And now no part of the land was desolate, save it were for timber; but because of the greatness of the destruction of the people who had before inhabited the land it was called desolate.
>
> And there being but little timber upon the face of the land, nevertheless the people who went forth became exceedingly expert in the working of cement; therefore they did build houses of cement, in the which they did dwell. (Helaman 3:5–7)

While New York is one of the coutry's leading suppliers of cement, both natural and Portland, a lot of timber would have been required to fuel the kilns needed to create the cement, and the land was already stripped of most of its timber. Why burn more to create cement? How then do we reconcile the construction of the cement houses the Nephites are said to have built? A look at what the word *cement* actually means is a good place to start. *The American Heritage Dictionary* describes cement as simply a building material made by grinding calcined limestone and clay to a fine powder, which can then be mixed with water and poured to set as a solid mass or used as an ingredient in making mortar or concrete. Limestone has been used as the binder in the construction of wattle and daub houses, which have been used by various populations around the world for thousands of years, including the British Isles, Ireland, and Mesoamerica. Wattle and daub houses are small circular, square, or rectangular houses made of a woven, or wattle, frame plastered, or daubed, over with a cement mix of clay, lime, chalk dust, or limestone dust and aggregates such as earth, sand, or crushed stone to give it stability, reinforced with straw or other fibrous material to give it strength. The reason the cement industry flourishes in New York is because of the prevalence of limestone in various areas, including the limestone cliffs of the Onodaga Escarpment that runs all across northern New York from east to west. Thus there is no reason to believe the Nephites could not have build a wattle and daub cement-like house, just like so many other people were doing around the world, for all the materials they needed were at the disposal right there in northern New York.

Wattle and duab (cement) house. cc Herb Rowe.

THE EVOLVING IROQUOIS AND ALGONQUIN TRIBES

The scriptures inform us that some of the people of Ammon, the Lamanites who had been converted by Ammon, also moved north. They too may have wanted to move away from the chaos in Zarahemla. Yet sadly, dissentions rose up in the land northward as well.

> And it came to pass that there were many of the people of Ammon, who were Lamanites by birth, did also go forth into this land.
>
> And now there are many records kept of the proceedings of this people, by many of this people, which are particular and very large, concerning them.
>
> But behold, a hundredth part of the proceedings of this people, yea, the account of the Lamanites and of the Nephites, and their wars, and contentions, and dissensions, and their preaching,

> and their prophecies, and their shipping and their building of ships, and their building of temples, and of synagogues and their sanctuaries, and their righteousness, and their wickedness, and their murders, and their robbings, and their plundering, and all manner of abominations and whoredoms, cannot be contained in this work.
>
> But behold, there are many books and many records of every kind, and they have been kept chiefly by the Nephites.
>
> And they have been handed down from one generation to another by the Nephites, even until they have fallen into transgression and have been murdered, plundered, and hunted, and driven forth, and slain, and scattered upon the face of the earth, and mixed with the Lamanites until they are no more called the Nephites, becoming wicked, and wild, and ferocious, yea, even becoming Lamanites. (Helaman 3:12–16)

When the people of Ammon, called the Anti-Nephi-Lehies, began to mingle with the Nephites after their conversion, their skins became white like the Nephites, for the curse of dark skin that had followed their more wicked brothers was taken from them.

> And it came to pass that they called their names Anti-Nephi-Lehies; and they were called by this name and were no more called Lamanites.
>
> And they began to be a very industrious people; yea, and they were friendly with the Nephites; therefore, they did open a correspondence with them, and the curse of God did no more follow them. (Alma 23:17–18)

The Lamanites who were converted to the Lord prior to his visit among them also became as white as their Nephite brothers—with the curse better defined in the following scripture:

> And it came to pass that those Lamanites who had united with the Nephites were numbered among the Nephites;
>
> And their curse was taken from them, and their skin became white like unto the Nephites;
>
> And their young men and their daughters became exceedingly fair, and they were numbered among the Nephites, and were called Nephites. (3 Nephi 2:14–16)

After moving away from their spiritual heartland in Zarahemla, both the Nephites and Lamanites who moved north lost their religious moorings, fell into the same old ways as their wicked Lamanite brothers, and were thus also classified as Lamanites (see Helaman 3:3–16). All the available evidence now leads to the common belief that the Iroquois evolved right there in New York from the earlier Point Peninsula populations (Nephites), with most living chiefly in the Finger Lakes region of north-central New York—the region the Book of Mormon teaches their Lamanite fathers destroyed their white Nephite brothers around the Hill Cumorah. The Onondaga branch of the Iroquois lived chiefly around Lake Onondaga, with the Cayuga and Seneca branches of the family to their west and the Oneida and Mohawk to their east. Being centrally located, the Onondaga were considered the "Keepers of the Fire." Thus, the Iroquois traditionally met together at Onondaga, just as their tribal chiefs do today.

As the men of Zion's Camp made their way west from Ohio to Missouri, they came across a burial mound in Illinois that contained the skeletal remains of a man. Joseph Smith prayed to learn more this man's remains and was shown in vision that the man was a white Lamanite by the name of Zelph, who was warrior and man of god under the prophet Onondaga, who was known from the Rocky Mountains to the Hill Cumorah, or the eastern sea. With so many of the Onondaga branch of the Iroquois living around Lake Onondaga over the centuries, a small lake just to the east of the of the Hill Cumorah, it is quite possible that both men hailed from this region.

FURTHER POINT PENINSULA MIGRATIONS

Some of the Nephites who moved north continued eastward all the way to New England. The area of distribution of the early point Peninsula culture is large, comprising most or all of southern Ontario eastward to Minnesota, east up the St. Lawrence River Valley to Lake Champlain and onward to Main and New Hampshire into New Brunswick, and south across southern New York and New England. All the available evidence—whether it be

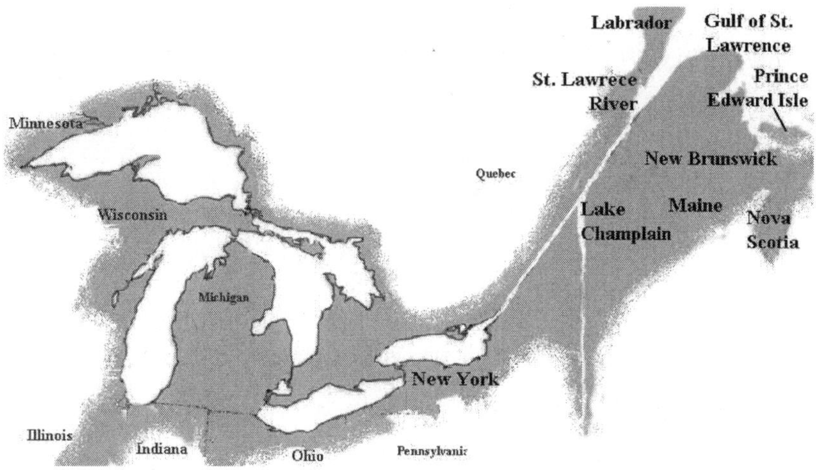

archaeological, linguistic, or genetic—strongly support the original expansion of the Point Peninsula people eastward from the Great Lakes region to the Atlantic coast, with those in the east being simply referred to as the *Anishnabe People*, a name which is thought to mean "first" or "original people." Another interpretation refers to their ideas about being good humans or a good people who are on the right road, or path, given them by their Creator, the Great Spirit.

The tribes who settled in Maine and the Maritime Provinces evolved into the Micmac branch of the Algonquin language family, with those in New Hampshire known as the Abenaki. Those who stayed closer to home (such as the Shawnee, Illini the Kickapoo, Menominee, Miami, Sac, and Fox) settled in Ohio, Indiana, Illinois, Michigan, and across the Mississippi into Iowa, Kansas, Minnesota, Missouri, Nebraska, North Dakota, South Dakota, and Wisconsin. Those in New England ultimately spread southward to the Delaware River and Chesapeake Bay and the coastal regions of Virginia and North Carolina, which they shared with some of their southern Iroquois brothers. Over the course of centuries, others moved back to the lands of their fathers around the great Lakes: the Ojibwa, Ottawa, Potawatomi, and Cree settling in Upper Michigan, Western Ontario, and in Minnesota, Wisconsin, and the Canadian Prairies.

From the *Oxford Companion to Archaeology: Iroquois and Algonquian Cultures*, we read,

> Algonquian tribes were once distributed widely through the central and eastern subarctic parts of Canada and the Great Lakes basin. Their adaptive radiation throughout this area is probably represented by what is referred to by archaeologists as Point Peninsula culture. The spread took place during the first millennium A. D. and was probably made possible by their acquisition of the bow and arrow, perhaps along with other innovations. . . . Eastern Algonquian tribes spread southward along the east coast from New England to as far as North Carolina. . . . At first contact with Europeans, the Massachusetts, Mohegan-Pequots, Mahicans, Delawares, and other fragmentary Eastern Algonquians, such as those known as the Powhatans, were living in villages of domed wigwams and subsisting on mixed economies of hunting, gathering, fishing, and cultivating.[1]

MI'KMAQ HIEROGLYPHIC WRITING

Early forms of communication among the Micmacs living in Maine and the Maritime Provinces included an elaborate system of runners who went from village to village relaying messages about recent or future events, treaties entered into, and even calls to war. Yet they also appear to have preserved the Nephite's ancient hieroglyphic style of writing. It was first recognized in 1610 when catholic monks began to teach the aboriginal tribes of the region about Christianity. It was while teaching them that they became aware that the Micmac wrote in a form of Egyptian hieroglyphics, which led to a considerable amount of controversy over the years. After extensive study of their hieroglyphics, the epigrapher Barry Fell could see a definite connection between the Algonquians and Egyptians. But, not knowing of the story of the Nephites or that they wrote in reformed Egyptian, he could only wonder if maybe Egyptians may have occupied the region at some remote time in history. It is from the scriptures that we learn the manner of writing used by the Nephites and their ties to the language of Egypt:

> Yea, I make a record in the language of my father, which consists

> of the learning of the Jews and the language of the Egyptians. (1 Nephi 1:2)

We learn further from Mormon, one of the last Nephite prophets to keep the sacred books of his people, that their language evolved over time, a language they taught the Mulekites once the two people merged. Both peoples thereafter spoke what apparently came to be known as Algonquin, a step up from the earlier Proto-Algonquin language spoken by the Mulekites living in Zarahemla and lower Ontario when they first arrived—a language the Nephites could no longer understand.

> And now, behold, we have written this record according to our knowledge, in the characters which are called among us the reformed Egyptian, being handed down and altered by us, according to our manner of speech.
>
> And if our plates had been sufficiently large we should have written in Hebrew; but the Hebrew hath been altered by us also; and if we could have written in Hebrew, behold, ye would have had no imperfection in our record.
>
> But the Lord knoweth the things which we have written, and also that none other people knoweth our language; and because that none other people knoweth our language, therefore he hath prepared means for the interpretation thereof. (Mormon 9:32–34)

Scholars have consistently insisted that the Micmac language is not related to ancient Egyptian but is a purely Native America language related to the Ojibway, Lenape, and Cree. Someday, they will recognize that it was a combination of both.

THE KEEPERS OF THE BOOKS AND SCROLLS

The Ojibway branch of the family were the keepers of the books and kept detailed and complex scrolls of events, history, songs, maps, memories, stories, geometry, and mathematics. The scriptures tell us that the records of those who moved north were kept chiefly by the Nephites. We read again,

> And now there are many records kept of the proceedings of this

> people, by many of this people, which are particular and very large, concerning them.
>
> But behold, a hundredth part of the proceedings of this people, . . . cannot be contained in this work.
>
> But behold, there are many books and many records of every kind, and they have been kept chiefly by the Nephites. (Helaman 3:13–15)

In speaking of the many cultural ties between the northeastern Ojibway and the tribes of Israel, William Warren said,

> The more I have become acquainted with their anomalous and difficult to be understood characters—the more insights I have gained into their religious and secret rites and faith, the more strongly has it been impressed on my mind that they bear a close affinity or analogy to the chosen people of God, and they are either descendants of the lost tribes of Israel, or they have had, in some former era, a close contact and intercourse with the Hebrews, imbibing from them their beliefs and customs and the traditions of their patriarchs.[2]

The founding DNA marker haplogroup X, which has been traced from the Middle East westward across Europe following the dispersion of Israel, has now also been discovered in America, where it shows up in frequencies as high as 10–40 percent in several modern Algonquin tribes. Although several related tribes across the country are known to carry the X haplogroup, it is found more frequently in the regions around the Great Lakes than elsewhere in North America.

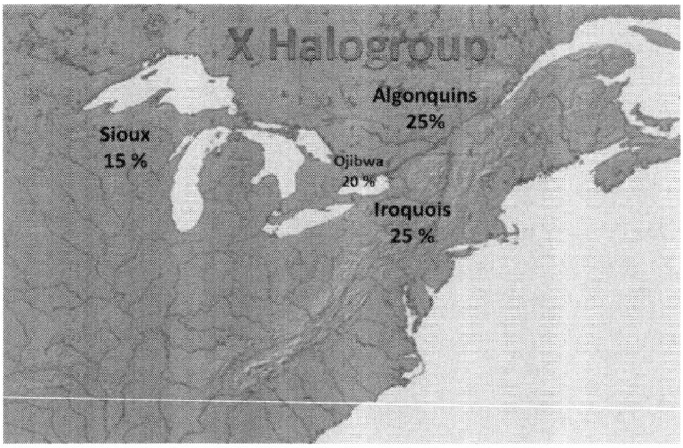

14

The Ohio Hopewell

While a large number of Algonquin speakers moved east to the Atlantic Coast, the Shawnee branch moved south into Ohio, with closely related languages found among the Sac, Fox, and Kickapoo. Shawnee oral traditions claim that they and the Kickapoo living in northern Ohio were once part of the same tribe, but when the Shawnee moved south to southern Ohio they became known as southerners. The word *Shawnee* comes from the Algonquin word *Shawun* (*Shawunogi*) meaning "southern," referring to their original location in the Ohio Valley relative to the other Great Lakes Algonquin.

While the relationship between the New York-based Nephites and the Adena populations in Ohio was minimal and confined to the exchange of a few trade items in the upper Ohio valley, those of their brothers who moved north into lower Ontario—where they became part of the Algonquin language family—appear to have been heavily involved with the Adena. Griffin theorized that the Adena culture developing in the Central Ohio Valley was so attractive to the people to the north that there was an actual movement of some of the people living in the New York area and lower Ontario into the Ohio Valley, where they blended with the Adena to produce what came to be called the Hopewell, after a farm where some of their artifacts were found. Scientists are now coming to believe that the Shawnee had much more to do with the emergence of the Hopewell culture than has hitherto been known, as did other related groups of the Algonquin language family; the hairstyle shown on Hopewell terra cotta figurines, the moccasins shown on male figurines, and the symmetrical designs in their artwork are all typically Algonquin. Olaf Prufer maintains that "Hopewell elements were something added to pre-existing local cultures."[1] Since the Ohio Hopewell are commonly believed to have emerged sometime between 100 and 50 BC, shortly before the time of Christ, we can suppose these changes were part of the catalyst that produced the culture of the emerging Ohio Hopewell.

The earlier Adena culture shows up in the archaeological record around AD 1000. While the origin of the Adena has long been debated, the archaeologist Don Dragoo believes that the Adena developed right there in Ohio from a mix of the people of the Central (Great Lakes) Basin, which we can take to be the merged populations of the Mulekites and Nephites who moved west around the Great Lakes, and the people of the Red Ochre Culture. After moving sideways from their parent colony in Illinois, the Red Ochre people merged with the Glacial Kame (Jaredites) living in Ohio to produce the hybrid race known as the Adena, some of whom would naturally have been of huge statures if they carried the blood of the Jaredites. DNA evidence has now proven Dragoo right, with their culture ultimately spreading into portions of Ohio, Indiana, West Virginia, Kentucky, and parts of Pennsylvania and New York.

The Adena went on to create various artistic works and pottery and carried on the tradition of their Red Ochre relatives of trade with distant regions, which supplied them with a variety of raw materials ranging from copper from the Great Lakes to shells from the Gulf Coast. Concern for their dead was a big issue with the Adena, who began to place burial treasures such as pottery vessels and jewelry made of copper and silver and other precious materials in the mounds alongside their dead. It is no wonder the Shawnee and other Central Algonquins found their culture so attractive that they moved south to join them.

THE MERGER OF THE ADENA AND THE IBERIANS

Evidence acquired over the years indicates that the Adena heartland was concentrated in a circle three hundred miles in diameter with its center in Chillicothe, Ohio. Two main centers existed, one on the Kanawha River in West Virginia and one on the Scioto River in southern Ohio. Minor centers existed in Indiana, northern Kentucky, western Ohio, and northwestern West Virginia, right where we find the huge Adena burial mound called the Grave Creek Mound, which is forty-five feet high with the circumference around the base of three hundred yards. Early excavation disclosed that thousands of human skeletons were interred within, some of huge stature. An engraved tablet found in the mound was totally different than other tablets attributed to the Adena, however, and appears to hold the answers to the identity of those interred within. Several attempts were made to decipher the script, but it wasn't until Barry Fell deciphered it in 1968 that a consensus was reached: it was Punic, written in a form of alphabet used in Spain (part of the Iberian Peninsula) during the first millennium BC. A typical burial mound on the west coast of the Iberian Peninsula is sixty feet high, similar to the Grave Creek mound in West Virginia. A similarly imposing mound is found in New Grange, Ireland. As early as 1892, Dr. Wilson noted that similarly imposing mounds found in Ireland and Britain were allied to the Iberians and that the sun-worshippers and serpent-worshippers of the Ohio River during the Hopewell era were similar to the class who left their symbols in Britain and Western Europe.

These new mound builders made a noticeable impact on the Adena culture, for those who first came to simply trade with the Adena initiated a new form of class distinction among the local populations with their hierarchy thereafter buried in colossal earthen mounds that were much higher and grander than those that housed the dead of the common folk and contained much more exotic grave offerings. Early Adena burials, which were marked by simple mound burials with a small amount of grave offerings, were now suddenly changed to include large mortuary/

ceremonial centers with more elaborate, "special," or elite burials. These elite burials included much more exotic grave goods, including a new type of ceramic and stone tablets with elaborate geometric designs. Even the mortuary traits of the Adena changed. The simple pit grave beneath mounds now gave way to large, elaborate log burial chambers beneath even larger burial chambers, where the bodies of the dead were painted with red ochre and laid in state while certain ceremonies were conducted and grave offerings were presented. The tomb was then covered with a mound of earth. Sometimes, several such burials were added to the first until the chambered mound often reached enormous heights. The archaeologist Don Dragoo noted that the changes in the Adena at this time were marked by sweeping and seemingly abrupt changes that seemed "as profound as the changes from Adena to Hopewell"[2] and suggested the arrival of new people into the land. Dragoo maintains that the expression and elaboration of the old Adena traits in the Robbins Complex in Kentucky, along with the addition of several new traits such as a new brachycephalic skull type, clearly distinguished it from the long-headed Algonquins who had already began to filter into the region from the north.

The Adena appear to have had friendly trade relations with these Iberian merchants early on and established trade routes through the Allegheny Mountains' gaps to the Tennessee River Valley, where trade was transferred back and forth between the two people. The culture of the Tennessee Cumberland area shows affinities to two regions, divided by a mountainous barrier: one in the area of the lower Wabash River across Kentucky into Tennessee and the other corresponding to eastern Tennessee and adjacent portions of Georgia, Florida, and the Carolinas. The burial sites and artistic work in the Tennessee Cumberland area are so different than those exhibited further north that it is now the common opinion that they were built by two separate races, one to the north of the Ohio River and one to the south, particularly along the Cumberland River, which spans portions of both Kentucky and Tennessee. The 688-mile-long Cumberland River drains 18,000 square miles and was once home to several racial stocks, including the Shawnee. Because the Tennessee and

Cumberland Rivers are so long, five or six cultures could live along their shores totally independent of each other with the short-headed, or brachycephalic, people in Kentucky and Tennessee as just one of the cultures.

FORT ANCIENT

Not far from Madisonville, Ohio, just to the north of the Ohio River, is the now famous Fort Ancient, the largest prehistoric hilltop enclosure in the United States. Fort Ancient is a series of earthworks that extend over three and a half miles around a high flat bluff along the Little Miami River in Warren County, Ohio, which is now thought to have been built during Hopewell times, between 100 BC and AD 400. Adjacent the Fort Ancient site, and for a considerable distance up and down the Miami River, evidence has been unearthed of a numerous population. Out of the 1,400 skulls found in Madisonville, Ohio, 1,200 of the skulls were brachycephalic, the same type skull represented just to the south of the Ohio River in Tennessee and Kentucky.

Exploration of their sites revealed that the people of Fort Ancient were widely spread throughout central and southern Ohio and for a considerable distance down the Ohio River and its tributaries into western West Virginia, Indiana, and Kentucky. A similar stone fort was discovered in Tennessee called Old Stone Fort. Their builders were likely the same people, for Roger G. Kennedy followed the route of the fort from its origins on the Scioto River in Ohio, across into Kentucky on its way to the Nashville, Tennessee, and then across the Cumberland River and up into the highlands to the Tennessee River and Georgia. Because much of this territory came to be Shawnee country, some believe the Shawnee were involved in the construction of Fort Ancient, since similarities in material culture, art, mythology, and Shawnee oral history all link them back to Fort Ancient times. But while Fort Ancient was constructed chiefly of fieldstones, the villages of the Shawnee that surrounded the fort were not. Moreover, Moorehead noted that all the graves that were explored in the vicinity of Fort Ancient contained the crania of the brachycephalic type, the same type Professor Putnam and General Thurston found in the graves of Tennessee. After his own careful study of the matter, Moorehead concluded that "these burials cannot be assigned, by any careful investigator, to the Shawnee Indians, either in Ohio, or Tennessee,"[3] for the Shawnee were decidedly doliocephalic. Such facts left researchers wondering whether a hierarchy of some kind ruled the Shawnee from their great hill forts in Ohio and Tennessee.

Hill forts such as Fort Ancient and the Old Stone Fort of Tennessee are imposing structures. They are generally large circular structures between one to forty acres in size and enclosed by a stone wall, or earthen rampart, or both. Some have multiple ramparts and are defended by multiple stone walls. Some hill forts have cairns or stone box graves inside their boundaries, some with a ditch cut out around the cairn. The hill forts were important tribal centers where the chief or king of the area would live with his extended family. Early scholars in the nineteenth century assumed that these enclosures were defensive in nature and most of them have been given names with the word *fort* in them, such as Fort Ancient. However, the ditches in Fort Ancient are located inside the walls rather than outside, as might be expected if it was an actual fort. In addition, there are over sixty gateways in the enclosure that would have provided easy access for any approaching enemy. Thus researchers are now of the opinion that the walls of Fort Ancient were designed for social and ceremonial purposes related to significant astronomical events, for the four circular stone-covered mounds in the northeast corner of the complex apparently function as a calendar, with the gaps in the walls aligned to highlight significant seasonal positions of the rising sun and moon. Old Stone Fort in Tennessee is now also thought to be an astronomical observatory, although evidence shows the forts may have been used for defense sometime later.

TWO ROYAL LINES MERGE

Warren King Moorehead found enough evidence to suggest that the brachycephalic race who encountered the doliocephalic race along the Scioto River and other places in southwest Ohio found them to be friendlier than those in the east (Iroquois) and ultimately absorbed them into their own cultures and tribes. Why not, for they may have been unsuspecting cousins, one line carrying the merged seed of Lehi and Mulek and the other perhaps carrying some of the blood of Mulek's sisters from either Iberia or Ireland. If so, the Hopewell living between 50 BC and AD 350 may prove to be a people of royal blood from the royal house of Judah—both the Perez line of Judah through the Mulekites, and the descendants of his twin brother, Zarah, through the Iberian Celts who arrive on the scene around 200 BC. Adding the Nephites to the mix who migrated west across Ohio, Indiana, and Illinois from their heartland in New York during their long sojourn in the land, a people carrying the royal seed of Joseph who held the birthright in Israel through his two sons, Ephraim and Manasseh, we find all the royals lines of Israel represented among the Hopewell.

MIGRATION INTO ILLINOIS

DNA evidence taken from the skeletal remains found in Hopewell mounds prove that as the regional expression of the Hopewell grew and spread, the Hopewell living in Ohio moved west into Illinois and intermarried with the existing cultures in that region, most of which were already physically and culturally related. Ties between the people in Illinois and those in New York have never been doubted. Dragoo claimed the similarities shared by the people in Illinois and the Point Peninsula people of New York were neither accidental nor the result of trade, but the result of a common physical and cultural heritage.

During the march of Zion's Camp, the Prophet Joseph Smith wrote a letter to his wife Emma, which mentions his delight at walking through the ancient lands of the Nephites. He said,

> We arrived this morning on the banks of the Mississippi . . . we left the eastern part of Ohio. . . . The whole of our journey, in the midst of so large a company of social honest and sincere men, wandering over the pains of the Nephites, recounting occasionaly

> [*sic*] the history of the Book of Mormon, roving over the mounds of that once beloved people of the Lord, picking up their skulls & their bones, as proof of its divine authenticity, and gazing upon a country the fertility, the splendor and goodness so indescribable.[4]

THE CULTURE OF THE SHAWNEE

Once in the south, the Shawnee acquired some of the traits of the Cherokee living in eastern Tennessee, but for the most part they remained typical Algonquin. Like the Ojibway branch of the Central Algonquin language family, the Shawnee divided themselves into twelve clans, each named after some animal, as was seen among the twelve tribes of Israel. They also practiced several seasonal festivals similar to those found in the law of Moses, such as their Green Corn dance and Autumn Corn dance, which celebrated the planting and harvesting of the grains they used in their religious ceremonies. Each subdivision of the Shawnee also maintains a sacred bundle of holy items bestowed upon them by the Master of Life, whose preservation they say is essential to the well-being of their people and the survival of the universe.

While the Shawnee did not engage in magic like the Druids who accompanied the Celts throughout their various regions, they nonetheless welcomed them into their congregations where they were noted among the Shawnee well into more historic times. Not only was their Druidic religion appealing but the Druids dedicated their lives to the protection of the earth and to guarding the Shawnee against evil creatures, and served them as healers and teachers and divine spellcasters. Under their carful tutelage, the Shawnee came to believe they were given the responsibly of maintaining the integrity of the earth by the Master of Life and considered themselves the keepers of its green heart, wandering the land and dutifully tending to their duties.

By the time of European contact, the Shawnee were one of the dominant groups of the old Northwest Purchase area, with village sites scattered as far east as Pennsylvania and as far south as the Carolinas, Kentucky, and Tennessee. In fact, the beautiful Tennessee River was initially called the river of the Shawnee on old maps until about 1770. The Shawnee leader, Tecumseh, brother of the prophet Tenskwatawa, became one of the greatest leaders of all time and had a huge love for his god, his people, and his land. Fallen from their early station in Israel, they were nonetheless God's people, with prophets rising among them and great leaders helping to mold the course of American history.

The great Hopewell Road of the Hopewell leads to their heartland in modern-day Chillicothe, Ohio. About two miles from its destination, the Hopewell Road climbs the side of Sugarloaf Mountain in Ohio's Great Seal State Park. Thousands of people have attended the Sugarloaf Amphitheater, where they watched the outdoor drama called *Tecumseh*, taking in the story of the great Shawnee leader and not realizing they may be strolling on the highway of Tecumseh's prehistoric ancestors, who may even have been among those who built the now famous Hopewell Road.

15

The LAMANITES

THE IROQUOIS PROVIDE the clearest link to the Lamanites. In fact, no other tribe could compare with the Iroquois in either bravery or ferocity. They possessed a high degree of both virtues and vices, which made them an object of mingled admiration and contempt. In bodily strength and physical endurance they were unsurpassed. It is said that Iroquois war parties roamed over half of America, and their name was a terror from the Atlantic to the Mississippi.

The wide distribution of the X haplogroup around the Great Lakes is thought by many to be linked to the New York–based Iroquois. While haplogroup X only showed up in about 4 percent of the remains studied in the northeast, once they studied the traditional lands of the Iroquois (New York), the X haplogroup showed up in nearly 25 percent of the Iroquois, as well as in the remains of their ancient ancestors. While all the evidence points to New York as the ancestral homeland of the Iroquois, various branches also moved south into some of the southeastern states. Linguistic and molecular studies are consistent with a proto-Iroquoian homeland in the Appalachian region, which stretches from the southern tier of New York State southward though what today would be Ohio, Pennsylvania, West Virginia, Maryland, Kentucky, Virginia,

North and South Carolina, Tennessee, Alabama, Mississippi, and Georgia.

While the Lamanites were generally known as warlike men, prone to wickedness and mayhem, many were righteous at times. In fact, sometimes the Lamanites proved to be more righteous than the Nephites. Some were even prophets, such as Samuel, who preached repentance to the Nephites when they had fallen into sin. In spite of the animosity between the Nephites and Lamanites, various Nephite missionaries went on extensive missions into Lamanite territory in hopes not only of converting them to the God of their fathers but also perhaps of stopping the constant feuding between the two people. Many were converted during such missionary excursions. Ammon and his brothers converted whole regions of the Lamanites during their long years of missionary service to them, including those in the lands of Ishmael, Middoni, Shilom, and Shemlon, and in the cities of Nephi, Lemuel, and Shimnilom. Those they converted were so fearful of shedding blood again and losing their souls that they laid down "the weapons of their rebellion, yea, all their weapons of war" (Alma 23:13).

The story of the Lamanite king Lamoni is a perfect example of how a Lamanite gave up his sins and turned back to the ways of the Lord. After spending three days in a spiritually induced, coma-like trance where he was taken to the abode of the Great Spirit and taught many things, he then brought back those teachings to his people (Alma 18–19). Many of his people followed him, yet others did not and fought continually against their more righteous brothers.

In the second half of the eighteenth century, an Iroquois prophet named Handsome Lake had a similar experience. He is said to have visited the upper world during a three-day trance, just like King Lamoni experienced so many years earlier. He was given a set of laws by a personage all agree must have been Jesus, for He showed Handsome Lake the nail prints in his hands. After carefully instructing him in many things, Handsome Lake was told to bring the information back to his people, which he did. This message, which was eventually published as the Code of

Handsome Lake, is still practiced by the Iroquois today and is known as their Long House Religion. Many of the Iroquois have since become Christians.

THE SIOUX

According to the Glossary of Indian Nations, the Siouan language group is believed to be related to the Iroquoian language. Mr. Lewis H. Morgan, who discussed Indian migrations in various interesting papers printed in the *North American Review,* believes "the Iroquois were separated very early on from the main stem which produced the great Dakota [Sioux] family." The French also recognized the Sioux as the same race as the Iroquois and called them *Iroquets*, or "little Iroquois." They both had similar forms of government and dialects, both were doliocephalic physical types, and both carried the X haplogroup in rather large proportions (the Iroquois at 25 percent and the Sioux at 15 percent). The Sioux branch of the family is the largest and most important Indian tribe north of Mexico, with the single exception of the Ojibway branch of the Algonquians. The Ojibway, a mix of both the Mulekites and the Nephites who moved north into Ontario, are scattered across both Canada and the United States. However, the Sioux of chiefly Lamanite stock, the parent stock from which all the Iroquois and Sioux tribes evolved, are virtually all within the United States, having settle an area from western New York southward as far as North Carolina and west up the Mississippi.

Although the more historic Sioux are best known in the western plains, linguistic and other evidence has led to the common belief that they originated in the east. An aged chief of the Osage, a well-known Sioux tribe, revealed to Major Sibley that

> the tradition had been steadily handed down from their ancestors that the Osage had originally emigrated from the east, because the population had become too numerous for their hunting grounds. He described the forks of Allegheny and Monongahela rivers and the falls of the Ohio at Louisville, where he said they had dwelt some time, and where large bands had separated from them and distributed themselves throughout the surrounding country. Those

> who did not remain in the region of the Ohio followed its waters until they reached the mouth, and then ascended to the mouth of the Missouri, where other separations took place, some going northward up the Mississippi, others advancing up the waters of the Missouri.[1]

Such history is consistent with the story of the Lamanites living in the lands of their first inheritance in western Pennsylvania and southwestern New York. Naturally, after a time they would have become so numerous that they would have begun to migrate outward in all directions. Sioux traditions have some of their people moving south and east into the Appalachia regions of Virginia, West Virginia, Kentucky, North and South Carolina, Georgia, Florida, and Louisiana. The Catawba, also known as Issa or Esaw, are considered the most powerful of the southeastern tribes of the Sioux nation. The Catawba live primarily along the borders of North and South Carolina. During the early years of the Restoration, the Catawba were contacted by Mormon missionaries, with the result that numerous tribal members were converted to the Church of Jesus Christ of Latter-day Saints, some of them migrating to Utah and neighboring states to be among the Saints. Even today, LDS church membership is said to remain high among the Catawba tribe.

Other branches of the Sioux moved west across the Mississippi to the Great Plains and then south through Texas and north to the Canadian border, where they are known as the Lakota and Dakota. In total, the Siouan language family encompassed over two million square miles, covering regions in Missouri, Arkansas, Iowa, Illinois, Minnesota, Wisconsin, Nebraska, Kansas, North Dakota, South Dakota, Wyoming, Montana, Idaho, and Colorado. From their mother tongue they devolved over 104 different languages and still speak of themselves as the "people of the parent speech."

THE CHEROKEE

The Cherokee were a powerful detached southern branch of the Iroquois. They are considered the largest and most important tribe in the southeast, although it is generally accepted that their early beginnings were farther north. In the nineteenth century, historians and ethnographers recorded the oral traditions of the Cherokee, who told them that they had migrated south from the Great Lakes region where other Iroquois-squeaking tribes were located. From their initial settlements along the Allegheny River, they came to dominate much of the mountain regions of southwest Virginia, western North and South Carolina, north Georgia, eastern Tennessee, northeast Alabama, and Ohio.

According to the Cherokee Chief Jahtiohi Rogers, MD, the Cherokee see themselves as children of God. The "One God" of the Cherokee is the Creator of all things, including the ability of men to choose their own path, the "white path of peace." According to Cherokee oral traditions, the Cherokee spoke the name of Jesus thousands of years before he appeared in the flesh 2000 years ago. Chief Jahtiohi Rogers claims Cherokee legends say they were visited by a spiritual being who taught principles of how to live in peace with animals and humans and how to have a proper respect for nature.

A young Irishman named James Adair was especially impressed with the Cherokee. Adair noted that they had one God whom they called Yohewah (Jehovah). They claim Yohewah was the head of their state and thus they had no other king. They had an ark— reminiscent of the ark of the covenant—that was carried on the back of a brave as they journeyed. They started their year at the first appearance of the new moon of the vernal equinox, according to the ecclesiastical year as outlined by Moses. Thus they continued with what they could remember of the law of Moses, although the law had been fulfilled with the coming of Christ. Adair maintained that the Cherokee were far more civilized than any of the neighboring tribes.

An impressive relic of the Cherokee was found in Tennessee called the Bat Creek Stone, which was discovered in 1889 in a burial mound where the Bat Creek and Little Tennessee rivers merge. The inscription found on the stone was initially thought to be a form of Cherokee loosely resembling the Cherokee alphabet, invented by a Cherokee named Sequoyah in the early nineteenth century. However, the early date of the inscription completely factors out the alphabet created by Sequoyah. Unfortunately, because so many of the pre-Columbian artifacts have indeed been arbitrarily classed as forgeries, the cry "fraud" went out immediately in regards to the Bat Creek Stone by those who were totally convinced that transatlantic migration did not existed before the time of Columbus. However, over the years, this particular stone and its inscription are constantly being evaluated in favor of their authenticity.

According to Chief Attakullakulla's ceremonial speech to the Cherokee Nation in 1750, the Cherokee were among those driven from the land from time to time, twice to Mexico and once to a Caribbean isle. After the isle was destroyed by violence and natural disasters, they made it back to the land of their fathers, where one group settled in the great Smoky Mountain range of what is now North Carolina, Virginia, West Virginia, and eastern Tennessee. There they officially became known as Cherokee, although a branch that settled in South Carolina, Georgia, and Alabama came to be known as the Tuscarora. A second group settled in New England, where they merged with another exiled Cherokee group to become the Oneida, while still a third group settled in what has become Nova Scotia to become the Naskapi.

CHEROKEE DNA

The Cherokee exhibit similar haplogroup frequency with the Iroquois populations and are considered the southernmost branch of the Iroquois-speaking tribes, all of which carry the X haplogroup with its ties to ancient Israel. The only place on earth where the X haplogroup is found at such an elevated level, other than among their northern Ojibway cousins, is among the Druze in the hills of Galilee in northern Israel and Lebanon. Although the Cherokees' ancestral father Lehi was living in Jerusalem when he left for the New World, he was of the lineage of Joseph, through Manasseh, whose line originated with the ten northern tribes. Further research confirmed that this region was indeed the center of the worldwide diffusion of haplogroup X.

DNA Consultants: Home of the DNA Fingerprint says that the

Cherokee exhibit several haplogroups not generally found among the western tribes of Indians. Testing among participants proved a high degree of interrelatedness and common ancestral lines among the Cherokee and the Israelites. Haplogroup T proved to be the largest lineage, followed by U, X, J, and H, all noted in populations of Egypt, Israel, and the Near East. In fact, the U, X, J, and H haplogroups found among the Cherokee are found in about the same proportion as those found in Egypt, Israel, and the Near East. The haplogroup T found in the Cherokee at 26 percent also approximates the percent found for Egypt, which carries it at 26 percent—one of the only places the T haplogroup attains a major position among the various mitochondrial lines. In Egypt the T haplogroup is three times more than that found in Europe, with the T haplogroup thought to have originated in the Fertile Crescent where so many of the earliest Semitic tribes originated.

Interestingly, the Y-DNA R1b has now been discovered in the same region where the mtDNA haplogroup X2 is found, chiefly around the Great Lakes, in the very regions the Nephites and Mulekites spread out across the land. While R1b is often associated with the Cimmerian children of Japheth, it has also now been tied to the pharaohs of Egypt, including King Tut. Although Israel was held captive in Egypt for 400 years with gene flow no doubt passing between both people to some degree, we might remember that Ephraim and Manasseh (from whom the Nephite civilization evolved) had an Egyptian mother. Joseph, the father of Ephraim and Manasseh, married an Egyptian princess while he was still in Egypt. In light of so much evidence linking the Native American tribes to the Near East, DNA consultants have now concluded that the DNA found among the Cherokee could not have been the result of a post-1492 European gene flow among the Cherokee Nation and other related tribes—one more validation of the story provided in the Book of Mormon, which asserts that these Indian tribes came from Jerusalem with the colony of Lehi at the time Jerusalem was destroyed.

16

The ZARAHITES and DANITES of MEXICO

SEVERAL EXOTIC CEREMONIAL centers whose style construction clearly belonged to the cultures of southeastern America and Mexico appeared in Ohio between 50 BC and AD 150. S. D. Peet maintains that the builders of the platform-mounds of southeastern America "were not wild Indians, like the Shawnees, but were a sedentary people more like the Muskogees, and yet they may have been older or earlier than the Muskogees and of the same stock with the Mayas or the Nahuas of the central province."[1] In fact, Edward V. McMichael claims to have found evidence that the flat-topped mounds found in Crystal River, Florida, were derived from Mexico's Veracruz by diffusion. In speaking of the Crystal River Complex, McMichael said, "It is this writer's position that much of the complex was derived from Mexico and that its occurrence in both the Crystal River and Ohio Valley Hopewell stemmed from this Mexican diffusion."[2] Veracruz was the homeland of the master architects/builders known as the Totonacs, who claim to have built the famous pyramids of the sun and moon in Teotihuacan, notwithstanding their Nahua neighbors also claiming ownership. Perhaps they were both involved, for it is said that they had close kinship bonds and were bilingual.

As to the architecture of the Teotihuacan temples, totally

different than those built in Egypt, they were more like the landscape forms seen in Mesopotamia, Crete, and Greece, where stepped pyramids or ziggurats are common. Early Mesopotamian temples, called ziggurats, were originally built on platforms, but by the second millennium BC, they began to build them even higher on stepped platforms. Each ziggurat was part of a temple complex that included other buildings. Such temples were built by the Sumerians, Babylonians, Elamites, Akkadians, and Assyrians for their local religions, each of which included many gods and goddesses who were identified with the sun and the moon and many other heavenly bodies. Their builders were a highly intelligent people who believed the earth was influenced by the movements of the other heavenly bodies. Using that formula, the priests and priestesses of the Babylonian area built up the theory of a close correspondence between the occurrences on earth and the phenomena in the heavens that closely resembled astrology.

Similar temples were also recently discovered just to the north of Greece in what today is Bosnia, an area once filled with a number of Illyrian and other Indo-European children of Japheth, the oldest son of Noah, with the Illyrians thought to be their builders. In fact, so similar were the Bosnian pyramids to the temples of the sun and the moon at Teotihuacan that were they named the pyramid of the sun and the pyramid of the moon after the pyramids at Teotihuacan. The Bosnian temple complex also had a pyramid of love, a pyramid of the dragon, and a pyramid temple of the earth. A paved entrance plateau was also discovered along with connecting underground tunnels. As to the builders, Professor John Wilkes of the University of London established the Bosnian temples as Illyrian, a people who descended from Japheth's fifth son, Mesheck.

While the early descendants of Mesheck were the original inhabitants of what came to be known as Illyria, it was another race that actually gave Illyria its name; a branch of Israel through the tribe of Dan who came to live all along the west coast of the Balkan Peninsula. The Illyrians occupied a wide swath of land adjacent the Adriatic Sea southward along both sides of the Dinaric Mountains to Macedonia in northern Greece and eastward to

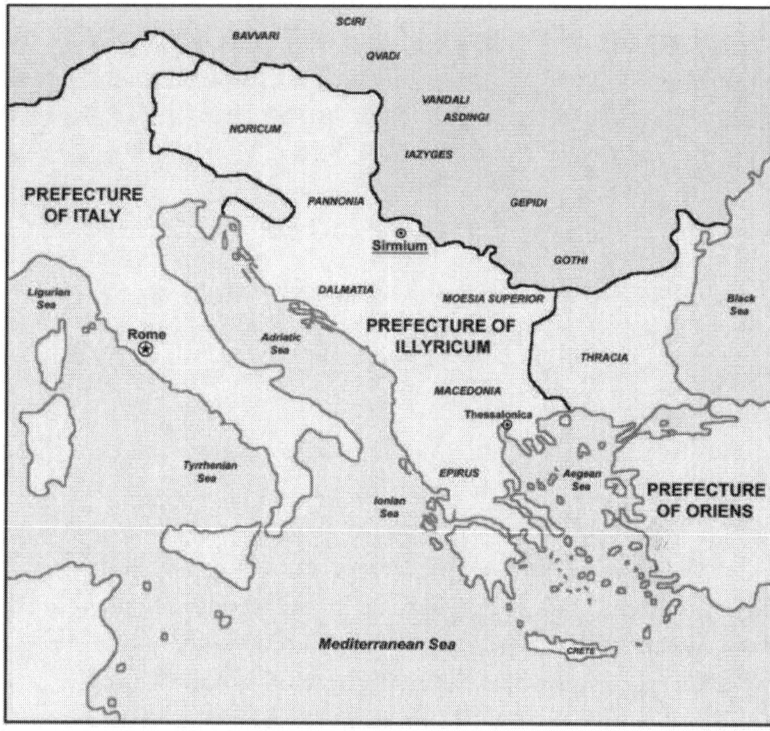

▭ - Prefecture of Illyricum, 318-379 AD

Thrace. The Greek historian Herodotus reveals that the Danites in southern Greece also became the ancestors of the Dorian princes through a certain "Danae, the daughter of Acrisus."[3] In fact, the Danites, under their leader Danaus, took over a number of Greek cities, including the cities of Argos, Pylos, Sparta, Mycenae, and others.

The Phoenician Cadmus, who arrived in Greece with Dardanus, the Zarahite who founded Troy, is said to have remained in Greece and introduced the Greeks to great variety of arts, including the alphabet and the art of writing. The Cadmus figure is prominent in Greek mythology, where we learn that Cadmus and his wife Harmonia were punished for their sins by the Greek god Zeus, who forced them to live out their days as serpents. Their son Illyrius was supposedly empowered by a serpent at his birth, thus establishing serpent worship as their divine symbol of worship, with the symbol of the serpent thereafter often worn on the forehead of Greek men. The priestly caste of the Illyrians was similar to that of the Druids who offered human sacrifice; observed the sky to predict the future; and created calendars, epic poems, and the doctrine of the immortality of the soul. The Danites, we will remember, were the first in Israel to take to idol worship and set up an apostate priesthood of their own from outside the tribe of Levi, who was given that charge by God.

> And the children of Dan set up the graven image: and Jonathan, the son of Gershom, the son of Manasseh, he and his sons were priests to the tribe of the Danites until the day of the captivity of the land (Judges 18:30).

While the Zarah-Judahites are best known in the annals of Tory, the Zarah-Judah line also played an important part in Greece. While Dardanus became the founder and king of Troy, his brother Calcol settled in Greece and founded and ruled as king of Athens. An excavated site in Mycenae, about 56 miles from Greece just to the southwest of Athens, covers a wide tract of land where a palace sits right at the base of Mount Zara. Thus the question has been posed about whether Mycenaean royalty also descended from Judah's son Zarah, the son of the scarlet thread.

The tribes of Dan and Judah were often found together as they were in Illyria. Some of the Zarahites from Troy even established a kingdom along the Thracian-Illyrian contact zone, with their descendants thereafter known as the Dardani (or Dardanoi or Dardanians), after Dardanus. When Troy fell around 1200–1100 BC, another group of Trojans arrived in the area, led by Helenus, son of king Priam of Troy, who after fleeing their beloved Troy in ships, came upon the coast of Epirus to the northwest of Greece, where they mingled with the native Illyrians. Thus a number of Danites and Zarah-Judahites were living and mixing together in the Balkan Peninsula. Both may even have been present at the building of the nearby Bosnian temples of the sun and moon. Could they also have been present at the building of the temples of the sun and the moon in Teotihuacan, built by those known as Nahuas in the New World? Considering how far and wide the merged Danites and Zarahites traveled and how many places they colonized, it would not be at all surprising. This is especially so since there are so many affinities between the Illyrians and Dardani living in the Balkans and the Nahuas in Mexico, including physical type, DNA, and language.

The Nahuas are described as a physically fine race, with a number of the old books describing them as being tall and well-formed with black hair and narrow receding foreheads. The historian Will Durant noted that an Egyptian papyrus mentions certain "Daradenui" as being among the allies of the Hittites. The mixing of the two people may have been what produced the receding forehead in the Nahuas that is found so prominently among the Hittites living in Anatolia. The Q haplogroup found among the Nahuas can also be found in Anatolia, whose people are thought to have been fathered by Togarmah, the only grandson of Japheth to carry the Q haplogroup. Because the Q haplogroup has also been found in a large percentage of Mexico's native populations, Togarmah is now also considered the father of both the Maya and the Nahuas.

As to physical type, the Danites and Zarahites living in the western Balkans may have taken on a Dinaric racial type that evolved among the people living adjacent the Dinaric Mountain range, a mix of both the Armenoid and Nordic races. While Judah carried the brachycephalic skull so prevalent among the Armenians, the Danites have always been classed among the tall, long-headed Nordic race. Yet the physical anthropologist Larry Angel, who measured hundreds of Greek skulls, identified the Dorians as being predominately brachycephalic and having a Dinaroid-Alpine Central trend. Jan Czkanowski noted that the Dinaric type is characterized by light skin, with hair that ranges from black to dark brown to dark blonde. They have a wide range of eye color, tall stature, a brachycephalic skull, long face, a large, narrow, and prominent curved nose, and a slender body, with the back of the head somewhat flattened—all traits noted among the Nahuas.

Along with racial type and DNA, linguistics also assists researchers in tying people together. In an effort to tie the Nahuas of Mexico back to the line of Zarah-Judah, we find that the

Nahuatl language has affinities with Finno-Urgic language spoken in ancient Troy, the Etruscan language spoken by the inhabitants of Italy that arrived from Troy, and the Guanche language spoken on the Canary Islands (which was likely one of the strongholds of Odin's Atlantic Empire, another descendant of Troy). It also shows affinities to the Basque or Euskara language of Iberia. All these nations had one thing in common: ties to the line of Zarah-Judah, the first true Christians of the ancient world, although they all fell in with the pagan tribes around them and began to worship foreign gods.

TYING THE STORY TOGETHER

In tying the ancient Danite/Illyrians and Zarahites of the Balkans to the American story, there must be a reason for a mass migration west. Any number might be given, for people migrate for a variety of reasons. Some move because of drought or some other natural disaster. But others move because of war, like the major war that broke out in Illyria around 400 BC, when 300,000 Celtic warriors moved into Italy and Illyria via two different routes. The political climate in Illyria played right into their hands, for the Illyrians had been busy warring with Greece at the time, which left their western flank open. By 310 BC, the Celts had succeeded in penetrating deep into Illyrian territory and subduing the Dardanoi, some of whom fled south into Macedonia where the young Macedonian king offered their former enemies protection. Attacks continued until neighboring Thrace fell under Celtic rule. In 280 BC, a great army of 85,000 warriors marched on Macedonia in central Greece with a large division aimed at the Macedonians and Illyrians, who suffered heavy losses when hoards of Celts descended upon them, burned their cities, and set up kingdoms of their own, which were now a mix of the Thracians, Illyrians, and Celts.

The Jewish communities of Greece are some of the oldest in Europe and date back to ancient times. After the fall of Israel, some of those from Israel's northern kingdom also came to live in Greece, probably including those of Ephraim. The place names given in Isaiah 66:19, such as Lydia and Tubal, clearly show that some of the northern tribes migrated into Greece and may have been among those the Celtic tribes attacked when they concentrated their efforts on Greece in 279 BC. A coalition of Greek men and even women went against the Celts, but only half returned. Thus, a large number of the royal seed took to sea, including Calcol's Greek descendants (those of the royal blood of the Dardanoi), the Illyrian Danites, and likely some of the Israelites living in the area. They likely traveled on Illyrian ships, for the tall, blonde, blue-eyed Danites were well-known sailors and ship builders and the first to build keeled boats that allowed them sail in deeper waters. Moving west from Greece would have taken them along the Mediterranean Sea to Iberia, then west around the Canary Island to Florida, where some appear to have landed before moving into Mexico.

THEIR ARRIVAL IN MEXICO

The records of the Nahua nation relative to the pre-Toltec period (when the bulk of the Nahuas moved south from the American southeast into Mexico in the fourth or fifth century) is obscure at best. Yet in his work on the primitive races of Mexico, Sahagun notes that the first settlers to arrive in Mexico came in ships by sea, which suggests a major migration. Interestingly, legends say these ships looked like serpents, with Illyrian coins showing that the bows of Illyrian ships were shaped in the form of a serpent's head.

E. H. Thompson describes their arrival along the east Gulf Coast as follows:

> The sides of their vessels shone like the scales of serpent's skins, and to the simple native who saw them approaching they appears to be great serpents coming swiftly toward them. In these crafts were light-skinned beings, and some of the traditions have it that they were tall of stature and blue-eyed. They were clad in strange garments and wore about their foreheads emblems like entwined serpents. The ordinary native who met them at the shore saw the manner of their coming with the symbol of the Sacred Serpent,

> which they worshiped, on their brows, and knew the strangers to be their gods come down from their home in the sun to teach and guide them.[4]

Interestingly, the date given for the Celtic invasion of Greece—279 BC—is the exact date given in an undocumented account by Brasseur de Bourbourg for the arrival of the Nahuas along the Gulf Coast of Mexico.[5] H. H. Bancroft also places them in Mexico in the two or three centuries before Christ. The Abbe Domenech also places the Nahuas on the Gulf of Mexico around 300 BC, adding that they came from out of the region where the sun rises or the east. The introduction of Bernardino De Sahagun's *Extracts Historia De Las Cosas De Nueva Espana* says they came from the direction of Florida, and "came coasting along the coast disembarking in the port of Panuco"[6] where in time they came upon the colony Votan had settled. The empire Votan had carved out for himself was divided into three main kingdoms, one in Yucatan, one possibly in Honduras, and the third extending across Chiapas. Thus he gave the newcomers the coastal regions of southern Mexico in what is referred to as Tamoanchan.

The historian Sahagun found an account of the arrival of the primitive Nahuas on the coast of Panuco in the Mexican state of Veracruz, with Tamoanchan the first home of the Nahua nations. He said,

> Countless years ago the first settlers arrived in New Spain. Coming in ships by sea, they approached a northern port; . . . now corruptly called Pantlan (Pánuco); And from this port they began to follow the coast . . . being guided by a priest carrying their god, with whom he continually took counsel respecting what they ought to do. They came to settle in Tamoanchan, where they remained a long time, and never ceased to have their wise men, or prophets, called *amoxoaque,* which means "men learned in the ancient paintings," who although they came at the same time, did not remain with the rest in Tamoanchan.[7]

Once they settled in Tamoanchan, only four of their prophets remained behind, who then had to decide among themselves how they were going to be governed. With no one else to give them direction, they went about the business of creating the various arts by which they would be governed, including the calendar, judicial astrology, and the art of interpreting dreams. As to their proposed efforts to invent astrology, while a study of the heavens and the revolving seasons were needed in their management of agricultural pursuits, a study of the stars was also often used for more superstitious reasons. Ixtlilxochitl said, "To a certain extent they were necromancers (related to magic or witchcraft), enchanters, sorcerers, astrologers."[8] Yet he added that they were also poets, philosophers, and orators. He noted that they used all the arts, the good as well as the bad.

After a careful study of this company, E. H. Thompson states that "in the passing of time . . . these wise men, the People of the Serpent, separated. . . . Some went north and some went south, each with a band of dark-skinned followers. Those who went north were known among the Chichimecas [who were living in northern Mexico] and even more northerly peoples [who were living about midway up the Mississippi River in a region known as Huehue Tlapalan], the savage tribes among whom they worked and taught and whom they left enlightened, as *Tultecas*—'teachers' or 'builders.'"[9]

H. H. Bancroft maintained that the Nahuatl language was once spoken to the east of the Mississippi. He noted the belief of Sahagun that the descending Apalachee tribes living in Florida around AD 700 spoke the Nahua language, extended their expeditions and colonies far into Mexico, and were proud to show the first conqueror of their country the great highway on which they traveled. The Apalachee were an agricultural people, which allowed them to settle in larger groups, increase their trading for both raw materials and finished goods, and specialize in the production of artisan goods. They are regarded as the most advanced of the indigenous population of Florida with a relatively dense population and a complex, highly stratified society and regional chiefdom. They had an expansive trade network that carried them from the Gulf Coast to the Great Lakes, throughout the Tennessee Cumberland area, and into much of the gold-bearing regions of Georgia.

THE TEMPLES OF THE SUN AND THE MOON AT TEOTIHUACAN

The overall powers of the Nahua living in southern Mexico extended north into the central valley of Mexico and embraced Teotihuacan, where, according to Sahagun's account, the Nahuas built the temples of the sun and the moon, the very same type of temples as those built by the Illyrians back in Bosnia. Sahagun said,

> From Tomoanchan they went to sacrifice at Teotihuacan, where they built two mountains in honor of the sun and the moon, and where they elected their rulers, and buried the lords and princes, ordering that tumuli, still to be seen, to be made over their graves.[10]

Frederick Peterson, in his *Ancient Mexico*, places the construction of Teotihuacan at around 150 BC, which then became the religious center of the Nahuas. Pilgrims came from every direction to consult the oracles, to worship in the temples of the sun and moon, and to place sacrificial offerings on the altars of their deities. The Nahuas refer to Teotihuacan as the birthplace of the gods, referring to their own birth in the land, a people so illustrious that prominent men among them were often worshipped as gods.

The Nahuas believed in a pantheon of gods, 200 in number, the same old gods of ancient Mesopotamia. While the Nahuas still venerated the Great Spirit, Bancroft found evidence in the most ancient and obscure legends that the inhabitants of old Mexico added to the idea of a Supreme Being the worship of the sun and the moon, offering them flowers, fruits, and the first-fruits of their fields, with "the most ancient monuments of the country, such as the pyramids of Teotihuacan, incontestably consecrated to these luminaries."[11]

Bancroft noted that they were close observers of nature. He said,

> Various divinities presided over the phenomena of nature, over the day, the night, the mist, the thunder, the harvest, the mountains, and so on. Souls, the place of the dead, warriors, hunters,

> merchants, fishing, love, drunkenness, medicine, flowers, and many other things had their special gods. A multitude of heroes and of illustrious kings, whose apotheosis had been decreed, also took their place among this vast pantheon where were besides seated two hundred and sixty divinities of inferior rank, to each of whom, nevertheless, one of the days of the year was consecrated. Lastly, every city, every family, every individual, had its or his celestial protector, to whom worship was rendered. The number of the temples corresponded to that of the gods; these temples were found everywhere, in the cities, in the fields, in the woods, along the roads, and all of them had priests charged with their service.[12]

THE QUICHE MAYA

The Quiche Maya are also tied to the early Nahua nation and formed as a separate entity in the Guatemala Mountains many centuries later. Of their most archaic populations little is known, but we learn from the natives that their ancestors came from where the sun rises, or the east. An obscure "manuscript of Don Juan Torres, the grandson of the last king of the Quichés [Maya of Guatemala], which was in the possession of the lieutenant-general appointed by Pedro de Alvarado" also notes that the Quiche Maya are tied to Israel, likely through the Danites among the Zarahites, for the Danites were the first in Israel to take to idol worship. It said,

> The Toltecas themselves descended from the house of Israel, who were released by Moses from the tyranny of Pharaoh, and after crossing the Red Sea, fell into idolatry. To avoid the reproofs of Moses, or from fear of his inflicting upon them some chastisement, they separated from him and his brethren, and under the guidance of Tanub, their chief, passed from one continent to the other, to a place which they called the seven caverns, a part of the kingdom of Mexico, where they founded the celebrated city of Tula.[13]

Israel's tribe of Dan left a serpent's trail wherever they went, for Jacob prophesied that Dan would be a "serpent by the way, an adder by the path" (Genesis 49:17), with the serpent being thereafter the tribal symbol of Dan. Interestingly, while it is commonly accepted that the emblem of Dan is a snake, Aben Ezra, a learned Jewish scholar of the 1600s, said the emblem of Dan was an eagle with a dragon (serpent) in its claw, which was passed down the Danite line to the Aztecs (one of the seven sub-tribes of the Nahuas). The flag of Mexico depicts an eagle with a serpent in its claws, the traditional emblem of Dan.

A high priest who sent an envoy to visit the Spartans of Greece, most of which were Danites, said,

> It is of the greatest interest to read that the seal on the letter from Sparta showed an Eagle holding fast a Serpent. Both these emblems are Israelites—of the tribe of Dan! The Spartans had preserved it for their official transactions.[14]

17

TRADE ROUTES *and* TIES

As THE CENTRAL Algonquins, of chiefly Nephite stock who moved north from Zarahemla into Ontario and became Lamanites, moved south into Ohio among the Adena, they began to utilize the trade routes initially set up by the Adena to expand out in various directions to acquire treasures to barter with one another and to inter their dead—a trait they learned from the Adena. Trade routes ultimately spread farther and farther south, with a particularly large center settlement found in Marksville, Louisiana, where trade and Hopewell ideas likely extended into Mexico. Olaf Prufer maintains that Hopewellian traits found at Santa Rosa-Swift Creek and St. Johns in Florida were clearly imported there directly from the northern centers. As people and cultures spread, those in outlying regions became acquainted with Hopewellian ideas, concepts, and material goods, and those in the north became acquainted with the customs and material goods of those in the south. The sheer volume of trade and extensive connections provided a degree of cosmopolitanism to the Hopewellian traditions that ultimately came to span most of the eastern third of America. The noted archaeologist Don Dragoo said there is no doubt that outside influences, cultures, and customs made their way north and fused with local Hopewell traits to create the full-blown Ohio Hopewell Complex.

INFLUENCE FROM MEXICO

Edward McMichael claims that it was actually the cultural traits from the Crystal River complex in Florida that provided the X-element that ultimately elevated the uninspired Hopewell to Climatic Hopewell. The Climatic Hopewell was distinguished by "elaborate ceremonial centers in Ohio, Indiana, and to a lesser extent, Illinois," and it included "platform mounds," "pottery figurines," and other material items unique to the south.[1] There are striking similarities between the truncated pyramid temple mounds in Ohio and the *Teocallis* of Mexico. The word *Teocalli* is the Nahuatl word for "God-house," a terraced pyramid surmounted by a temple, with some of the most important religious rituals in pre-Columbian Mexico taking place in the temple atop the pyramid, including human sacrifice. High status chiefs or priests lived atop the flat-topped mounds spreading across the south and up into Ohio, with the mound serving the same function as the stone Mayan and Aztec pyramids in Central America and Mexico. The people buried in the Crystal River mounds in Florida were buried with copper tools and other artifacts that arrived from Ohio through the widespread Hopewell trade network, with platform mounds rising in each of the regions they traded with on their way to the Cumberland River and then into Ohio. Because of the importance of trade relations between the north and the south, much of which trade was transported by watercraft along the Mississippi, the pyramid builders of the southeastern states also utilized overland trails that connected the two regions, particularly the gap in the Cumberland Mountains, which led directly into the lucrative trade centers along the Tennessee and Ohio rivers and the adjacent Hopewell centers in Ohio and Illinois. The gap in the Cumberland Mountains thus became a thoroughfare for merchants, with the tokens they left behind indicating that those in the Gulf Coast States frequented this woodland highway often to do business with Ohio Hopewell trade centers. Certain customs that germinated in the south thus ultimately spread north, where traditions such as mounds and flat-topped mounds associated with lodge circles and fortified village sites found their way into Ohio. The platform builders of the south found a large community of tribes among the Hopewell that provided them with the additional hands they needed to build up various ceremonial centers, with the elite among them taking control of the indigenous populations by introducing them to the caste system with its attending ancestral worship. Dragoo believes they then turned the river-bottom settlements into workshops to produce the wealth that went into the mounds of their great chieftains and employed the less cultured populations (of likely Algonquin stock) as cheap labor to build them.

Thus, while the Algonquins made up the bulk of the Hopewell populations, the Zarah-kings of both Tennessee and Florida were once again creating an empire like the others they had created. Each king built upon the basic structure and customs of the indigenous populations with whom they merged and added customs of their own until a culturally superior society of elite priests and kings rose up to rule over the local populations of farmers, workers, artisans, craftsmen, and merchants. It was obvious to Olaf Prufer that all the burials in Hopewell territory were the elite, or *special* people, the *privileged*, whose bereaved survivors could marshal the amount of community labor and the wealth needed to construct colossal mounds.

From an old Indian prophet called Dee-Coo-Dah, we learn a little more about one ceremonial mound center of an elite group whose tribal history was recorded by great circular earthworks. He said,

> You observe in the centre of this group, a large mound with no small mound near it; this once stood in the centre of an ancient city, the home of a great king. . . . This central monument was called the king's tower, and was daily used as a place of look-out. . . . The inner circle memorializes the race of legitimate sovereigns, ancestors of the founder of this metropolis; the second circle memorializes, numerically, the great chiefs that signalized themselves during the reign of those sovereigns; and the outer circles give the number of loyal tribes under the control of the founder of the metropolis at the time of its erection, each tribe constructing its own monument. Thus, you read . . . the rise and progress of a

> great nation under the sovereignty of twelve kings, sustained by sixteen great war-chiefs, commanding forty-four tribes. The four residentials, or large mounds, that surround the inner circles were occupied by dignitaries in power during the primitive occupancy of the metropolis. The north residential was occupied by the king, the south by the commanding war-chiefs, the eastern by the prince entitled to succession, and the western by the holy prophet. [2]

The Indian prophet Dee-Coo-Dah claimed to belong to the Elk Nation, likely of Sioux origins. The Sioux were very much involved with the evolving Hopewell society and remained sun worshipers until the later days when they were finally converted to Christianity.

THE YUCHI

One of the most important intertribal traders in the region was the Yuchi. A number of researchers link the Yuchi to an offshoot branch of Votan's island empire that was destroyed in some terrible natural catastrophe. The Yuchi lived chiefly in Tennessee but had scattered villages from Florida to Illinois and from the Atlantic coast to South Carolina. They called themselves *Tsoyaha*, or "the children of the sun, from far away." Dr. Covey maintains that the Yuchi were a white race who assumed a supervisory role over the Algonquins in the Ohio Hopewell regions, speaking both the Algonquin language among the native populations and their own tongue among themselves. They were particularly close to the Shawnee, whom they bordered in Tennessee. They were a powerful tribe and claim to have been the middlemen in trade between the north and south. Trade relations took the Yuchi throughout the northeast, including along the Ohio River and up and down the Mississippi, where trade routes connected the Gulf States and Mexico to Lake Superior (where the copper industry provided an important element in the earlier Adena confederacy, of which the Yuchi were a part). The powerful position the Yuchi held in what was a very cosmopolitan culture, and their status in a rather sophisticated society of priests, leaders, and traders, made them an important part of the emerging Hopewell society and its ties to sun worship, with each independent region led by a "Great Sun." Three types of nature worship prevailed in the southeast in which the fire, the serpent, and the sun were all seen as divinities. The monuments they built implied a widespread religious system under a powerful priesthood, with their altar-mounds suggesting sacrifice (burned human bones, human sacrifice), all to their supreme lord, the sun god. While there is no region in the southeast United States that did not practice sun worship, it ultimately found its highest development in southern Ohio among groups or clans scattered along the various rivers that were brought together in one grand confederacy.

Far too much evidence proves that the Hopewell tradition did not incorporate just one race or culture but many, with Ohio being the swarming place where a number of tribes and cultures merged to create one of the greatest economic and cultural centers in eastern North America. With the added input of regional artisans and cultures and the powerful influence of an elite cult of priests and powerful rulers who were able to persuade others to agree with them on matters of trade and religion, a highly stratified social-political organization emerged and spread rapidly through Hopewell centers. Under the direction of such powerful leaders, the tentacles of the Hopewell began to stretch out in all directions to accommodate foreign merchants who were bringing wealth and prosperity into the region, as well as needed exotic materials to trade and barter with in outlying networks. Thus Hopewell settlements and trade centers began to rise in southern Illinois and Indiana, western Michigan, Kentucky, West Virginia, Tennessee, Alabama, Mississippi, Iowa, Missouri, Quebec, Louisiana, Arkansas, and Florida. DNA taken from some of the participants in the widespread Hopewell trade network link them to the ancestors of the various Algonquin tribes, particularly the Chippewa/Ojibway and Kickapoo of the Great Lakes region, with genetic ties also found with one or more individuals as diverse and widespread as the Apache, Iowa, Micmac, Pawnee, Pima, Seri, Southwest Sioux, and Yakima.[3]

Unfortunately, during their sojourn in the north, various cult leaders and regional chiefs were able to successfully corrupt the long-headed Hopewell, who also began the unholy practice of worshiping the sun and indulging in human sacrifice. The religious system of the southern mound-builders was much more elaborate than those of the Hopewell, suggesting that they belonged to an entire different race or received their religion from an entirely different source, which of course they did. Thus it is no surprise that little evidence exists to label the people in New York "Hopewell." The Nephite dissenters and Lamanites who moved from Ontario among the Adena and morphed into Hopewell knew they would not be welcomed back into Zarahemla—and if they did come, war would follow. So little evidence of the Hopewell culture exists in New York, except for a short period following the 200 years of peace the region experienced after the death of the Savior, that the archaeologist Don Dragoo could only conclude that the people in New York must not have participated actively the formation of the Ohio Hopewell and its large ceremonial centers. In fact, he felt it sad "that the Point Peninsula populations in New York were never to become active in or to share the full fruits of the Ohio Hopewell Culture which their western cousins were to establish after their intrusion into the Adena area." Of course, he was right, for the Hopewell had all totally corrupted the ways of God and had turned to sun worship. It is no wonder only the record of the Nephites living in the limited regions of Western New York were preserved for those of our day, for they were the only people in the area that continued to revere the Lord.

Baldwin said,

> It has heretofore been stated that remains of this people [the mound builders] exist in Western New York, but a more intelligent and careful examination shows that the works in Western New York are not remains of the Mound-Builders. This is now the opinion of Mr. Squier, formed on personal investigation since the great work of Squier and Davis was published.[4]

Sad as it is to say, the hill country of New York has been ascribed to a military class, not a mound-building class. New York was filled with defensive and military works, not earthen mounds. Over three hundred were found in the state of New York alone.

Nowhere in the scriptures is the erection of prodigious earthen monuments implied. Warfare fills the pages of that sacred work, just as the archaeological record testifies.

Although the Hopewell are now extinct, the ghosts of their dead can still be felt across the land. William F. Romain said,

> They're all dead now. But sometimes in the early morning, when the fog is still hovering there in the valley and the ground is wet with dew, one can almost make out the ancient encampments of the Hopewell there in the shifting, changing mist. Other times it happens at night, when shadows from the fire flicker and dart about like wandering ghosts from some ancient, forgotten burial ground.
>
> Spirits of the Old Ones who lived here? Powerful warriors or medicine men who once knew this land as their home? No—surely such images are tricks of the brain, illusions of the mind's eye. . . .
>
> Still, this is the land of the Hopewell—Native Americans whose powers of mind and spirit reached deep into unexplored realms. Indeed, the Hopewell were a special people, who, to a greater extent than any of the peoples in eastern North America who preceded them, unlocked the secrets of geometry, developed a sophisticated system of measurements, and even came to understand the great cycles of the sun and moon. These were tremendous accomplishments of the mind and spirit that have almost been forgotten, almost lost in the shadows of time. [5]

18

The Great Destruction

The period leading up to the birth of Christ was filled with conflict. Satan did his best to bring the righteous to a point of no return before the prophesied signs destined to accompany the Savior's birth and death came to pass; that time finally came and with it the cleansing of the wicked from the land. The scriptures tell us that the mighty hand of chastisement came down upon the unrepentant in the form of a terrible tempest and an earthquake. It speaks of a storm arriving, the likes of which had never been seen in the land before. In fact, it was accompanied by a tornado-producing tempest with whirlwinds that carried away people who were never heard from again. This was a storm of biblical proportions, with the quaking of the earth so terrible that some cities sank beneath the sea and mountains slid down and covered others. The Clarendon/Linden earthquake fault, running parallel the north-south trending Tonawanda Creek (the Nephites' east border) must have slipped at this time, for the city of Moroni is said to have slid down into the sea, likely Java Lake, a local lake to the east of the creek from which it draws much of its waters.

> And the city of Moroni did sink into the depths of the sea, and the inhabitants thereof were drowned. (3 Nephi 8:9)

The Clarendon/Linden earthquake fault has had many small earthquakes in the past, most not more than 4 or 5 on the Richter scale. But the one that hit near Attica, about midway along its course, registered 5.6 in 1929. This quake had an intensity of 8 on the Modified Mercalli Scale and was one of the largest to rock the western New York area. The earthquake was felt over a 100,000-square-mile area. Combine a local earthquake with that of a larger worldwide quake, and it is no wonder the land southward was devastated. Much of eastern New York has been broken by long fractures in the earth just like in the unstable regions of California and Japan, with faults found in several places in the state. In the last two hundred years, New York has experienced the third highest earthquake activity of all the states east of the Mississippi River. Although most of the earthquakes are not very great, the intensity of such earthquakes are felt over a greater area than might be felt in the western states because the crust and upper mantle of New York is more rigid than it is elsewhere.

A great deal of earthquake activity has also taken place on the US/Canadian border near Messina in northern New York, with the greatest one in recent years occurring in 1944. Even though it registered only a 6 on the Richter scale, it had a maximum intensity level of 8, which is massive. Now, if the epicenter of the earthquake that shook the land at the time of the Savior's death was in that same location, it might help to explain why there was more destruction in the land northward than in the land southward. There are some similarities between earthquakes in California and New York State. However, the crust and upper mantle in New York are older, cooler, and more ridged than California. As a result, an earthquake in New York is felt over a much larger area than one of the same size in Californian.[1]

THE TERRIBLE TEMPEST

Tornado-producing storms from the Midwest have also been known to sweep across the central Great Lakes as far as the east end of Lake Ontario. Some are as impressive as those found in Oklahoma or Kansas, which are capable of great damage.

Hurricanes are best known in the open waters of the Atlantic, yet some move inland as far as the Great Lakes and do terrible damage along the shores bordering the lakes, where major flooding takes place. One newspaper report of such a hurricane and the flooding it caused said, "It was a gigantic flood with smashed houses and uprooted trees bobbing like corks, everything going down the river so fast. Houses crashing into the sides of other houses, people everywhere screaming. And then you couldn't even hear the screams anymore."[2]

Hurricane Hazel, the most famous hurricane in Canadian history, struck southern Ontario on October 15, 1954. Hurricane Hazel was projected to dissipate, but instead it reintensified unexpectedly and pounded the Toronto region with 11.23 inches of rain in just 48 hours. Bridges and streets were washed out and homes and trailers were washed into Lake Ontario. Three hundred million tons of water fell during the Hurricane Hazel, with winds reaching 155 miles per hour in the Caribbean, making it a category 4 hurricane. The death toll from the hurricane was staggering. Four thousand people died in Ontario alone, with 1,868 families left homeless.

In 1996, Hurricane Huron also hit the area. In addition to the eye of the hurricane, as the convective clouds began to form, the eye wall of a tropical cyclone was also formed. Cyclone circulation persisted over the eastern shores of Lake Huron with another center north of Lake Ontario, the perfect description of the whirlwind activity the scriptures say ravaged so much of the Nephites' land northward at the time of the Savior's death (see 3 Nephi 8:12).

The terrible tempest that hit the area was apparently only the precursor to even more terror, for darkness ultimately encompassed the area as well.

> And it came to pass that when the thunderings, and the lightnings, and the storm, and the tempest, and the quakings of the earth did cease—for behold, they did last for about the space of three hours; and it was said by some that the time was greater; nevertheless, all these great and terrible things were done in about

> the space of three hoursand then behold, there was darkness upon the face of the land. (3 Nephi 8:19)

The Nephites could hardly see their hands before their faces. They could not even light a candle, so thick was the vapor of darkness that blanketed the land for the next three days, blotting out the sun and the moon and the stars. There was apparently more going on in Nephite territory than just a storm, for fire reportedly destroyed a number of Gadianton cities because of their wickedness. While lightning may have caused much of the destruction in Zarahemla, one of the Gadianton leaders called Jacob built up his kingdom in the north, where another type of fire may have destroyed his cities.

> Therefore, Jacob . . . commanded his people that they should take their flight into the northernmost part of the land, and there build up unto themselves a kingdom. (3 Nephi 7:12)

The northernmost territory occupied by the Nephites was along the St. Lawrence River as far as Maine and New Hampshire—where some of the early Celts are also said to have lived—with New Hampshire perhaps one of the original strongholds of the Gadiantons.

> And behold, that great city Jacobugath, which was inhabited by the people of king Jacob, have I caused to be burned with fire because of their sins and their wickedness, which was above all the wickedness of the whole earth, because of their secret murders and combinations; for it was they that did destroy the peace of my people and the government of the land; therefore I did cause them to be burned, to destroy them from before my face, that the blood of the prophets and the saints should not come up unto me any more against them. (3 Nephi 9:9)

Considering the three days of darkness the Nephites speak of, we might wonder if an undocumented volcanic episode took place in the area, for regions along the St. Lawrence River in Quebec and parts of New Hampshire have nearly every type volcano found on earth. In fact, at one time the volcano in New Hampshire, called the Ossippee Mountain Ring Dike Complex today, was once as high as 10,000 feet and looked something like Mt. Vesuvius or Mt. Fuji. Three major eruptions changed the volcano into the famous Ossipee ring dike seen today.

Most of the volcanic activity that impacts the United States comes from Alaska along the Pacific Coast and from Iceland. Forty-six active and extinct volcanoes have been documented on Iceland, with the Hekla volcano considered the most active in the world. Yet underwater volcanoes located in the Atlantic Ocean have also impacted the area. In a US geological survey for the National Oceanic and Atmospheric Administration, Dan Scheirer claims that if we were to drain the ocean's basins, we would see tens of thousands of underwater volcanoes called "seamounts" or sea mountains.[3] As isolated plumes of hot material rise from the mantle below the tectonic plate, it forms magma that may erupt at the surface in volcanoes, known as hotspots.

The Monteregian Hills, a series of volcanic buttes on both sides of the St. Lawrence River between Quebec and New York, are the remnants of eight extinct volcanoes that stretch across the St. Lawrence River to the Appalachian highlands. They are the eroded remnants of the oldest volcanoes in the New England hotspot track that extends into the Atlantic, where thousands of underwater volcanoes extend along the ocean floor clear to Africa. The Monteregian Hills are part of the Great Meteor hotspot track, formed as a result of the North American Plate sliding westward over the long-lived New England hotspot that has been interpreted as the feeder intrusion of long-extinct volcanoes. While these volcanoes' last eruptions are thought to have been thousands of years ago, clay deposits containing volcanic ash found all across most of central New York prove volcanic activity reached into Nephite territory, with one or another of the volcanoes in the area (or those further up the St. Lawrence River) perhaps erupting at the time of the Savior's death.

Still further north we come to the Black River System, where we find not just a volcano but a super volcano similar to the one found in Yellowstone, which spans a huge area along the borders of Quebec and Ontario. Within that huge complex are a cluster of calderas, one of which is similar in size to Lake Toba in

Indonesia. Still another caldera exists along the Ottawa River at Lake Timiskaming, which interestingly produced diamonds.

While all the volcanoes in the area have been extinct for untold ages, scientists are now discovering that some of the volcanic rocks in the area are younger than they previously supposed and now believe an earthquake may have allowed some of the magma to surface through faults weakened by a quake in more recent times. Could such a thing have happened during the terrible earthquake that shook Nephite territory at the time of the Savior's death?

While most of the volcanic activity noted in the region is thought to have taken place in the far distant past, the traditions of the Indians tell a different story, as does an eyewitness to an eruption somewhere along the St. Lawrence River in the late 1800s. The traditions of the Indians speak of a "fire mountain" in Quebec that was active until at least a few centuries ago. White settlers living in the region also carried such tales. Stories circulated about possible eruptions in New Hampshire as well. While most accounts referred to rather insignificant eruptions accompanied by nothing more than great booming noises, earthquakes, and a small amount of ash and lava flow, reports by settlers living along the St. Lawrence River spoke of earthquakes followed by periods of (1) profound darkness, (2) violent gusts of winds, (3) rain, and (4) lightning—the same phenomena mentioned in the scriptures.

A report noted in *The Historical Magazine* spoke of a strange period of "dark days" and "extensive earthquake" activity in lower Canada. The *Quebec Gazette* of October 20th, 1785, covered the event when it happened, along with the minutely detailed report of Chief Justice Sewell, who was president of the Library and Historical Society of Quebec at that time. A short period of darkness was experienced the day before around four o'clock in the afternoon, with a luminous glow noted in the sky to the northeast, turning to yellow along the horizon. On the 15th, the same phenomenon took place, but a little earlier in the day, and just as it had on the 9th, it was accompanied by violent gusts of wind, lightning, thunder, and rain. The next morning was perfectly calm, except for a thick fog that covered the area (a thick vapor of darkness?).

By nine o'clock a light wind from the northeast entirely dissipated the fog, which was soon replaced with black clouds that came in so rapidly from the northeast that by ten thirty ordinary print could not be read. "'The darkness lasted for about ten minutes. At twelve, a second period of obscurity took place; then a third, and a fourth, and fifth, at intervals: at half-past four [in the afternoon] it was as dark as midnight.'"[4]

John Shea, editor of *The Historical Magazine*, 1864, suggests the dark days reported in Canada may have simply been the result of a great conflagration that swept rapidly across the land from Hudson Bay to the St. Lawrence River, feeding principally upon dry caribou moss, which burns rapidly and emits dense volumes of smoke. Chief Sewell disagreed and suggested Canada's dark days were the result of volcanic eruption rather than an extensive conflagration, saying, "It seems impossible to suppose that the conflagration of a forest could have produced a mass of smoke so dense and so extensive as to overspread, as it did in October 1785, the surface of a territory exceeding certainly 300 miles in length and probably 200 miles in breadth, and producing at its utmost longitudinal extremity, and at mid-day the obscurity of the darkest night."[5]

One man appears to have been an eye witness to such an eruption that was later included in an obscure article found in *The Historical Magazine, Notes and Queries Concerning the Antiquities, History and Biography of America*, vol. VIII. The editor, John Gilmary Shea, reported the record of Messr. Gognon, who detailed his firsthand account of seeing a volcanic eruption in the rear of St. Paul's Bay, situated on the north shore of the St. Lawrence River halfway between Quebec and the Saguenay River on Tuesday, December 6, 1791.[6] Although his report is too long to include here, in short, he said,

> Tuesday, December 6, 1791 at St. Paul's Bay, and at neighboring places, at about a quarter after seven, a severe earthquake was felt; the whole night was disturbed by small ones, repeated at intervals, and by a sudden shaking running toward the east. The shocks were felt for forty-one days, from two (shocks) to five a day. . . .
>
> Two mountains near my dwelling, at some 401 northwest

> have a valley between them, so that you may see beyond them. It is by this valley or passage, that I saw a continual eruption, mixed with smoke and flame which appeared very plain on the horizon, and at other times struggling among themselves as if too oppressed in their issue. . . Finally, on the night of the 26th and 27th, a most beautiful spectacle was produced. The whole atmosphere was in flames and agitated, one's face suffered from the heat. The eruption continued the whole night with flames. [7]

Whatever caused the destruction at the time of the Savior's death, whether it be a meteorite strike, a volcanic eruption, or some other phenomena of nature, the earthquake, whirlwinds, tempest, and dense vapor of darkness produced a scene of indescribable terror for those involved. Death and destruction were everywhere; friends, neighbors, and relatives were taken home to God to await an awful judgment, and the land was torn up from one end to the other. And if anything could top that, the voice of the Savior spoke to them from out of heaven as one man speaks to another, not in a dream, nor vision, but an audible voice. How were they to absorb it all? The Lord said,

> Wo, wo, wo unto this people; wo unto the inhabitants of the whole earth except they shall repent; for the devil laugheth, and his angels rejoice, because of the slain of the fair sons and daughters of my people; and it is because of their iniquity and abominations that they are fallen! (3 Nephi 9:2)

The words of Dickens—"It was the best of times, it was the worst of times"—come to mind at this point, for even after such terrible destruction, which was surely the worst experience of their lives, the best experience any of them could ever even have imagined would shortly come to pass, a visit from the Savior. The Book of Mormon provides us with the most amazing documented account yet known to man of the Savior's visit to any group of people after his death and resurrection. The Savior's appearance to his faithful flock near the temple in Bountiful was so glorious that words alone cannot express the grandeur of that occasion, for it was the Lord God Omnipotent Himself who introduced His Son Jesus Christ. His voice was so soft the crowds barely heard it the first time around or the second, but once God had their full attention, He introduced his beloved Son, saying,

> Behold my Beloved Son, in whom I am well pleased, in whom I have glorified my name—hear ye him. (3 Nephi 11:7)

19

The Golden Age *of* Christ

After the great destruction of the wicked, the voice of the Lord was heard "upon all the face of this land," chastising them for their wicked behavior and explaining why so many of the people were destroyed (3 Nephi 9:1). Silence followed "for the space of many hours," during which time the Nephites had ample time to ponder those sobering words (3 Nephi 10:1). Later, another voice was heard, a voice so soft the crowds could barely hear it. Then it came again, a little louder this time, but still not fully understandable. Then, when the great Father of us all had their full attention, He introduced His Beloved Son, Jesus, saying,

> Behold my Beloved Son, in whom I am well pleased, in whom I have glorified my name—hear ye him. (3 Nephi 11:7)

After hearing the Father announce His Son, the stunned crowd watched as the Savior slowly descended and stood in their midst and said, "Behold, I am Jesus Christ, whom the prophets testified shall come into the world" (3 Nephi 11:10). The name of Jesus Christ is the very name we covenant to remember in the sacrament prayer, a name that has been an integral part of His identity from the beginning of time and will continue to be throughout the eternities. But of equal importance, it is by His name and none other that salvation comes to the children of man (see Mosiah 3:17).

> Behold, I am Jesus Christ, whom the prophets testified shall come into the world.
>
> And behold, I am the light and the life of the world; and I have drunk out of that bitter cup which the Father hath given me, and have glorified the Father in taking upon me the sins of the world, in the which I have suffered the will of the Father in all things from the beginning. (3 Nephi 11:10–11)

A similar manifestation took place in Palmyra, New York, many centuries later, not more than 80 miles from ancient Bountiful, when the Father presented His Son to young Joseph Smith and told him about the sacred records of the ancient Nephites. From that sacred record we learn that after descending upon that ancient scene, Jesus walked among the Nephites, blessed their children, healed the people, and organized His Church among them. His prayers were so wondrous they could not be written. Fire encircled their little ones as angels ministered to them, and numerous others were blessed and healed. The Savior even provided the name whereby His church should be known—His name, for it is His church and thus should be named after Him and no one else. He gave them instructions on daily living almost the exact same as the Beatitudes and commanded them to be baptized in His name—all save little children, who were exempt from that ordinance until the age of accountability, they being innocent and thus naturally saved by virtue of His Atonement. He predicted the future and told of the rise of a free people in the land of promise and of the coming forth of the Book of Mormon. He foretold the rise of the New Jerusalem, the gathering of Israel, and the return of the tribes who have been lost. He told of the last days when nations would be in distress, the righteous would gather to Zion, and He would return to save the righteous and to burn the wicked. In fact, He expounded all things from the beginning to the end, things that could not be written. The Savior's appearance to his faithful flock in Bountiful was one of the most wondrous events to take place in world history (see 3 Nephi 11–18).

During the Savior's visit He ordained twelve disciples and commanded them to spread the glad news of the gospel and to cry repentance, for the children of Lehi and Mulek, and even those of Zarah-Judah, were His people—the children of Abraham, Isaac, and Jacob—and it was time to reclaim them and bring them back into the fold. The twelve disciples had their hands and hearts full. In fact, they were full to overflowing with love for their Savior and an overwhelming desire to tell the world about the Lord's great plan of happiness and to encourage them to repent and to be baptized. Even the locals who had not been present at the temple site in Bountiful heard of the Savior's visit from others and were caught up in the excitement of it all, adding their voices to those who were spreading the happy news of that sacred occasion throughout the land. We can even imagine throngs of people heading for the temple in hopes of absorbing some of the Spirit that might have lingered in the area after the Savior departed. Oh, the joy that must have been felt in the land as runners went from city to city and village to village to tell the people of the Savior's wondrous visitation and the profound gospel doctrines He imparted to them for their benefit and salvation.

As the missionary effort of the Lord's disciples moved across the land, teaching and preaching of Christ, many of the Zarahites were also no doubt converted, as were the Druid priests who made some of the greatest missionaries of the early Christian world. "When the Druids adopted and preached Christianity, their universities were turned into Christian colleges and the Druid Priests became Christian ministers; the transition was to them a natural one."[1] An old Indian prophet spoke of a prophet's residence that may well have been a Druidic center not far from one of the large platform mounds at Chillicothe, Ohio. He called it the Holy City, the Celestial City, and the Royal Union City. The old Indian explained that it was a prophet's metropolis, "a holy seminary of priests or prophets that included holy circles, festival square, secluded walks, private avenues, funeral-pynes, and five residential circles that were the permanent abode of the senior fathers who were appointed by the people to important instruction to the junior prophets."[2] Who these priests and prophets were is unknown, but the entire complex with its circles and squares sounds very much like a Druidic ceremonial center—perhaps from their place of origin in West Virginia, having arrived with the Iberians Celts. Numerous writers have commented on the similarities between Christianity and Druidism, with this group likely also converted to the worship of Christ. Unfortunately, Christianized Druids often mingled their faith with a large element of the original Druidic cults, thus tainting the pure religion of Christ. Newly Christianized Druids turned their universities into Christian colleges, and their Druid priests became Christian ministers and openly preached of Christ. The culture-hero Quetzalcoatl of Mexican fame, who may himself have been a Christianized Druid, is said to have arrived in Mexico from someplace to the north—perhaps the Celestial City.

With religious fervor spreading through the land, Christian converts from all walks of life and from all the various cultures and tribes in the land likely numbered in the tens of thousands. Yet sadly, the traditions carried along by many of the descendants show their old ancestral religions were never entirely forgotten. The Creek, for instance, who are thought to be the descendants of the mound builders of the southeast, say that at some unknown period in time (likely the time of Christ), their polytheistic religion was changed to a monotheistic religion. This new religion included a single invisible omnipotent Creator, a heavenly place for the righteous and a hell for evildoers, but lurking beneath the their new monotheistic religion were traces of their old religion with its many gods, with the sun god and moon god at its top. But for a time Christ reigned as the supreme God of the land, and Christian churches began to dot the landscape—fragile churches built of wood that ultimately succumbed to the ravages of time. McMichael believed the long-headed Hopewell never fully accepted the idea of using a platform mound as part of their temple structure. The reason why is explained in the Book of Mormon, which tells us that the Nephites built their temples after the manner of Solomon's (2 Nephi 5:16). Their churches were not built atop "high places" such as those found in Canaan but on places set apart here and there across the land in the midst of their towns and villages.

> And it came to pass that the thirty and fourth year passed away, and also the thirty and fifth, and behold the disciples of Jesus had formed a church of Christ in all the lands round about. And as many as did come unto them, and did truly repent of their sins, were baptized in the name of Jesus; and they did also receive the Holy Ghost. (4 Nephi 1:1)

THE CONVERSION OF THE LAMANITES

The scriptures say that over the course of the two or three years following the Savior's visit to the region, all the various branches of the Nephites and Lamanites—which we can take to include the Hopewell—were converted to the Church of Jesus Christ. While the Zarahites had been separated from the ancient prophets of Israel for centuries and thus from the teachings of Jehovah, the Nephites had always been taught of Christ. In fact, the Nephites had been looking forward to His arrival among men for quite some time. Even the Lamanites, who had all gone astray, knew who the God of their ancient fathers was and thus were pulled up short when they heard about the Savior's visit and what had happened to the more wicked among them.

> And it came to pass in the thirty and sixth year, the people were all converted unto the Lord, upon all the face of the land, both Nephites and Lamanites, and there were no contentions and disputations among them, and every man did deal justly one with another. (4 Nephi 1:2)

THE CIRCLEVILLE EARTHWORKS

A second witness to the conversion of the Lamanites comes to us from the words of the old Dakota Prophet Dee-Coo-Dah, who spoke of a time his people lived in Circleville, Ohio, along the Scioto River near what today is Columbus, Ohio, south of Lake Erie—the land southward of the Nephites or their land of first inheritance. The Circleville earthworks consisted of two concentric circles, the larger circle being approximately 1,100 feet in diameter, with an adjoining square approximately 900 feet on each side and a few accompanying mounds. At the center of the concentric circles was a mound about 15 feet in height and about 60 feet in diameter. When excavated, it was found to contain a number of burials and artifacts.

Once again we have a center that falls in line with those built by the Druids. While the Druidic circles themselves were never considered temples in the true sense of the word but were rather places simply set apart from the world and dedicated for the use of sacred things, the old Indian prophet Dee-Coo-Dah spoke of a time when the earthworks "at Circleville [were] traditionally dominated by the Temple of Peace."[3] He remembered being told that the blood of neither man nor beast had stained the earth within that circle. Thus we can assume that the human burials in the mound occurred sometime later when peace had been taken from the land, for to inter the dead in or even beneath a sacred temple would have desecrated the setting according Mosaic law and rendered it unholy and unfit for the Savior to rest His holy feet upon. Was it a pure setting anciently? Only time will tell! Yet how glorious a place it may have been at one time, at least if we can trust the recollection of the old prophet Dee-Coo-Dah, who said of the Circleville works:

> The Great Spirit rested on the central mound, and thence gave oracles to the prophets at the appearance of each new moon.
>
> Once a year the neighboring nations met together to sing songs about the sacred circle and to receive, through the prophets the blessings of their fathers.
>
> So great a sacred a temple is not often seen; but this was erected by the union of four nations that lived for many years at peace with each other, and met annually in festive union."[4]

As to who the four nations may have been during this time of peace, which we can take to be the Nephite's golden age, Dee-Coo-Dah trembled with emotion when Walter Pigeon spoke of Circleville and explained that a city now rested within the old enclosure. After composing himself, the old prophet asked, "Do the bones of my father rest in peace?"[5] Because Dee-Coo-Dah was a member of the Dakota branch of the Sioux language family, a language linked to that of the Iroquois, we can suppose the Sioux were one the four nations. The other three were also likely descendants of Lehi, for their prophets spoke of the blessings they were to receive through their fathers, which suggests they were all part of the same ancestral line. They likely included the Erie branch of the Iroquois who settled along Lake Erie, the Cherokee living along the Allegheny River in western Pennsylvania and parts of neighboring Ohio, and the Shawnee living in Fort Ancient in southern Ohio.

In Forest Hill Cemetery, in Utica, New York, an interesting relic of the Iroquois can be seen: a stone that came to be known as the Stone of the Oneidas. The Iroquois explain that two brothers left the Onondagas and settled along the north shores of Lake Oneida, where they kept the celebrations commanded by the Great Spirit that placed them in His favor. One morning a stone appeared among them unlike any others in the vicinity. They were told it was to be the altar around which their councils and festivals should take place and that it would follow them from place to place, which it did. Each time they moved to a new location, they discovered the stone in their midst. Thus they took the name, The People of the Upright Stone.

NEW INSIGHTS INTO FORT ANCIENT

As more and more research is done on Fort Ancient, more and more researchers are coming to believe the Shawnee played some pivotal role in its construction. The old prophet Dee-Coo-Dah said that the real name for Fort Ancient was Moon City and that its walls "were constructed by successive labors of a long line of kings and rulers."[6] Sometime during the first two weeks of the month, often at the end of the Sabbath, Jews recite a blessing over the moon in gratitude for having been given the cycles of time. The Zarahites of New England who arrived from Iberia were likely the initial architects of the huge hill fort, yet researchers are coming to believe the Shawnee either played a part in the construction of part of it or were at least present at the time. While Fort Ancient, which shows evidence of ancient warfare, may have been fortified against an enemy at some later point in time, researchers are now coming to believe that part of the great hill fort was built for ceremonial purposes. In 2005, a remote sensing survey revealed traces of a large circular structure beneath the surface in the north part of the fort that appears to have incorporated three rings of posts. The southern half of the circle is filled with 15 concentric shallow trenches alternating with prepared floors, some of which were partially covered by limestone slabs. Small wooden posts had been set into both the trenches and the floors. These features are thought by some to be the remains of bleachers for those attending a worship service. Considering its construction is thought to have taken place two thousand years ago around the time of Christ, one cannot help but tie the two together, especially after Jack Blosser suggested we think of the Fort Ancient earthwork as a church. Evidence indicates it was not just built for the local populations but for pilgrims from hundreds of miles away. The Creek Indians speak of their ancestors making such pilgrimages in the spring and in the fall to a similar hill fort in Tennessee. The importance of Fort Ancient as a place of power endured long after the end of Hopewell, with pilgrimages continuing to the area well into recent times. Simon Kenton often observed groups of Shawnee visiting the place en route to Ohio to pay homage to the spirits of those of their ancient fathers.

THE GOLDEN AGE

The visit of the Savior to the Nephites in Bountiful was the singularly most important event to take place in America in pre-Columbian times, making the region as holy as the lands of His nativity. Yet the only remaining hint of His presence in the land, other than the account given in the Book of Mormon, is evidence of the widespread trade network that sprang up among the Hopewell, which prevailed in the land for over two centuries. All the available evidence places the Hopewellian Climax shortly after AD 1 until around AD 150. The Ohio Hopewell and their counterparts in Indiana and Illinois attained their zenith during this golden age. With the destruction of the wicked and the survivors acquainted with their Savior, the Nephites mingled freely with the Lamanites during a golden age of peace the scriptures say lasted for an unprecedented period of two hundred years. During this golden age, the trade network of the Hopewell grew to nearly continental proportions, capable of amassing resources from the Rocky Mountains to the Appalachians and from the Great Lakes to the Gulf of Mexico. Four roads of commerce were noted: (1) along the various rivers in the region, (2) along the mighty Mississippi, (3) to the east across the mountains to where ships traveled along the shores of the Atlantic, and (4) west on the highway that led to Mexico. Trade with such regions brought ideas and merchandise back to local populations in the north, who then incorporated those traditions into their own until the entire region was a filled with beauty, culture, and wealth.

Robert Silverberg considered the Hopewell "the first empire builders of the United States. . . . Some archaeologists have written of an actual Hopewell state, ruled from a central capital in southern Ohio and extending its grasp westward across Indiana and Illinois into southeastern Iowa, northward to Wisconsin and Michigan, and southward down the Mississippi past St. Lewis." However, "a younger school of archaeologists has introduced the idea of a Hopewell 'interaction sphere,' held together by a common religion rather than by any central government," an idea which has more merit than they knew.[7]

20

The Culture Hero Quetzalcoatl

While Brasseur de Bourbourg places the first colony of Nahuas in Mexico in the few centuries before Christ, a second company of white men was about to join them, a company of Toltecs from Huehue Tlapalan. The entire region was flourishing by the time the second company arrived, led by the illustrious Quetzalcoatl, who, after leaving their original northern home in Huehue Tlapalan, chose Tulla, north of Anahuac, as the first capital of their newly founded kingdom. Torquemada's account confirms that they came from the north and were led by the celebrated Quetzalcoatl, a name-title given all their ruling high priests. He said,

> Certain people came from the north by way of Panuco. These were men of good carriage, well-dressed in long robes of black linen, open in front, and without capes, cut low at the neck, with short sleeves that did not come to the elbow. . . . They brought with them as their chief and head a personage called Quetzalcoatl, a fair and ruddy complexioned man, with a long beard. . . . These followers of Quetzalcoatl were men of great knowledge and cunning artists in all kinds of fine work; not so good at masonry and the use of the hammer as in casting and in the engraving and setting of precious stones, and in all kinds of artistic sculpture, and in agriculture.[1]

Other accounts say he was a white man, with a strong formation of body, broad forehead, large eyes, black hair, and a heavy beard. Yet all the accounts agree that Quetzalcoatl was venerable, just, and holy, and taught by precept and example the paths of virtue in all the Nahua cities, particularly in Cholula. He was said to have been the "father of mathematics, metallurgy, and astronomy and was said to have measured the earth," another Druid practice. He also founded productive agriculture. As a great doctor and master of medicines, he was patron of healers and diviners and disclosed to the people the mysteries of the properties of plants. In addition, he was revered as a lawgiver, as a protector of craftsman, and as a patron of all the arts—all characteristics of a Druid high priest of exceptional capacity. For the sake of modesty, he is said to have worn white robes that reached down to his feet, with a blanket covering it sewn with either black or red crosses.[2]

The date Quetzalcoatl enters Mexico has been a matter of much discussion over the years, with some claiming he came with the first Nahua company in the two or three centuries before Christ, and others insisting he came later in time. While both Ixtlilxchitl and Bourbourg believed Quetzalcoatl showed up around the time of Christ, H. de Charency believed he came around 68 AD.[3] In light of such confusion, all we can do is pinpoint the rule of the first Quetzalcoatl of importance as sometime in the two or three centuries before or during the time of Christ, with him being as great a religious leader as early Mexico had known to that point.

It is said that during Quetzalcoatl's season in Mexico, the Nahuas built fine and beautiful houses and temples, with Quetzalcoatl filling the position of ruling high priest. The old records claim his rule was mild, although he insisted on a strict performance of all religious duties. His people loved him for many reasons, including that (1) he taught the silversmith's art, a craft which the people greatly prided themselves in; (2) he desired no sacrifice of the blood of men or animals but delighted only in offering of bread, roses, and other flowers and of perfumes and sweet odors; and (3) he prohibited and forbade all war and violence. Now, if Quetzalcoatl's rule came in the years prior to the time of Christ as some suppose, his forbidding animal sacrifice would have been a grave error on his part, for many of the Nahuas were Israelites under command to follow the law of Moses until its fulfillment with the sacrifice of the unblemished Lamb of God. On the other hand, if, as Ixtlilxochitl believed, Quetzalcoatl came in the years following the life, death, and resurrection of Christ, then we would have to assume the law had been fulfilled, and thus his doing away with animal sacrifice, along with human sacrifice, was appropriate.

Quetzalcoatl's desire to be a worthy servant of God often led him up the slopes of Cotcitepec, or Tzatzitepec, a volcano near his beloved Tulla where he would subject himself to long and numerous penances. Interestingly, the name of the volcano means "mountain of outcry," for it is said that when Quetzalcoatl gave laws, he sent a crier to the top of the mount where his voice could be heard for three hundred miles in every direction, as some say, which the Spanish fathers insist was not an exaggeration. While tales of a crier's voice being heard for three hundred miles still seems excessive, regardless of those who insist otherwise, the Book of Jasher claims the sons of Jacob actually did have certain extraordinary physical abilities, including the ability to cry out so loud that it caused fear in all who heard them. In one instance, when the sons of Jacob were fighting the men of Gaash, Judah let out a shriek so loud that many of the men of Gaash fell from the walls of the city to their deaths. The frightened men of Gaash thus agreed between them that "they could not stand against the sons of Jacob, for fright and terror had seized them at the shriek of Judah . . . whose cry was heard at a great distance" (Jasher, pp. 111, 112).

Once in his sanctuary atop the mount, it is said that Quetzalcoatl drew blood from his tongue, thigh, or ears with a maguey thorn or cactus to atone for his sins, and as an example of penance to the priests and those who followed after him. Such a ritual is also not in keeping with the worship of the Savior. Even if the law had been fulfilled and blood sacrifice done away with, the Lord required nothing more than a broken heart and a contrite spirit as a token of one's repentance—a more satisfactory form of penance the Lord taught the Nephites back in Zarahemla during his visit to Bountiful.

> And behold, I have given you the law and the commandments of my Father, that ye shall believe in me, and that ye shall repent of your sins, and come unto me with a broken heart and a contrite spirit. Behold, ye have the commandments before you, and the law is fulfilled. (3 Nephi 12:19)

Regardless of so many lingering questions about Quetzalcoatl, the fact that he was a *Lord Par Excellence* goes without question, for under his care their capitals soon became flourishing cities where all branches of art received their fair share of attention. Quetzalcoatl's disposition and character were so lofty that while the temporal rule of Tula was still in the hands of a lord named Vemac, in all their spiritual and ecclesiastic matters Quetzalcoatl was supreme and was considered the chief pontiff and reverenced in the same way they would a king.

It is said Quetzalcoatl lived during a veritable golden age, which is just as it was in Nephite territory after the time of Christ when evidence shows trade was flourishing throughout the land. While Zarahemla was the spiritual center of the Nephites, Teotihuacan was still the religious center in Mexico, with construction of all types of structures reaching new heights. Thus Teotihuacan quickly became the largest and most populous urban center in the new world.

The story of Quetzalcoatl becomes more difficult to follow from here, for some of the incidents attributed to Quetzalcoatl were similar to incidents attributed to two other high priests called Quetzalcoatl who came later in time: Ceacalt Quetzalcoatl and Topiltzin Quetzalcoatl. Bancroft is inclined to attribute these incidents to the earliest, as do others, since the last Quetzalcoatl's return to Huehue Tlapalan (that being Topiltzin) took place during a time of war and secrecy. With the understanding that they cannot be attributed to one or the other with any sense of certainty, they will be presented here in the review of the affairs of the original Quetzalcoatl, he being the high priest of Tula in probably the first century, who in time wanted to go home to Huehue Tlaplan, which many have been somewhere along the Mississippi Valley.[4]

As his journey homeward continued, it is said he passed by

numerous cities and villages, leaving the memory of his visit indelibly imprinted in the minds of those he taught along the way. From town to town he traveled, leaving many signs along the way until he finally reached Cholula, where the people enticed him to stay for a time, which he did—for twenty years. It was said the people there adored him, just as they had in Tula, so much so that they revered him as their chief god and temples were erected everywhere in his honor, even by the enemies of the Cholulans. No wonder his memory lived on through the ages.

After twenty years of devoted service in Cholula, Quetzalcoatl resumed his long journey homeward toward Huehue Tlapalan. The *Codex Chimalpopoca* claims he died "four days after his return."[5]

21

The Post-Christian Decline

Quetzalcoatl's ministry in Mexico is an indication of the way the Nahuas in Huehue Tlapalan in the mid-Mississippi Valley embraced Christianity, as did all the surrounding regions who all became one in Christ. What a blessing for the Nephites, who had worked so hard and fought so many battles to maintain their rights and liberties and the right to worship the Lord God of Israel as they pleased.

> There were no robbers, nor murderers, neither were there Lamanites, nor any manner of ites; but they were in one, the children of Christ, and heirs to the kingdom of God. (4 Nephi 1:17)

While the Lord may not have visited the sun worshipers in the land, the missionary efforts of the Lord's newly appointed disciples, who were instructed to take the glad news of the gospel to every person in the land, would certainly have made an impact on the region.

> For behold, thus said Jesus Christ, the Son of God, unto his disciples who should tarry, yea, and also to all his disciples, in the hearing of the multitude: Go ye into all the world, and preach the gospel to every creature. (Mormon 9:22)

It would be wonderful to have an account of the conversion of some of those who lived during that wondrous time, likely through the ministries of the Lord's twelve disciples, each of whom must have been every bit as anxious to spread the word of God as Alma had been in the years before, who cried,

> O that I were an angel, and could have the wish of mine heart, that I might go forth and speak with the trump of God, with a voice to shake the earth, and cry repentance unto every people!
>
> Yea, I would declare unto every soul, as with the voice of thunder, repentance and the plan of redemption, that they should repent and come unto our God, that there might not be more sorrow upon all the face of the earth. (Alma 29:1–2)

Unfortunately, the records of such missionary excursions remain hidden, perhaps to preserve them from the kind of distortion that has obscured so many of the visits of Quetzalcoatl. To add to the mystery, no books of the Hopewell survived either, undoubtedly having been burned right along with the books of the Nephites. Thus we must draw upon archaeological evidence what little information has been gleaned from the earth to help us learn what took place in the northeast following the time of Christ. While Satan was bound for a time because of the righteousness of the people, peace was not destined to go on indefinitely. Time was proving to be a real enemy, for the tales of the visit of the Savior were quickly fading into the mists of time, and people began to fall into apostasy again.

In prophesying about the time of Christ's visit to the faithful in Bountiful and the decline that followed, Jacob, the brother of Nephi, said,

> But the Son of Righteousness shall appear unto them; and he shall heal them, and they shall have peace with him, until three generations shall have passed away. (2 Nephi 26:9)

Evidence indicates that the decadent ways of the Hopewell began to resurface and make their way into New York sometime within a century or two either side of AD 160, according to New York Archaeologist, William. A. Ritchie, who added,

> In brief, to varying degrees within the affected region the existing

> social groups were suffused with Hopewellian religious ideas, practices and material cultural elements, some of which were no doubt cult-related.[1]

While no traces of sun worship show up in New York during their earlier years, evidence of a mixed culture began to surface during this phase, a culture that branches off the Hopewell culture. This new culture moved from southern Ohio up the Allegheny River into western New York and then up the Genesee River, where E. G. Squire discovered a number of ancient sites high up in the Genesee River Valley. The entire area was so thoroughly occupied by modern man that remnants of that ancient time in history were hard to find. Yet reports were made of the discovery of a circular mound found about four miles above the village of Portageville. It has been described as rising probably a hundred feet above the surrounding land, with the Genesee River curving around its base, creating a semicircle, before sweeping along its course and cascading over the falls below Portageville. Two prominent sites were also noted near Mount Morris, one on Squawkie Hill, a name subsequently given the Point Peninsula populations living during Hopewell times in this region, a region that became infused with the Hopewellian religious practice and the material culture and elements from Ohio.

Regional centers with these same cultural traits as the Squawkie Hill phase of the Nephites were also found in northwestern Pennsylvania and adjacent southwestern New York in the lands of Nephi and Zarahemla but particularly in the land of Nephi among the Lamanites. It was the addition of certain relics in their sites that revealed their connections to the Ohio Hopewell centers and their subsequent intrusion into the area via the Ohio, Beaver, and Allegheny Rivers. Not having the Book of Mormon as a guide, archaeologists could only conclude that because those along the Genesee were so far away from their parent colonies, they must have settled the area after being deposed from their own lands through warfare, migration, or expatriation by their own kind.

The scriptures say that by AD 201 new churches appeared in the land and, for the next ten years, spread like wildfire—and no wonder, with the arrival of so many Hopewell into the area with their corrupt form of worship that they began to perpetuate among the Nephites. While the scriptures make it clear that the new churches rising up in the area were Christian, they nonetheless denied much of the doctrines of Christ, just as many of the newly converted Druids did, even after their conversion.

> And it came to pass that when two hundred and ten years had passed away there were many churches in the land; yea, there were many churches which professed to know the Christ, and yet they did deny the more parts of his gospel, insomuch that they did receive all manner of wickedness, and did administer that which was sacred unto him to whom it had been forbidden because of unworthiness.
>
> And this church did multiply exceedingly because of iniquity, and because of the power of Satan who did get hold upon their hearts.
>
> And again, there was another church which denied the Christ; and they did persecute the true church of Christ, because of their humility and their belief in Christ; and they did despise them because of the many miracles which were wrought among them.
>
> Therefore they did exercise power and authority over the disciples of Jesus who did tarry with them, and they did cast them into prison; but by the power of the word of God, which was in them, the prisons were rent in twain, and they went forth doing mighty miracles among them.
>
> Nevertheless, and notwithstanding all these miracles, the people did harden their hearts, and did seek to kill them, even as the Jews at Jerusalem sought to kill Jesus, according to his word. (4 Nephi 1:27–31)

> Nevertheless, the people did harden their hearts, for they were led by many priests and false prophets to build up many churches, and to do all manner of iniquity. And they did smite upon the people of Jesus; but the people of Jesus did not smite again. And thus they did dwindle in unbelief and wickedness, from year to year, even until two hundred and thirty years had passed away. (4 Nephi 1:34)

The second church mentioned in this scripture did not even

believe in Christ. By the time 230 years had passed away "there was a great division among the people" in Zarahemla, with the righteous referred to as Nephites and the wicked referred to as Lamanites again, regardless of their race or color; by now it was a matter of political view rather than ancestry (see 4 Nephi 1:35–36).

By the time 244 years had passed away from the time of Christ's visit among them, the wicked "were more numerous than were the people of God" (4 Nephi 1:40). The scriptures tell us they continued to build churches and drew away still more of the people until 260 years passed away. Unfortunately, the situation worsened when the wicked began to seek out the secret works of Gadianton again and the righteous began to be puffed up in pride because of their wealth and became vain and haughty. The addition of astrology and certain occult practices accelerated the people's downward spiral. Archaeological evidence suggests the people of the region went from using the priesthood to heal the sick and perform their miracles to depending upon shamans and magicians, who used hallucinogenic drugs to produce the state of consciousness they wanted. These practices were particularly abhorrent to the Nephites, who mentioned them when lamenting their various woes.

> For behold no man could keep that which was his own, for the thieves, and the robbers, and the murderers, and the magic art, and the witchcraft which was in the land. (Mormon 2:10)

By the time 300 years had passed away, both the Nephites and Lamanites had become equally wicked, for they had once again begun to embrace the secret works of the Gadiantons. The only righteous left in the land were the three Nephites, whom the Lord ultimately led away, along with any other pocket of righteous Nephites still living in the land (see Jacob 3:4). Thus, after 320 years had passed away, Amaron was constrained by the Holy Spirit to hide up the sacred records of his people (see 4 Nephi 1:48).

The archaeologist Olaf Prufer claims the Hopewell went through a long and piecemeal degeneration, which most now agree ended around AD 350, very close to the time with the scriptures place the demise of the Nephite nation, AD 384.

Alma prophesied,

> Behold, I perceive that this very people, the Nephites, according to the spirit of revelation which is in me, in four hundred years from the time that Jesus Christ shall manifest himself unto them, shall dwindle in unbelief.
>
> Yea, and then shall they see wars and pestilences, yea, famines and bloodshed, even until the people of Nephi shall become extinct—
>
> Yea, and this because they shall dwindle in unbelief and fall into the works of darkness, and lasciviousness, and all manner of iniquities; yea, I say unto you, that because they shall sin against so great light and knowledge, yea, I say unto you, that from that day, even the fourth generation shall not all pass away before this great iniquity shall come. (Alma 45:10–12)

As the never-ending war between the Nephites and Lamanites escalated toward the end of the fourth century, the Gadiantons and Lamanites had taken over much of the land and finally pushed the Nephites out of Zarahemla and into the land northward. Unfortunately, the Lamanites were not content with the acquisition of just the land southward; they wanted the land northward as well. Because the Nephites had deteriorated into a bloodthirsty people and had thus lost the assistance of the Lord, the Lamanites were about to succeed in their desires.

The Nephites had been battling the Lamanites for nearly a thousand years but only to defend themselves, for it was the strict command of the Lord that they not take the offensive in the war with their brethren. They were only assured of His divine assistance if they obeyed that long-standing edict. But, now fueled by their hatred for the Lamanites, they cast aside their trust in the Lord and His council and swore between themselves that they would avenge the blood of their brethren to the ultimate destruction of every last Lamanite in the land.

22

The FALL of the HOPEWELL CIVILIZATION

MANY OF THE elite among the Ohio Hopewell populations were Nahuas, whose own center of activity along the Mississippi River may well have factored into the fall of the people in both regions. While the Chichimecs lived to the west of the river in a region known as Huehue Tlapalan, the Nahuas settled to the east, with their Creek descendants spreading along the banks of several rivers in Georgia, Alabama, Florida, Mississippi, Louisiana, and Tennessee. The Creek people are descendants of the pyramid builders who constructed magnificent earthen pyramids and ceremonial complexes throughout the entire southeastern United States. At some point in the early centuries AD, after the Nephites' golden age, the Nahuas were sent packing by the wilder Chichimecs tribes living in Huehue Tlapalan, a region Humboldt places at a longitude that corresponds with the region along the Mississippi River parallel to the mouths of the Arkansas and Missouri rivers.

Conant (quoting Humboldt) defined the regions occupied by the Chichimecs and Nahuas, or Toltecs, with one tribe among them known later in time as the Aztecs. He said,

> The Toltecs, the Chichimecs, and the Aztec pretended to have issued

> successively, from the sixth to the twelfth century, from three neighboring countries situated toward the north. . . . Where, it may be asked, must be places that parent land? . . . The country between the 33rd and 41st degrees of latitude, parallel the mouth of the Arkansas and the Missouri, is considered by the Aztec historians as the ancient dwelling of the civilized nations of Anahuac.[1]

In speaking of the widespread empire known as Huehue Tlapalan, John Thomas Short, said that "the State of Louisiana and the valleys of the Arkansas and Red Rivers are not only the most thickly populated wing of the mound-builders' domain, but also furnished remains which present affinities with the great works of Mexico so striking that no doubt can longer exist that the same people were the architect of both."[2]

Short said in his *North Americans of Antiquity:*

> The most reasonable conjecture as to the locality of Hue hue Tlapalan is that which places it in the Mississippi Valley, and assigns the works of our Moundbuilders to the Nahua nations. . . . We have shown the close resemblance of the mound crania to the ancient Mexican, and have pointed out the gradual transition from the rude and simple mounds of the north to the truncated pyramid of the south, constructed on strict geometrical principles, having one or more graded ways, and so closely resembling the Mexican teocallis. Besides the testimony of Sahagun that the first settlers of Mexico came from towards Florida, and the universal report of a northern origin prevalent among the Aztecs at the time of the conquest, there are other evidences of a racial identity common to Moundbuilders and Mexicans, such as pottery, sculpture.[3]

A large city in Huehue Tlapalan called Tlachicatzin, which had a numerous population and was renowned throughout the regions, appears to have played a pivotal role in the forced migration of the Nahuas southward into Mexico. The city was apparently founded by a man named Toltecatl, and according to the tradition of the time, the people became known as Toltecs after their founder and chief. Because of the ability, industry, and skill of his people, both in cultivating the fields and in the exercise of the arts, the Toltecs living in Tlachicatzin grew to be a mighty nation, to the degree that they began to desire the entire kingdom for themselves. As Veytia relates the story, "some 2,379 years after Huehue Tlapalan was first founded by the Chichimecs, two great lords of the Toltecs rebelled against the rightful sovereigns of the land in hopes of gratifying their desires. Thus, a revolt broke out which was quickly and decisively quelled by the Chichimecs who drove them from the land with the ousted Toltec princes and their many allies."[4]

Legends of the long and toilsome migration of the Toltecs, which is said to have taken 104 years to complete, make repeated mention that some arrived in Mexico by land, others by sea, but always from the northeast. J. D. Baldwin quotes Brasseur de Bourbourg as saying,

> Previous to the history of the Toltec domination in Mexico, we notice in the annals of the country. . . the existence of an ancient empire known as Huehue-Tlapalan, from which the Toltecs, or Nahuas, came to Mexico in consequence of a revolution or invasion, and from which they had a long and toilsome migration.[5]

Few details are given of the rebellion, except to note that they were fleeing the Chichimecs who were united under one great leader. Foster claimed that there was a terrible struggle, but that after thirteen years of conflict, the Toltecs were no longer able to resist successfully and were thus obliged to abandon their country to escape subjugation. H. H. Bancroft said:

> In its ancient centre—not Anahuac . . . —the primitive Nahua power was overthrown, or from that centre it was transferred to be re-established by exiled princes and their descendants on the Mexican plateaux. This transfer, whose nature we may vaguely comprehend, but of whose details we know nothing, is the event or series of events referred to by various migration-traditions.[6]

The peace that lasted from the time of the earthquake after the Savior's death (AD 33) and visit to the land came to an end with this royal company's departure from the city of Tlachicatzin.

> Three hundred and five years later, when the empire had been long at peace, . . . [two] chief descendants of the royal house of the Toltecs, raised a revolt for the purpose of deposing the legitimate successor to the throne. The rebellious chiefs were after long wars

> driven out of their city Tlachicatzin in Huehue Tlapallan, with all their numerous families and allies. They were pursued by their kindred of the city or country . . . for sixty leagues, to a place they named . . . "little" Tlapalan. . . . And they were accompanied on their forced migration by five other chiefs.[7]

Various early writers have proposed a variety of dates for the departure of this colony, doing their best to decipher the confusing mass of information found in the old books of Mexico, many of which have conflicting accounts. Most favor a time between the fifth and sixth century for this particular company, although one obscure writer proposed their exodus came as early as 181 BC and others as late as AD 700. Brasseur de Bourbourg, on the other hand, found a date which placed the exodus at the close of the fourth century in AD 387—surprisingly close to the exterminating battle of the Nephites at Cumorah in AD 384. The Mexican historian Ixtlilxochitl places the revolt in AD 338, a date that corresponds remarkably well with the date given in the Book of Mormon for the start of the 47-year war between the Nephites and the Lamanites that began around AD 327 (see Mormon 2:1–3).

The migration of the Toltecs into Mexico is noted in many of the old books of Mexico, although they often say little more than some came by sea, others by land. Baldwin said,

> All the accounts say the Toltecs came at different times, by land and sea, mostly in small companies, and always from the northeast. This can be explained only by supposing they came by sea from the mouth of the Mississippi River or from the Gulf coast near it, and by land through Texas. But the country from which they came was invariably Huehue Tlapalan.[8]

In reference to their ancient homeland, Cabrera instructs us that its simple name was Tlapalan, but they called it Huehue, or Old, to distinguish it from three other Tlapalans founded in the districts of their new kingdoms. According to Torquemada, the distinction was also made to perpetuate their attachment to their ancient country and their grief at being expelled from it after so long a time. Thus, where before it bore the simple name of Tlapalan, it was ever after referred to as Huehue Tlapalan, meaning old, old Tlapalan.

The Toltecs are always referred to in the same way, as men of great knowledge and cunning artists in all kinds of fine work, such as the casting of silver and the engraving and setting of precious stones. They were also known for their understanding of agriculture and good government.[9] It must have been hard to leave their new homeland and the many improvements they had made. Yet the number and strength of the Chichimec was just too much for them, and they had to flee if they were to survive. Legends say the fleeing Toltecs were never safe from the Chichimecs, who were never far behind. Yet there is safety in numbers, and legends claim that all their numerous families and allies from the city of Tlaxicoluican joined them along the way. Thus there was quite a company who fled with the princes who ultimately came to settle a place they also called Tlapalan, although referring to it as *little Tlapalan*.

Following the Toltec princes and their large company further, we learn that during their three-year stay in little Tlapalan, seven of their numbers counseled together as to what to do next. Their astronomer prophet, Huematzin, probably a Druid priest, reminded them that although they had been suffering great persecutions from heaven, such times were always followed by a period of great prosperity. Moreover, his astrology taught him that the land was now free for the taking and urged them to go forward, especially since the Chichimecs were not far behind. He counseled them further that the planets which ruled their destinies were not destined to cause disruption for another century, and they and their descendants could enjoy a time of peace. Such information pleased the seven chiefs. Thus after a three-year stay in *little Tlapalan*, eleven years from the time they left Huehue Tlapalan, they continued on their journey.

A variety of dates have been given for the Toltec's ultimate arrival in Mexico, which has also been the source of much controversy. But after their arrival, Heumatzin gave a prophecy that informed the Toltecs that ten cycles (of fifty-two years each) from the time they left Huehue Tlapalan, a ruler would appear upon the scene whose right to the throne would be challenged, a prophecy that was fulfilled with the crowning of Topiltzin Quetzalcoatl in the early years of the tenth century. Thus their arrival must have been in the fifth century (the time period from 401 to 500), with Alfred Chavero placing their arrived sometime in 442–443 AD. This date seems the most reasonable, for the date of 338 AD given for the revolt, plus a 104-year migration, would have them arriving in Mexico in 442 AD. Ixtlilxochitl said:

> In the year . . . ce Calli the Tultecas, or rather the Huetlapalanecas, arrived in Tula. . . .
>
> And having arrived at this place and land, the Tultecas thought it very good, and especially Huematzin, the astrologer that led them. . . . And seeing the location so good for their purpose and the temperateness of the land, and the other things which he found in his astrology to be good for a city, they began to build it.[10]

The Huetlapanecas toiled for six years, building magnificent edifices, palaces, and temples, which formed the basis of a great empire, with the grand city of Tollan as its capital. When their city was completed, the sacerdotal supremacy attributed to the priesthood of Tollan came under the name of Huematzin. But it was really exercised by the priests of the sun at Teotihuacan, where their deliberations were held, and their first king probably received the rights of the coronation. By the fifth century of our era, the Toltecs had been successfully transferred from Huehue Tlapalan to the Mexican plateau, with the broad extent of land around it gradually occupied by numerous Nahua nations of varying power and numbers and of varying degrees of civilization. Bancroft explains that some quickly became wild, nomadic, and terrorizing of their neighbors, while others lived by agriculture and retained much of their former greatness. The most advanced in culture settled in the center of the valley where grand cities began to dot the land, with their residents thereafter spoken of as Toltecs—a name associated with everything that is skillful and excellent in art. The more barbarous tribes lived outside the cities and were referred to as Chichimecs, although those who moved back into the cities and attained a measure of polish were once again distinguished as Toltecs.

Thus rose the magnificent Toltec Empire, which was classed

as one of the greatest and most powerful kingdoms of the ancient world. It was said to have been over 1,000 leagues long and 800 wide. Even the highest mountains were covered with houses and cultivated lands, with no span of land left unpopulated or uncultivated. As the Toltecs grew in number, so did their empire, patterned after the one from which they came, with the Nahuatl language becoming the dominant stock language of Mexico from the Pacific Ocean to the Gulf Coast.

Over the course of centuries, the Toltecs came to settle in what has come to be known as Chichen Itza, one of the greatest Mayan centers of the Yucatán peninsula. Merging Mayan construction techniques with Toltec elements from central Mexico made Chichen Itza a prime example of the Mayan-Toltec civilization in Yucatán.

It can hardly be doubted that a large number of Lehi's seed was among the friends and allies of the Nahuas who escaped to Mexico, with many now returning to the lands of their fathers through our southern borders, both legally and not.

THE COLLAPSE OF THE HOPEWELL CIVILIZATION

With much of the hierarchy among the Hopewell populations sent packing along with all their various allies and neighbors—many of whom were no doubt their Zarah-Judahite cousins living in Tennessee and Kentucky—the Hopewell civilization collapsed, and the local populations went back to the tribal way of living that existed before Hopewell times. Brasseur de Bourbourg had always believed that the Toltecs and the mound builders of the Ohio and Mississippi valleys were the same people. Even Bancroft noted a connection between the two people. The long period of peace Ixtlilxochitl mentions before the forced migration of the Nahuas seems to fit right into the Hopewell scenario. Olaf Prufer suggests that the large unprotected ceremonial centers in Hopewell territory represented a long period of peace and stability (the two-hundred-year golden age of the Nephites), while the forts were built in times of trouble. It was as if the people rather suddenly took to the hills and abandoned their centers in the wake of some danger.

Prufer also noted that the New York–based Iroquois also began to construct fortified sites around this time, which suggested to him a common but unidentified cause that may have led to the violent end of the Ohio Hopewell. The southern tribes were continually growing, expanding, and threatening to take over the entire region, something the Iroquois, Sioux, and Cherokee were not likely any more pleased with than the Chichimecs were and thus likely aided them in their fight. Baldwin went so far as to suggest it was the Iroquois and their related tribes who expelled the mound builders from their border settlements, cut them off from the copper mines, and finally pushed them down the Mississippi.

Salvatore Michael Trento noted the comments of Colonel Joseph Brant, a Dartmouth-educated Mohawk sachem whose biography was written by William Tone in 1838, which suggest the same scenario.

> In the book Stone cites a lengthy and informative conversation between Brant and a questioning scholar:
>
> "Among things relating to the western country," says Mr. Woodruff, "I was curious to learn in the course of my conversation with Captain Brant, what information he could give me respecting the *tumuli* (mounds) which are found on and near the margin rivers and lakes from the St. Lawrence to the Mississippi. He stated, in reply, that the subject had been handed down time immemorial, that in an age long gone by, there came white men from a foreign country, and by consent of the Indians established trading-house and settlements where these *tumuli* are found. A friendly intercourse was continued for several years; many of the white men brought their wives, and had children born to them; and additions to their numbers were made yearly from their own country. These circumstances at length gave rise to jealousies among the Indians, and fears began to be entertained in regard to the increasing numbers, wealth, and ulterior views of the new comers; apprehending that, becoming strong, they might one day seize upon the country as their own. A secret council, composed of the chiefs of all the different nations from the St. Lawrence to the Mississippi, was therefore convoked; the result of which, after long deliberation, was a resolution that on a certain night designated for that purpose, all their white neighbors, men, women, and children, should be exterminated. The most profound secrecy

> was essential to the execution of such a purpose; and such was the fidelity with which the fatal determination was kept, that the conspiracy was successful, and the device carried completely into effect. Not a soul was left to tell the tale."[11]

While some attribute this to a later time in history, it certainly seems to fit a pattern they probably used again and again. The Iroquois were likely those who, along with various related brothers, gathered their forces together and totally annihilated their Nephite brothers around the Hill Cumorah in 385 AD.

Joseph Smith sought answers to the identity of the bones of what turned out to be the white Lamanite Zelph. One of the accounts of Joseph's vision said, "His name was Zelph. He was a warrior and a chieftain under the great Prophet Onandagus. The curse was taken from Zelph—at least in part" (suggesting the reversal that took place when the people of Ammon moved north and fell into wickedness), and "he was killed in battle by an arrow found among his ribs, during the last great struggle of the Lamanites and Nephites."[12]

With so many of the Nephites settled throughout Ohio, Indiana, and Illinois, what struggle could he have been referring to other than the war that sent the Hopewell packing on a long migration south to Mexico? The Iroquois were likely involved with the Chichimecs in their struggle for land and power—the Chichimecs keeping the lands along the Mississippi in their control once the Hopewell civilization collapsed, and the Lamanites keeping all the lands around the Great Lakes. This was not the final battle at Cumorah but simply one of the far-reaching struggles that gave supremacy of the land to the Lamanites after their nine-century-long struggle with their Nephite brothers. The final battle at Cumorah was yet to come. By the time they got to Cumorah, few Nephites were left, with only 230,000 men (along with their families) left on the battlefields around the Hill Cumorah to testify of their long existence in a land they had colonized across thousands of miles. It is no surprise at all that it took more than one battle to do away with them all.

Archaeological matters were of great interest to William Henry Harrison, ninth President of the United States, who made his own assessment of the end of the Ohio Hopewell. Robert Silverberg, speaking of President Harrison, said,

> He saw the mounds as relics of a great race; he imagined stirring battles, sweeping migrations of tribes under attack, mighty swarms of civilized people streaming through the heartland of what one day would be the United States of America. To learn of them, he wrote, "we must search amidst the remains which are still before us. . . . We learn first, from the extensive country covered by their remains, that they were a numerous people. Secondly, that they were congregated in considerable cities. . . . Thirdly, that they were essentially an agricultural people; because, collected as they were in great numbers, they could have depended on the chase (hunting) but for a small portion of their subsistence." He was of the opinion that the Mound Builders "were compelled to fly from a more numerous or a more gallant people. No doubt the contest was long and bloody. . . .' The attackers, he thought, came from both the north and the south, and the Mound Builders made their last stand on the banks of the Ohio River; ". . . it was here that a feeble band was collected . . . to make a last effort for the country of their birth, the ashes of their ancestors, and the altars of their gods. That the crises was met with fortitude, and sustained with valor, need not be doubted. . . . But their efforts were in vain, and flight or death were the sad alternatives. . . ."[13]

Shetrone believed "no people in stage of civilization, would willingly have abandoned such a country; endeared to them as it must have been, by long residence and the labor they had bestowed up on. . . . If they had been made to yield to a more numerous or more gallant people, what country received the fugitives, and what has become of the conquerors?"[14] In 1850, Walter Pidgeon said, "It can no longer be doubted . . . that there has been a day when this continent swarmed with millions of inhabitants, when the arts and sciences flourished, when men lived, and labored, . . . and fought, and were in turn conquerors and conquered, subjects and kings, where now the deep silence of the forest has overcome all such evidence of life and civilization."[15]

23

The Fall of the Nephite Civilization

Just as the Chichimecs rose up against the Nahua nations along the Mississippi, so the Lamanites rose up against the Nephites in Zarahemla, and with the same end in mind: destruction. While a good number of the Nahuas and their allies escaped total annihilation, the Lamanites were determined to kill every last Nephite in the land; total victory was the goal this time. Not one Nephite was to be left alive no matter how long it took or how many battles they had to fight.

Mormon spent much time on his knees during those terrible years, for the wickedness of his own people ultimately exceeded that of the Lamanites; the more wicked the Nephites became, the more the Spirit of the Lord withdrew from them. Thus over the course of the next few decades, the Lamanites were successful in their strategy of systematically destroying the Nephites, one city at a time and one Nephite at a time. In fact, the situation was so serious that the Lord's beloved disciples were taken from the land, and miracles among the people stopped.

Although Mormon knew why the Lord had withdrawn His Spirit from the Nephites, he may not have been totally prepared for the success the Lamanites were enjoying now that the Lord had withdrawn His help and support from his wicked countrymen. While the Nephites fought with the strength of lions and succeeded in driving the Lamanites back at times, the Lamanites ultimately succeeded in pushing the Nephites from Zarahemla and Bountiful into the land northward, where they found sanctuary in the various cites built around the seashore. As one city was attacked, those who survived the onslaught took refuge in the next city, and then the next, and the next, until they were ultimately driven to the city of Joshua, which lay along the seashore near their western borders. As more and more people arrived, Mormon was able put together a fighting force of forty-two thousand men to stand against the Lamanite army of forty-four thousand. This time victory favored the Nephites, who then retook their lands in the south.

Unfortunately, peace did not follow, for although the Lamanites had been driven back into their own lands, the Nephites continued to be set upon by robbers and murders and those who practiced the magic arts and witchcraft. Thus a great lamentation was heard among the Nephites, who surprisingly began to repent at that point in hopes that God would help them through their many troubles. In fact, their sorrowful lamentations could be heard all across the land, which gave Mormon hope that perhaps the Lord would spare his people. Unfortunately, in time he came to see that his people were not sorrowing over their sinful behavior but because the Lord refused to prosper them in their wickedness. The Nephites had become so wicked that Mormon, who commanded the entire Nephite army, even gave up his command, for his people were completely without feeling. Even so, when the war worsened, he repented of his oath to refrain from leading the army and took up his command again, knowing that their only hope of survival rested in his hands. But it was no use, for the superior numbers of the Lamanites succeeded in driving the Nephites eastward from city to city until they were finally driven into the land of many waters for one final showdown. Mormon sent an epistle to the king of the Lamanites and asked for permission to gather his people into one body and prepare them for battle. The king granted his request, for such was the custom of the time.

So many Nephites had already been slain in Nephite villages and cities across the land that it took four years to gather out the remainder of their people. The land of Cumorah was chosen as their gathering place because of the vast number of small drumlin hills in the area and the abundance of natural resources which would give them a certain advantage—especially the great Montezuma marsh, which lay just to the east of the Hill Cumorah. The Hill Cumorah itself was chosen as a command center, for although it was not much taller than the numerous other hills in the area, it was still the most prominent hill there, which made it possible for those posted on top to see the enemy approaching from any and all directions. Neighboring hills were also fortified, each near some unfailing water supply. Walls were thrown up, ditches dug, and battle gear and weapons created. Fires burned day and night as weapons and shields were forged and their people were outfitted for war. Even little children were fitted with breastplates and weapons. The nearby mountain range had plenty of iron ore for such a project, and the nearby flint mines provided the material they needed to make arrowheads.

From *Life of Heber C. Kimball, An Apostle*, by Orson F. Whitney, we read,

> I have visited the fortifications on the tops of those hills frequently, and the one near Bloomfield [New York] I have crossed hundreds of times, which is on the bluff of Honeyoye River, at the outlet of Honeyoye Lake. . . .
>
> The Hill Cumorah is a high hill for that country, and had the appearance of a fortification or entrenchment around it. In the State of New York, probably there are hundreds of these fortifications which are now visible. . . .
>
> Readers of the Book of Mormon will remember that in this very region, according to that sacred record, the final battles were fought between the Nephites and Lamanites. At the hill Cumorah, the Nephites made their last stand prior to their utter extermination, A.D., 385.[1]

Along with gathering his people and preparing them for battle, Mormon also had the responsibility of transferring the sacred records of their people to safer territory. He wrote in his record of this terrible time:

> And when three hundred and eighty and four years had passed

> away, we had gathered in all the remainder of our people unto the land of Cumorah.
>
> And it came to pass that when we had gathered in all our people in one to the land of Cumorah, behold I, Mormon, began to be old; and knowing it to be the last struggle of my people, and having been commanded of the Lord that I should not suffer the records which had been handed down by our fathers, which were sacred, to fall into the hands of the Lamanites, (for the Lamanites would destroy them) therefore I made this record out of the plates of Nephi, and hid up in the hill Cumorah all the records which had been entrusted to me by the hand of the Lord, save it were these few plates which I gave unto my son Moroni. (Mormon 6:5–6)

When the terrible hour arrived to stand and face the Lamanites in one final showdown, the Nephites stood in groups of ten thousand each along the plains surrounding the Hill Cumorah. In our mind's eye, we can almost see Mormon standing in front of the troops, his red cape whipping about in the wind and his eyes trained on the western horizon, which was simply black with approaching warriors. Not a sound was heard from the troops. Each stood rigid in place, sword in hand, gripped with unbelievable terror, and not without cause, for once they saw the innumerable army of the Lamanites they knew they were doomed. So many Lamanite warriors had rallied to the call of their king that the army of the Nephites paled in comparison. As the Nephites looked out over the horizon and saw that host of Lamanites coming toward them, they were nearly paralyzed with fear. Yet in spite of their trembling knees, their hatred for their dark-skinned brothers overcame their panic, and they planted their feet firmly in place and braced themselves for battle, fully convinced that they would prevail.

There are no words to describe the awful scene that followed as sword clashed against sword and the troops of Mormon began to fall. No amount of practice or pre-battle war talk prepared them for what they encountered, for the Lamanites far outnumbered them. The Nephites fought with more strength than they even knew they had, but as one Lamanite went down in battle, two more took his place. Tragically, the anticipated battle went in favor of the Lamanites, with the ten thousand of twenty-three Nephite captains lying lifeless on the ground after the battle ended. Even the women and children had been slain. It was a terrible scene, one no one should ever have to look upon. It must have been all Moroni could do to hold back his emotions as he gazed in horror over the battlefield and heard his father's heart-wrenching cry for the loss of his people:

> O ye fair ones, how could ye have departed from the ways of the Lord! O ye fair ones, how could ye have rejected that Jesus, who stood with open arms to receive you!
>
> Behold, if ye had not done this, ye would not have fallen. But behold, ye are fallen, and I mourn your loss.
>
> O ye fair sons and daughters, ye fathers and mothers, ye husbands and wives, ye fair ones, how is it that ye could have fallen!
>
> But behold, ye are gone, and my sorrows cannot bring your return. (Mormon 6:17–19)

The things they witnessed that day were things no man should ever have to see, not even God. Yet the angels of death were busy that day.

In spite of the tragic end of his people, the prophet Moroni still had one more job to complete. He was divinely commissioned to record not only the events leading up to the final battle but the ultimate end of his nation as well. Not surprisingly, he found it nearly impossible to describe the awful depravity that led up to the ultimate annihilation of his people. Thus he touched upon it only lightly as he began recording upon the plates, not daring to give too full an account of the things that he had seen, lest some future reader be harrowed up in inconsolable sorrow because of their unspeakable wickedness.

In contemplating the events of that terrible time in history, Oliver Cowdery, who stood gazing upon the Hill Cumorah, recited his own version of the tragic events that took place there. In speaking of the hill known as the Hill Cumorah by the Nephites and Ramah by the Jaredites, he said,

> In full view from the top of this same hill, one may gaze with astonishment upon the ground which was twice covered with the dead and dying of our fellow men. Here may be seen where once

> sunk to nought the pride and strength of two mighty nations; and here may be contemplated, in solitude, while nothing but the faithful record of Mormon and Moroni is now extant to inform us of the fact, scenes of misery and distress—the aged, whose silver locks in other places and at other times would command reverence; the mother, who in other circumstances would be spared from violence; the infant, whose tender cries were regarded and listened to with a feeling of compassion and tenderness; and the virgin, whose grace, beauty and modesty, would be esteemed and held inviolate by all good men and enlightened and civilized nations, alike disregarded and treated with scorn!—in vain did the hoary head and man of gray hairs ask for mercy; in vain did the mother plead for compassion; in vain did the helpless and harmless infant weep for verry [*sic*] anguish, and in vain did the virgin seek to escape the ruthless hand of revengeful foes and demons in human form—all alike were trampled down by the feet of the strong, and crushed beneath the rage of battle and war! Alas, who can reflect upon the last struggle of great and populous nations, sinking to dust beneath the (hand of Justice and retribution without) weeping over the corruptions of the human heart, and sighing for the hour when the clangor of arms shall no more be heard, nor the calamities of contending armies no more experienced for a thousand years? Alas, the calamity of war, the extinction of nations, the ruin of kingdoms, the fall of empires and the dissolution of governments! O the misery, distress and evil attendant on these![2]

During the sad days that followed, Mormon used what little strength he had left to record the terrible destruction of his people. After a few more words of counsel to the Lamanites and Gentiles, Mormon's strength was spent; he could write no more and gave the plates over to his faithful son, Moroni. We don't know how long Mormon lived after the battle at Cumorah. But when the terrible time came that he closed his eyes for the last time, we can imagine that Moroni carried his father's body to a beautiful forest glen and buried him in some secluded spot, knowing full well that he was not alone but was being welcomed home by a host of angelic beings, his family who had gone on before, and that great Jehovah who had been watching over him these many, many years.

After burying his father, Moroni became the guardian of the

plates. In an effort to preserve his life so that he could complete his mission to finish the record, he hid himself away from the Lamanites for the next thirty-six years until the plates were finished and safely deposited. Moroni was grateful to know that the records his father had entrusted to him would carry their story. Not only did they testify of Jesus Christ but also of the history of both the Nephite and Jaredite nations, including their fall from grace. In the latter days, this story was destined to be revealed to the great Gentile nation in hopes that they might learn from the mistakes of the past and not fall victim to same sins. He could only pray they would listen.

From the writings of Joseph Fielding Smith we read,

> From all the evidence in the Book of Mormon, augmented by the testimony of the Prophet Joseph Smith, these final battles took place in the territory known as the United States and in the neighborhood of the Great Lakes and hills of western New York. And here Moroni found the resting place for the sacred instruments which had been committed to his care.[3]

Brigham Young Jr. and George Q. Cannon went to the Hill Cumorah and wrote an account that was published in the Millennial Star. In part they said,

> Undoubtedly great changes had occurred in the appearance of the surrounding country[side] since the days when Mormon and [his son] Moroni had trod the spot where we stood. Still we could readily understand, even now, how admirable a position this would be [from the hilltop] for a general to occupy in watching and directing the movements of armies and in scrutinizing the position of the enemy.
>
> Around Cumorah is yet a land of many waters, rivers and fountains [just] as Mormon said it was in his day. Our emotions on treading on this sacred hill were of the most peculiar character. They were indescribable. . . .
>
> From the summit of this hill, Mormon and his great son Moroni had . . . witnessed the gathering of hosts of the Nephites, and the dusky and myriad legions of their deadly enemies, the Lamanites. Around this hill they had marshaled their forces—their twenty-three divisions of ten thousand men each, commanded by

> the most skillful of their generals, all to be swept away except Moroni.
>
> It was here that [Mormon] hid the abridgment which he made of the records [of his people], and which is now known by his name [the Book of Mormon]. And it was here, thirty-six years after this tremendous battle, that his son Moroni also hid his abridgment of the book of Ether, and the record which he had made from which we learn the fate of his father, Mormon, and his other companions.
>
> It was to this spot that about fourteen hundred years after these events, Joseph Smith, the Prophet, was led by Moroni in person, and here the records, engraved on plates, were committed to him for translation. Who could tread this ground and reflect upon these mighty events, and not be filled with indescribable emotions?[4]

EVIDENCE OF WAR

The numerous bone pits discovered in western and central New York are evidence enough that terrible wars once raged across the Cumorah lands, since hurriedly-dug graves were created to facilitate the burial of hundreds and thousands of the dead. Remnants of numerous oak fortifications have also been found, left behind by the Nephites as they made their final stand against the enemy, fortifications exactly like those described in the Book of Mormon. More than one thousand fortified sites were found in Ontario, Livingston, Genesee, and Monroe Counties alone, those counties closest to the battle of Cumorah. Professor E. G. Squires's *Aboriginal Monuments* is filled with such discoveries. He noted that there were "nearly 500 sites charted in Monroe Country alone. In Geneses County are over 100 fortified holltops and strongholds, and similar number of burial sites, and nearly 50 true mounds." He went on to say, "It thus appears that long before the coming of the white man, this region was settled by active and vigorous peoples. Their villages were along the rivers, creeks, and lakes, their camps upon the hill, their fortifications in strategic places difficult to assault. There is not an area of like size in all the

United States east of Ohio, and north of the Mason and Dixon Line where evidence of aboriginal occupation are so abundant."[5]

No other region in the Americas provides more evidence of ancient warfare than western New York.

> The museums in New York State are filled with the instruments of warfare that had been fashioned by the red men and so freely used in that historic area. The opinion is expressed in all those relic halls that western New York was the site of an ancient battlefield. There is more evidence of a well-planned defensive warfare in that locality than there is in any other region on the American continent. It is the opinion of most scholars that the defenses on the drumlin hills were prepared by a people more civilized than the Indians and were exterminated by the inferior race who were still in possession of the country when Columbus discovered this land.[6]

While the Nephites spread out into a number of other regions, the story of the Nephites' long sojourn in the promised land began in this region and ended in this region after over nine centuries of intrigue and warfare. During that long span of time, righteous men were raised up to record the history of their day and age and to preserve for us a legacy of prophecy and religious insights worthy of our attention and instruction and to impress upon our minds the fact only those who worship God will prosper in the promised land.

24

After Cumorah

Although everything Moroni held near and dear had been taken from him, his mission did not end with the battle at Cumorah but continued for another thirty-five years. Moroni witnessed many things during his thirty-five years of wandering. He witnessed the grandeur of God's handiwork firsthand as he walked the land from one end to the other and witnessed sunrises and sunsets in many different parts of the country. He sat atop great mountains, swam in countless lakes, and marveled at the land and the Sculptor who formed such a magnificent landscape. During his wanderings, he no doubt also had a chance to witness, from the seclusion of nearby forests, what village life was like for his dark-skinned brothers, noting on a number of occasions how blissfully their children scampered unafraid about their villages and how carefully their elderly were cared for and respected. After years of reflection, and after experiencing the softening effects of the pure love of Christ, Moroni actually began to look upon the Lamanites as brothers. Indeed they were—wayward and in need of sore repentance to be sure, but brothers nonetheless. Thus, just as each of the prophets who preceded him had done, Moroni pled with the Lord for their ultimate return to the fold, for he knew that only repentance and a return to God could bring them true happiness. Moroni's father had similar concerns and thus included a strict admonition to the Lamanites on his own plates, instructing them to set aside their animosities and join with the Saints. He reminded them that they were of royal lineage and that God was waiting for their return. Moroni could only hope and pray that such counsel would one day impact their descendants and bring them to a greater understanding of their Redeemer, that they might enjoy all the blessings the Lord has in store for those who love Him and keep His commandments.

The golden plates were precious to Moroni. He had been working on them so long that he almost hated to part with them. But knowing of their importance in bringing about the latter-day Restoration, he quickly made an end of writing, knowing that the day would surely come when this work would come forth to the inhabitants of the earth. The only thing left for him was to seal up the plates for the last time, plates that included an abridgment of the history of the Nephites and a small abridgment of the Jaredites. Other matters of importance were also included, such as the fact that children under the age of accountability need no baptism, being alive in Christ. He felt that his father's epistle on faith, hope, and charity should also be added. He also felt to include the Lord's position on the proper method of preparing the sacrament and the proper mode of baptism. He felt issues relevant to Church discipline should also be included, lest those in the latter days flounder over such matters and lose the faith, like so many of his own countrymen had done. His own farewell would complete the record. He wrote:

> And now I bid unto all, farewell. I soon go to rest in the paradise of God, until my spirit and body shall again reunite, and I am brought forth triumphant through the air, to meet you before the pleasing bar of the great Jehovah, the Eternal Judge of both quick and dead. Amen. (Moroni 10:34)

Thus ends one of the greatest yet saddest sagas of all time: the saga of a man whose mission, both in life and as a resurrected being, would lead to the salvation of innumerable souls.

THE LAMANITES AFTER CUMORAH

In spite of their wicked ways, God continued to watch over the Lamanites in deference to the many prayers that had been offered up in their behalf by so many of Nephite prophets: Enos, Moroni, Mormon, and particularly those who were Lamanites by birth; the Lord had promised the Lamanites continued existence in the land. In an effort to preserve the more righteous from the hands of their wicked brothers, some were even led away from time to time. For instance, the oral traditions of the Lenni Lenape speak of living in a land of cold and snow for a time before being urged through visions and dreams to return to the ancient lands of their fathers. They ultimately settled in New Jersey along the Delaware River and came to be known as the Delaware.

The Lord was also mindful of the Ojibway or Anishnaabe branch of the Algonquin language family, those chiefly of Nephite blood who moved north from Zarahemla and then east to the Atlantic. The New England tribes speak of seven spiritual beings, or prophets, who warned them of the future and encouraged them to move farther inland. Each prophet had a different set of instructions. The sixth prophet revealing that the indigenous people of the land would be attacked by a light-skinned race in the future and that a great period of suffering would follow. Thus began a long migration west. It is said that 10,000 canoes could be seen traveling west along the St. Lawrence River to the Ottawa River to Lake Nipissing and then to the Great Lakes, with several stopping places noted along the way. Various branches of those moving west came to be known by a variety of names, with the most notable being the Algonquin, the Nipissing, the Mississaugas, the Ojibway, the Odawa, and the Potawantomi. The Ojibway settled near Sault Ste. Marie in Ontario, Canada, and from there southward along the Ohio and Illinois Rivers and westward along Lake Superior and the northern Great Lakes, where they incorporated many of their relatives still living in the area into their own tribes.

WHITE CONQUEST IN NORTH AMERICA

The Micmac were among some of the first of the northeast coast to be encountered by Europeans. When Sebastian Cabot landed in 1497, he took three natives back to England with him, which are believed to have been the Micmac. The Book or Mormon speaks of such encounters:

> And I looked and beheld a man among the Gentiles, who was separated from the seed of my brethren by the many waters; and I beheld the Spirit of God, that it came down and wrought upon the man; and he went forth upon the many waters, even unto the seed of my brethren, who were in the promised land. (1 Nephi 13:12)

There is no reason to suppose that Columbus, who discovered the West Indies, was the only man moved upon by the Holy Spirit to explore the lands to the west. Many of our early explorers were Christians, including John Cabot, a member of the religious fraternity of St. John. The scripture found in 1 Nephi 13:13 makes it clear that others were also moved upon by the Holy Ghost to explore the lands to the west: "And it came to pass that I beheld the Spirit of God, that it wrought upon other Gentiles; and they went forth out of captivity, upon the many waters."

True to the scriptures, many more followed, including Giovanni da Verrazano, who followed Cabot westward. His encounter with the Indians in Maine led to rumors of a rich and powerful native kingdom, which brought still more people to the area. Samuel de Champlain soon followed and founded Quebec for the French. Another English sea captain, Henry Hudson, believed he could find a northwest passage to Asia. After exploring the waters off the east coast of America, he sent word back to the Netherlands that the mainland was rich in natural resources, which brought still more Gentiles into the area. Jesuit priests also arrived from the old world. However, they were much more interested in converting the Indians than feeding them, for the French Catholic Church wanted to establish a utopian Christian community in the colony. Little did they know that the Savior Himself had once walked these lands. These were His people, remnants of the house of Israel, and this was their promised land, a land the Lord would not take from them, notwithstanding the upcoming trials they were about to endure.

Just as prophesied, once the whites arrived, trouble was not far behind, followed by death from disease and the sword. Others wanted to rob the Indians of the land. Treaties were made with the Indians as early as 1817 that offered them unoccupied lands beyond the Mississippi River, which would become known as Indian Territory. One treaty was made with the Iroquois living on four reservations in New York. But because of fraudulent dealings on the part of the US government, the shrewd Iroquois living in New York were able to buy back the land their people had been living on for centuries with the money they were initially given by the government to move west—land many of them still live on today.

Their Cherokee brothers agreed to make the move, however, and were taken to unoccupied territory west of the Mississippi in present-day Oklahoma, bordering Missouri, which was the fringe of the newly formed United States. Unfortunately, true to the stubborn nature of so many Lamanites, not all their brothers followed. Thus in 1830 the Indian Removal Act was authorized by President Andrew Jackson, and during the fall and winter of 1838 and 1839, the last of the Cherokee were forcibly moved west by the United States government. Approximately 4,000 Cherokee died on that forced march, which became known as the Trail of Tears.

During the 1860s most of the Lenape were also displaced and taken to portions of Oklahoma. Some of the Shawnee were also relocated to Oklahoma. After wars with the Americans and settlers of the Ohio Valley, the Kickapoo signed treaties in 1819, ceding their lands to the government, and were relocated to southern Missouri. Those who refused to leave were forcibly removed by the military in 1834. Thus a large number of Lamanites were living just beyond the bounds of the early United States, far from the lands of their fathers. But the Lord knew where they had been taken. In a revelation given through the Prophet Joseph to Newel Knight in Doctrine and Covenants 54:8, the Lord instructed him

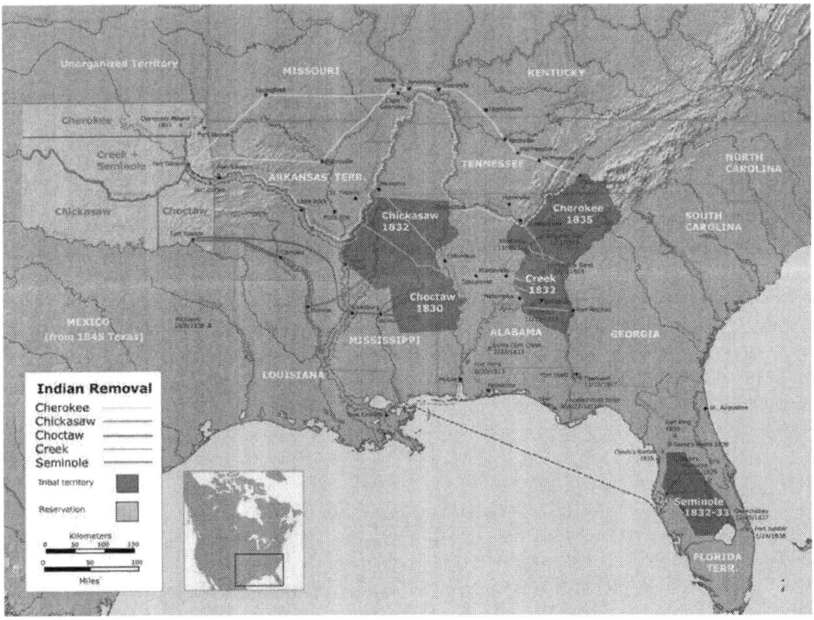

to flee his enemies and go west to Missouri—the borders of the Lamanites.

THE SEED OF LEHI IN MEXICO

From the Anishnaabe history of the Shawnee, we learn that some of the Shawnee made it all the way to Mexico. Along with the tribes in Oklahoma, there is a Shawnee Anishnaabe reservation in west Texas, another in the Mexican state of Coahuila, and still another in the Mexican state of Sonora—about seventy miles south of the United States border.

The Kickapoo were also on the move. Fewer than half stayed on their Missouri reserve, several bands wandering south and west until the Kickapoo were spread from Oklahoma, through Texas, and all the way to Mexico. During the late 1820s, a group of Cherokee, Delaware, Shawnee, and eight hundreed Kickapoo was permitted by the Mexican government to relocate themselves from where they were living in Arkansas to a spot in eastern Texas. There they established farms and villages and were allowed to raise large herds of livestock. Their time of peace was short-lived, however, for the Mexican government offered a land grant policy. It was so attractive to those looking for lands to settle that early American colonists began to arrive by the thousands. In time, the settlers rebelled against the Mexican government, which led to the ultimate takeover of what would become known in 1835 as the Republic of Texas. Because Indian involvement was feared by both sides during the rebellion, treaties and promises were made with the Indians. They were later broken by those who were vehemently opposed to "rights" for Native Americans. As a result, a number of tribes, including the Kickapoo, fled southward into Mexico. By 1865, all of the remaining Kickapoo, with the exception of those residing in Kansas, were now located in Mexico. Yet between 1873 and 1878 half the Mexican Kickapoo returned to the United States and were sent to Oklahoma.

Nearly a century later in the 1960s, as many as 98 percent of the Kickapoo still living in Mexico migrated back into the United States each spring and spread from California through Colorado, Utah, Wyoming, Montana, North Dakota, and New York as agricultural workers, returning to their villages in Mexico in late fall after the last harvest. The nomadic lifestyle of the Kickapoo, the low wages of the migrant workers, and the fringe existence in two nations took its toll on the Mexican Kickapoo, who lived in a continual state of poverty. Due to the assimilation of the tribes through marriage and language, it has become increasingly difficult to identify the Kickapoo carrying Native American blood from those of strictly Mexican descent. Intermarriage with the local US citizens also clouds their identity. But the recognizable tribes of the bands who were first encountered in the Great Lakes include (1) the Kickapoo tribe of Kansas, (2) the Kickapoo tribe of Oklahoma, (3) the traditional Kickapoo tribe of Texas, and (4) the band of Mexican Kickapoo living in Coahuila, Mexico.

THE LAMANITES ARE ISRAELITES

When looking at the big picture, we can see that the Lamanites played a big part in both the ancient and modern history of America, though not altogether a very happy history. But the time will come when they will wake from the sleep of ages and come to recognize that they are destined to play a big part in the rise of the New Jerusalem. Things are destined to get better for Lehi's children of the forest.

Although a large number of those with Lamanite blood have long since melted into the mainstream of America, those who made their way into Mexico over the course of centuries due to famine, war, pestilence and any number of other reasons are slowly being returned to the lands of their ancient fathers. In 2008, over 11.4 million Mexican immigrants resided in the United States, accounting for 30 percent of all US immigrants. It is impossible to say how many are literal descendants of Lehi, but his bloodline has no doubt spread throughout a wide expanse of territory after so great a time span. While still more trials lay ahead for the seed of Lehi, who was a literal descendant of that Joseph who was sold into Egypt, we can trust that the time will come when they will know who their ancient fathers were and will one day stand proudly in the shade of future Zion and proclaim: "We, too, are Israel."

In the 1845 Proclamation of the Twelve Apostles, the Apostles declared that God would ultimately "assemble the Natives the remnants of Joseph in America; and make of them a great, and strong, and powerful nation; and he will civilize them and enlighten them and will establish a holy city, and temple, and a seat of government among them, which shall be called Zion."

The declaration continued:

> The despised and degraded son of the forest, who has wandered in dejection and sorrow, and suffered reproach, shall then drop his disguise, and stand forth in manly dignity, and exclaim to the Gentiles who have envied and sold him: Joseph: does my father yet live? Or, in other words: I am a descendant of that Joseph who was sold into Egypt. You have hated me, and sold me, and thought I was dead. But lo! I live. (Proclamation of the Twelve Apostles, April 6, 1845)

Those of pure Mexican descent are also of Israel, chiefly through the Zarah line of Judah's twin sons. While his brother

Perez's line is destined to return to Jerusalem to rebuild their temple and to wait upon the Lord in the Old World, the Zarah line of Judah never lived in Jerusalem. They may simply be numbered among America's Israelite populations who are destined to assist in the building of the New Jerusalem. Speaking of the role the Gentiles will play in the rise of the New Jerusalem, the Lord said,

> And they shall assist my people, the remnant of Jacob, and also as many of the house of Israel as shall come, that they may build a city, which shall be called the New Jerusalem. (3 Nephi 21:23)

Without question, Joseph's seed will be major players in its construction of the temple, under the guidance and direction of the First Presidency of the Church of Jesus Christ of Latter-day Saints, who holds the keys of temple building. Yet we must not forget that there are other descendants of Joseph in America besides the seed of Lehi. The tribe of Ephraim, the son of Joseph, has been gathered out from among the gentile nations by the thousands by early Latter-day Saint missionaries and make up the bulk of The Church Jesus Christ of Latter-day Saints today. These Ephraimites are being used as a perpetual missionary force to gather out the remainder of Israel and have been given the charge to bring them back into the fold through baptism, including the Lamanites. While the scriptures make it clear that the Lamanites will help in the construction of the New Jerusalem, they will do so under the direction and guidance of the First Presidency of The Church of Jesus Christ of Latter-day Saints and its members, who are chiefly of Ephraim, the birthright son of Joseph.

The land now called America has quite a history, with even greater things yet to come, notwithstanding the trials and struggles it is yet destined to endure. During its long history three bodies of Christian Saints have occupied the same territory: (1) The Jaredite civilization, (2) the Nephite/Mulekite civilization, and (3) the Gentile nation. In the very same lands the first two civilizations lived and died, the early Latter-day Saints have been gathered out from among the Gentiles and organized into the formal Church of Jesus Christ of Latter-day Saints.

The question that must now be answered is what will become of our nation? Will we remain a Christian-based society and receive all the blessings promised those who live in the land righteously? Or will we follow the same dark paths the Jaredites and the Nephites followed, which led to their ultimate destruction?

Joseph Fielding Smith said,

> This country was founded as a Christian nation, with the acceptance of Jesus Christ as the Redeemer of the world. It was predicted by a prophet of old that this land would be a land of liberty and it would be fortified against all other nations as long as its inhabitants would serve Jesus Christ; but should they stray from the Son of God, it would cease to be a land of liberty and his anger be kindled against them.[1]

Current events in our nation lead us to fear and tremble lest the latter scenario be true. Yet in spite of the rocky road that appears to lie before us, this nation will endure, for it is the place the New Jerusalem will be built and where the Lord will rule and reign over the entire earth for a thousand years of peace.

Harold B. Lee said,

> Men may fail in this country, earthquakes may come, seas may heave beyond their bounds, there may be great drought, disaster, and hardship, but this nation, founded on principles laid down by men whom God raised up, will never fail. This is the cradle of humanity, where life on this earth began in the Garden of Eden. This is the place of the new Jerusalem. This is the place that the Lord said is favored above all other nations in all the world. This is the place where the Savior will come to His temple. This is the favored land in all the world. Yes, I repeat, men may fail, but this nation won't fail. I have faith in America; you and I must have faith in America, if we understand the teachings of the gospel of Jesus Christ. We are living in a day when we must pay heed to these challenges.
>
> I plead with you not to preach pessimism. Preach that this is the greatest country in all the world. This is the favored land. This is the land of our forefathers. It is the nation that will stand despite whatever trials or crises it may yet have to pass through.[2]

25

Final Thoughts *and a* Voice *of* Warning

In the sad hours and years that followed the horrific battle at Cumorah, Moroni recorded not only the epilogue to his own people's destruction but the fate that befell the Jaredites as well. In so doing, he was quick to remind us that their destruction came about because they had forsaken the Lord and had all turned to wickedness.

> For behold, they rejected all the words of Ether; for he truly told them of all things, from the beginning of man; and that after the waters had receded from off the face of this land it became a choice land above all other lands, a chosen land of the Lord; wherefore the Lord would have that all men should serve him who dwell upon the face thereof;
>
> And that it was the place of the New Jerusalem, which should come down out of heaven, and the holy sanctuary of the Lord. (Ether 13:2–3)

The Nephites were next to inherit the land, and they, too, were warned of the terrible consequence if they turned from God.

> Wherefore, this land is consecrated unto him whom he shall bring. And if it so be that they shall serve him according to the commandments which he hath given, it shall be a land of liberty unto them;

> wherefore, they shall never be brought down into captivity; if so, it shall be because of iniquity; for if iniquity shall abound cursed shall be the land for their sakes, but unto the righteous it shall be blessed forever. (2 Nephi 1:7)

Many promises were made to both nations, but in each instance, the children of the promised land ultimately turned their backs on God and served the devil instead. Over and over again the Lord reminded them that they must keep the promised land clean so that at some future time the great Gentile nation, which was destined to rise in the latter days, would be able to fulfill its mission in preparing the way for the restoration of all things in anticipation of the Savior's Second Coming. Unfortunately, neither nation remained faithful and were thus totally wiped away—including almost all evidence of their very existence, lest others desire the land for its riches before the appointed time of the Gentiles. The Jaredites were all destroyed, excepting two men: Coriantumr and the prophet Ether. Only Moroni survived among the Nephites slaughtered at Cumorah, and, of course, the victorious Lamanites survived who, in deference to certain prophets who pled their case, were permitted continued existence in the land. Because the Nephites had been given greater light and knowledge than the Lamanites and then turned away from it, they were not privileged to remain in the land.

With the fall of the Nephite nation, the Lord began the process of preparing the way for the influx of Gentiles who were next in line to inherit the promised land. But just like the Nephites and Jaredites before them, the blessings they would subsequently enjoy would be conditional upon their righteousness and their faith and worship of the Lord, Jesus Christ.

> Behold, this is a choice land, and whatsoever nation shall possess it shall be free from bondage, and from captivity, and from all other nations under heaven, if they will but serve the God of the land, who is Jesus Christ, who hath been manifested by the things which we have written. (Ether 2:12)

Just as in days of old, living in the land of promise carries with it the responsibility to remember the Lord our God and to live righteously upon the land, for this great land of liberty cannot stand without the blessings of the Almighty. But most important of all is His counsel to remember Him, for those who forget the Lord or set him at naught will surely fall. The destruction of both the Nephites and Jaredites provides ample evidence of his seriousness about the matter.

It is no wonder such emphasis is placed on reading the Book of Mormon, for within its pages we find prophetic warnings for our day, especially in respect to defiling the promised land. Far too many scriptures describe the greatness of the latter-day Gentile nation to have questions about the location of the promised land any longer. Right from the beginning, it was destined to rise with an influx of pilgrims from many nations under the care of founding fathers who would formulate a constitution of the people, by the people, and for the people.

President Ezra Taft Benson tells us the Lord raised up such honorable men to assure this land remain a land of freedom. He said,

> Nearly two hundred years ago some inspired men walked this land. Not perfect men—but men raised up by the perfect Man to perform great work. Foreordained were they to lay the foundation of this Republic. Blessed by the Almighty in their struggle for liberty and independence, the power of heaven rested on these Founders as they drafted that great document for governing men—The Constitution of the United States. Like the Ten Commandments, the truths on which the Constitution were based were timeless; and also with the Decalogue—the hand of the Lord was in it. They filled their mission well. From them we were endowed with a legacy of liberty—a Constitutional Republic.[1]

Great blessings have been bestowed upon the Gentiles of this generation. Yet the scriptures make it clear that tragedy awaits them if they reject the Lord after all he has done to sustain them and bring them to their present state of greatness, notwithstanding their various trials along the way. The blessings and cursings pronounced upon those who occupy the land of promise were rehearsed to the Nephites during their earliest years in the land so that throughout the generations they would know that the promised land was holy ground and must not be defiled. We learn of its status as holy ground from Enos.

> And while I was thus struggling in the spirit, behold, the voice of the Lord came into my mind again, saying: I will visit thy brethren according to their diligence in keeping my commandments. I have given unto them this land, and it is a holy land; and I curse it not save it be for the cause of iniquity; wherefore, I will visit thy brethren according as I have said; and their transgressions will I bring down with sorrow upon their own heads. (Enos 1:10)

The prophecies pertinent to this holy land of America were directed not just to the ancient Saints but also to those of our day, so that we, too, might know of our responsibility to keep the promised land free from sin. Knowing this land is the promised land is far more important than we might otherwise have supposed. This knowledge is critical to our very survival as a nation and as individuals who may suffer untold misery in years to come if we allow the nation to become ripe in iniquity. The Lord's decree that all who inhabit this promised land must serve him or be wiped away is an everlasting decree, just as pertinent to those of our day as it was to the Nephites or Jaredites. According to the Lord himself, this glorious land of America, the place of the New Jerusalem, is the land of promise, and who shall dispute His word?

Wherefore, this is the land of promise, and the place for the city of Zion (D&C 57:2).

Ezra Taft Benson, also makes it clear where the promised land is and who the various nations were who occupied the land anciently.

> Many great events have transpired in this land of destiny. This was the place where Adam dwelt; this was the place where the Garden of Eden was; it was here that Adam met with a body of high priests at Adam-ondi-Ahman shortly before his death and gave them his final blessing, and the place to which he will return to meet the leaders of his people (D&C 107:53–57). This was the place of three former civilizations: that of Adam, that of the Jaredites, and that of the Nephites. This was also the place where our Heavenly Father and his Son, Jesus Christ, appeared to Joseph Smith, inaugurating the last dispensation.

> The Lord has also decreed that this land should be "the place of the New Jerusalem, which should come down out of heaven, and the holy sanctuary of the Lord" (Ether 13:3). Here is our nation's destiny! To serve God's eternal purposes and to prepare this land and people for America's eventual destiny, He "established the Constitution of this land, by the hands of wise men whom [He] raised up unto this very purpose, and redeemed the land by the shedding of blood (D&C 101:80).[2]

In speaking across the pulpit in general conference in November 1987, President Ezra Taft Benson said, "Two great American Christian civilizations—the Jaredites and the Nephites—were swept off this land because they 'did not serve the God of the land, who is Jesus Christ' (Ether 2:12). What will become of our civilization?"[3]

President Benson also said,

> For centuries the Lord kept America hidden in the hollow of His Hand until the time was right to unveil her for her destiny in the last days. "It is wisdom that this land should be kept as yet from the knowledge of other nations," said Lehi, "for behold, many nations would overrun the land, that there would be no place for an inheritance" (2 Ne. 1:8).
>
> In the Lord's due time His Spirit "wrought upon" Columbus, the pilgrims, the Puritans, and others to come to America. They testified of God's intervention in their behalf (see 1 Ne. 13:12–13). The Book of Mormon records that they humbled "themselves before the Lord; and the power of the Lord was with them" (1 Ne. 13:16).
>
> Our Father in Heaven planned the coming forth of the Founding Fathers and their form of government as the necessary great prologue leading to the restoration of the gospel. Recall what our Savior, Jesus Christ said nearly two thousand years ago when He visited this promised land: "For it is wisdom in the Father that they should be established in this land, and be set up as a free people by the power of the Father, that these things might come forth" (3 Ne. 21:4). America, the land of liberty, was to be the Lord's latter-day base of operations for His restored church.[4]

The great men who were instrumental in setting up our form of government were very much aware of the Lord's part in its formation and of the necessity of keeping God in the forefront of our lives if the nation were to survive. The words of Dr. Daniel Webster, who spoke to the New York Historical Society on February 22, 1852, is as pertinent to those of our day as it was to those of his. He said,

> Unborn ages and visions of glory crowd upon my soul, the realization of all which, however, is in the hands and good pleasure of Almighty God; but, under his divine blessing, it will be dependent on the character and the virtues of ourselves, and of our posterity. . . .
>
> And let me say, gentlemen, that if we and our posterity shall be true to the Christian religion—if we and they shall live always in the fear of God, and shall respect his commandments, if we and they shall maintain just, moral sentiments, and such conscientious convictions of duty as shall control the heart and life—we may have the highest hopes of the future fortunes of our country; and if we maintain those institutions of government and that political union, exceeding all praise as much as it exceeds all former examples of political associations, we may be sure of one thing—that while our country is furnishing materials for a thousand masters of the historic art, it will afford no topic for a Gibbon. It will have no Decline and Fall. It will go on prospering and to prosper.
>
> But, if we and our posterity reject religious instruction and authority, violate the rules of eternal justice, trifle with the injunctions of morality, and recklessly destroy the political constitution which holds us together, no man can tell how suddenly a catastrophe may overwhelm us, that shall bury all our glory in profound obscurity. Should that catastrophe happen, let it have no history! Let the horrible narrative never be written! Let its fate be like that of the lost books of Livy, which no human eye shall ever read; or the missing Pleiad, of which no man can ever know more, than that it is lost, and lost forever! [5]

It is sad to note that both the Nephites and Jaredites learned just how serious the Lord was about keeping the promised land clean and firmly rooted in its Christian foundation, both nations having been totally destroyed. Both learned the hard way that as people grow they follow one of two paths: up toward God or down to destruction. President Ezra Taft Benson noted that history itself proves nations progress "from bondage to spiritual faith/ from spiritual faith to courage/ from courage to freedom/ from freedom to abundance/ from abundance to selfishness/ from selfishness to complacency/ from complacency to apathy/ from apathy to fear/ from fear to dependency/ from dependency to bondage."[6] We might ask ourselves, where on this scale do we as a nation stand today?

> Yea, and we may see at the very time when he doth prosper his people, yea, in the increase of their fields, their flocks and their herds, and in gold, and in silver, and in all manner of precious things of every kind and art; sparing their lives, and delivering them out of the hands of their enemies; softening the hearts of their enemies that they should not declare wars against them; yea, and in fine, doing all things for the welfare and happiness of his people; yea, then is the time that they do harden their hearts, and do forget the Lord their God, and do trample under their feet the Holy One—yea, and this because of their ease, and their exceedingly great prosperity.
>
> And thus we see that except the Lord doth chasten his people with many afflictions, yea, except he doth visit them with death and with terror, and with famine and with all manner of pestilence, they will not remember him.
>
> O how foolish, and how vain, and how evil, and devilish, and how quick to do iniquity, and how slow to do good, are the children of men; yea, how quick to hearken unto the words of the evil one, and to set their hearts upon the vain things of the world! (Helaman 12:2–4)

Our own history books are filled with instances of success by those who had God on their side. For example, those who fought to preserve our freedom to worship Almighty God as our hearts so dictated—such as the men who fought during the Revolutionary War—were spared and ultimately went on to build a nation that prospered beyond all other nations on earth. In contrast, the last generations of the Nephites and Jaredites—who fought only for worldly gain, power, and possessions—lost their final battles and were consigned to the arms of Mother Earth to await a day of reconciliation. Thus a constant study of the rise and fall of the Nephites and Jaredites can be a powerful tool in learning from the past the course we should take today. Once we become familiar enough with the characters in the Book of Mormon to feel the pains of those who lost everything and recognize their folly in rejecting God, we will be more inclined to avoid the same mistakes and take every measure needed to stay the hand of the devil, whose dark minions are moving all too quickly across this land.

If only a movie could be made of the journey of the golden plates, we would be amazed by the struggle it took for the various prophets and scribes to keep them out of the hands of the Lamanites and those who wished to destroy them. They hid them in caves and in hillsides and were careful to allow only those they felt confident were guided by the Spirit to ever come in contact with them. The scriptures tell us they were polished and kept bright through each generation so that those of our day could see the workings of God among men and learn from the mistakes of those who turned away from him and were ultimately destroyed (see Alma 37:5).

These records show the devil at work, trying every way he can think of to tear down and debase the children of God and turn them from their Savior. But these things are happening in our day as well, and his minions will increase in numbers and strength until the Lord himself destroys the wicked from off the face of the earth. Thus searching the Book of Mormon for clues on how to win the battle between good and evil is vital to those of our day. More often than not, the trials of today are simply a repeat of those of yesterday, with the stories in the Book of Mormon revealing the rewards of those who either succumbed to evil and lost their souls, or obeyed the commandments and found eternal life.

Searching the Book of Mormon for the enlightenment we need to survive the coming storms is not just a request from our living prophets but from the Lord Himself. Moreover, it is a plea from Nephi and from Alma and from Helaman and from his sons Nephi and Lehi. It is a plea from Mormon and Moroni and all those who fought and died in battle to preserve these records so that those of our day might learn from the mistakes of the past and not fall victim to Satan's wiles. Hopefully, with the scriptures to guide us, this generation can avoid the pitfalls that caused so much sorrow and destruction in the past and can look forward with joyful anticipation for the Savior's triumphant return and His reign as King of kings and Lord of lords during a millennium of peace.

Chapter Notes

THE JAREDITES

1. Albert Tobias Clay, *Amurru, the Home of the Northern Semites* (HardPress Publishing, 2013), 153.

2. Ronan James Head, "A Brief Survey of Ancient Near Eastern Beekeeping" *The Farms Review* 20/1, (Provo, UT: Brigham Young University, Neal A. Maxwell Institute for Religious Scholarship, 2008), 62–63.

3. Flavius Josephus, 93 C.E., William Whiston, Tran., *The Works of Flavius Josephus: Antiquities of the Jews* I, VI (Scholar's Choice, 2015); emphasis added.

THE JOURNEY BEGINS

1. Irving Finkel, "Was Noah's Ark Round? 3,700-year old clay tablet reveals giant boat was made out of reeds and bitumen," *Daily Mail*, www.dailymail.co.uk/sciencetech/article-2545494/.

2. Herman LeRoy Fairchild, *The Geologic Story of the Genesee Valley and Western New York* (Rochester, NY: Herman LeRoy Fairchild, 1928), 159.

THE JAREDITES' EARLY KINGDOM

1. Hugh W. Nibley, "The Moving Host" *The Collected Works of Hugh Nibley: Jared on the Steppes* ch. 3 (Provo, UT: Neal A. Maxwell Institute for Religious Scholarship, Brigham Young University).

2. Herman LeRoy Fairchild, *Geologic Story of the Genesee Valley* (Rochester: Herman LeRoy Fairchild, 1928), 199.

3. Parker E. Calkin and Carlton E. Brett, *Ancestral Niagara River Drainage: Stratigraphic and Paleontological Setting* 89 no. 8 (GSA Bulletin, Aug 1978), 1140-1154.

4. O. Turner, quoted in E. Cecil McGavin & Willard Bean's, *The Geography of the Book of Mormon,* (Salt Lake City: Bookcraft, 1949), 11.

5. Ibid., 13.

6. William A. Ritchie, *The Archaeology of New York State*, revised edition (Garden City, NY: Natural History Press, 1965), 183.

7. William A. Ricthie, *Indian History of New York State: Pre-Iroquoian Cultures*, Educational Leaflet no. 6 (Albany, NY: New York State Archeological Association), 23.

8. William A. Ritchie, *The Archaeology of New York State*, revised edition (Garden City, NY: Natural History Press, 1965), 200.

9. Ibid.

10. Papworth, quoted in Joseph E. Granger, Jr., Granger's *Meadowood Phase Settlement Pattern in the Niagara Frontier Region of Western New York State*, anthropological papers (Ann Arbor, MI: , 1978), 25-6.

11. J. R. Jochmans, "Strange Relics from the Depth of the Earth," *Ancient American* no. 43 reprint (1979), 9.

12. Josiah Priest, *"And Discoveries in the West" American Antiquities* (Albany: Hoffman and White, 1838), 265

THE CELTIC CHILDREN OF JAPHETH

1. Steffasson, quoted in Roger L Jewel's, *The Ancient Mines of Kitchi-Gumni*, (Fairfield, PA: Jewel Histories, 2004), 113.

THE JAREDITES' SECOND RISE AND FALL

1. William A. Ritchie, *The Archaeology of New York State,* revised ed. (Garden City, NY: Natural History Press, 1965), 164.

2. Joseph E. Granger Jr., *Meadowood Phase Settlement Pattern in the Niagara Frontier Region of western New York State*, (Ann Arbor, MI: University of Michigan Press, 1978), 55.

3. William A. Ritchie, *The Archaeology of New York State*, revised ed. (Garden City, NY: Natural History Press, 1965), 156.

4. Joseph Fielding Smith, *Doctrines of Salvation* vol. 3 (Salt Lake City: Bookcraft, 1956) 233-234; emphasis in original.

5. Oliver Cowdery, *Joseph Smith Papers* vol. 1 (Salt Lake City: Deseret Book), 79-81.

6. Josiah Priest, quoted in E. Cecil McGavin and Willard Bean's, *The Geography of the Book of Mormon*, (Salt Lake City: Bookcraft, 1949), 16.

7. E. Cecil McGavin and Willard Bean, *The Geography of the Book of Mormon* (Salt Lake City: Bookcraft, 1949), 12–13.

8. Ibid.

THE MIGRATION OF PRINCE ZARAH

1. L. Taylor Hansen, The Anceint Atlantic, (Amherst Press, 1969), 35.

2. Jewish Encyclopedia, Full-text, Unedited, (1906).

ZARAH-JUDAH IN NEW ENGLAND

1. Paul H. Andree, III. *Israelology: The Birthright, House of Israel, Kingdom, and Sons of God* (Paul H. Andree, 2008).

2. Barry Fell, *America B.C.: Ancient Settlers in the New World* (Muskogee, OK: Hoffman Printing, Artisan Publishers, 2005), 64.

3. Ibid., 5, 6.

4. Ibid., 193.

THE ROYAL LINE OF JOSEPH

1. Arthur Caswell Parker, *Archaeological History of New York* (NY: The University of the State of New York).

2. Don Dragoo, Joseph R. Caldwell and Robert L. Hall, eds., "The Development of Adena Culture and its Role in the Formation of Ohio Hopewell," *Hopewellian Studies* vol. 12 (Springfield, IL: Dept. of Registration and Education, Illinois State Museum, 1964), 16.

3. Ibid., 19.

THE ROYAL LINE OF JUDAH

1. *Proto. Algonquin Language.* Wikipedia the free encyclopedia.

2. William A. Ritchie, *The Archaeology of New York State* revised edition (Garden City, NY: Natural History Press, 1965), 201.

3. Susan Alfson, *The Stone of Israel and the Two Witnesses: Destiny's Epilogue* (Writers Club Press, 2000), 66, 67.

4. Barry Fell, *America B.C.: Ancient Settlers in the New World* (Muskogee, OK: Hoffman Printing, Artisan Publishers, 2005), 99.

5. James P. Whittall, quoted in William F. McNeil, *Visitors to America*, (Jefferson, KY: McFarland and Company, 2005), 225.

ZARAH-JUDAH IN TENNESSEE

1. Salvatore Michael Trento, *The Search For Lost America: The Mysteries of the Stone Ruins* (Chicago IL: Contemporary Books, 1978), 103.

2. Ibid., 120.

3. Joseph Jones, quoted in Salvatore Michael Trento's, *The Search For Lost America,* (Chicago IL: Contemporary Books, Inc., 1978), 135, 136.

4. Stephen D. Peet, *The Mound Builders* (Chicago, IL: Office of the American Antiquarian, 1892), 108; insert added.

5. M. Viollet. le. Duc, quoted in Hubert Howe Bancroft's, *The Works of Hubert Howe Bancroft: The Native Races* vol. 5 (San Francisco: A. L. Bancroft and Co., 1883), 233, https://archive.org/details/worksofhuberthow05banc.

6. Hubert Howe Bancroft, *The Works of Hubert Howe Bancroft: The Native Races* vol. 3 (San Francisco: A. L. Bancroft and Co., 1883), 727.

BACK TO THE THE LAND OF NEPHI

1. John and Evangeline Griswold and Co., Ruth Griswold 1979, Marsia Painter with Sue Gullo, *1829-1979 Arkwright Sesquicentennial: History of the Town of Arkwright*, (Town56@frontiernet.not: Nathan Towne 2008), http://www.rootsweb.ancestry.com/~nychauta/HISTORY/Arkwright/ArkwrightTownHistory.html; insert added.

THE LAND NORTHWARD

1. *Oxford Companion to Archaeology: Iroquois and Algonquian Cultures*, "Algonquian Cultures," 2014, http://www.answers.com/topic/iroquois. and. algonquian. cultures#ixzz37pPAKsmj

2. William A. Warren, *The History of the Ojibway People*, *Collections of the Minnesota Historical Society* vol. 5 reprint (St. Paul: Minnesota Historical Society Press, 1984), 63.

THE OHIO HOPEWELL

1. Don Dragoo, Joseph R. Caldwell and Robert L. Hall (eds.), "The Development of Adena Culture and its Role in the Formation of Ohio Hopewell," *Hopewellian Studies* vol. 12 (Springfield, IL: Dept. of Registration and Education, Illinois State Museum, 1964), 40.

2. Ibid., 20.

3. Moorehead, quoted in Stephen Denison Peet, *The Mound Builders: their Works and Relics, Prehistoric America* vol. 1 ch. 7, (Chicago: Office of the American Antiquarian, 1892), https://archive.org/details/moundbuilders00peetrich.

4. Joseph Smith, quoted in Dean C. Jessee, ed., *The Personal Writings of Joseph Smith*, (Salt Lake City: Deseret Book, 1984), 344–46.

THE LAMANITES.

1. "Siouan Migrations and Iroquois Conquests" *Access Genealogy*, www. accessgeonalogy.com /native/siouan/east/siouan.migration.

THE ZARAHITES AND DANITES OF MEXICO

1. Stephen Denison Peet, *The Mound Builders: their Works and Relics, Prehistoric America* vol. 1 ch. 7 (Chicago: Office of the American Antiquarian, 1892), 180, 181, https://archive.org/details/moundbuilders00peetrich.

2. Don Dragoo, Joseph R. Caldwell and Robert L. Hall (eds.), "The Development of Adena Culture and its Role in the Formation of Ohio Hopewell," *Hopewellian Studies* ,vol. 12 (Springfield, IL: Dept. of Registration and Education, Illinois State Museum, 1964), 128.

3. Herodotus, VI, I, iii.

4. Edward Herbert Thompson, *The People of the Serpent: Life and Adventure Among the Mayas* (Boston, NY: Houghton Mifflin, 1932), 78, 79, note 1.

5. Hubert Howe Bancroft, "The Native Races: Primitive Races," *The Works of Hubert Howe Bancroft*, vol. 5 (San Francisco: A. L. Bancroft and Co., 1883), 233.

6. Ibid., 191

7. Sahagun, quoted in Hubert Howe Bancroft, "The Native Races:

Primitive Races," *The Works of Hubert Howe Bancroft,* vol. 5 (San Francisco: A. L. Bancroft and Co., 1883), 189.

8. Hubert Howe Bancroft, "The Native Races: Primitive Races," *The Works of Hubert Howe Bancroft,* vol. 5 (San Francisco: A. L. Bancroft and Co., 1883), 189.

9. Edward Herbert Thompson, *The People of the Serpent: Life and Adventure Among the Mayas* (Boston and New York: Houghton Mifflin Co, 1932), 78.

10. Sahagun, quoted in Hubert Howe Bancroft's, *The Native Races: Primitive Races, The Works of Hubert Howe Bancroft* vol. 5 (San Francisco: A. L. Bancroft and Co. Publishers, 1883), 190.

11. Hubert Howe Bancroft, *The Native Races: Myths and Languages, The Works of Hubert Howe Bancroft* vol. 3 (San Francisco: The History Company, 1886), 187.

12. Ibid., 188.

13. Don W. Dragoo, *Mounds for the Dead: An Analysis of the Adena Culture*, *Annals of Carnegie Museum*, vol. 37 (Granville, OH: McDonald and Woodward, Carnegie Museum, September 1963).

TRADE ROUTES AND TIES

1. Edward V. McMichael, "Veracruz, the Crystal River Complex, and the Hopewellian Climax," Paper 5, in *Hopewellian Studies*, Joseph R. Caldwell and Robert L. Hall (ed), *Illinois State Museum Scientific Papers*, vol. 12 (Springfield: State of Illinois, 1964), 132.

2. William Pidgeon, William De-coo-dah, *Traditions of De-Coo-Dah: And Antiquarian Researches* (New York: Horace Thayer, 1858), 143.

3. Hopewell Ancient DNA Research http://www.friendsofpast.org/earliest. americas/030807OhioDNA.html

4. John D. Baldwin, "The Mound-Builders" *Ancient America in Notes on American Archaeology* (Montana: Kessinger Publishing Co, 1872), 32.

5. William F. Romain, *The Mystery of the Hopewell*, (Akron Ohio: The University of Akron Press, 2000), 1.

THE GREAT DESTRUCTION

1. Yngvar W. Isachsen, *Geology of New York: A Simplified Account: Educational Leaflet* no. 28 2nd Edition (NY: New York State Museum, 2000), 236.

2. Bryan Mitchell, *Toronto Star*, (October 14, 1984).

3. Dan Scheirer, "A Hundred-Million Year History of the Corner Rise and New England Seamounts," *Ocean Explorer*, 2005, http://oceanexplorer.noaa.gov/explorations/05stepstones/background/geologic_history/geologic_history.html.

4. John Shea (ed), "The Dark Days and Earthquakes in Canada" *The Historical Magazines and Notes and Queries Concerning the Antiquities, History, and Biography of America*, vol. 5, 1864.

5. Ibid.

6. *Transaction of the Library and Philosophical Society of Quebec*, 1830, vol. 5 no. 2.

7. Messr. Gognon, quoted in J. W. Dawson, LLD., F.G.S., *Notes on the Earthquake of October*, vol. 8 (1860), 39, 40.

THE GOLDEN AGE OF CHRIST

1. Isabel Elder, *Celt Druid, and Culdee*, p. 99.

2. William Pidgeon, William De-coo-dah, *Traditions of De-Coo-Dah: And Antiquarian Researches* (New York: Horace Thayer, 1858), 257.

3. Ibid., 98.

4. Ibid., 99.

5. Ibid., 98

6. Ibid.

7. Robert Silverberg, *The Mound Builders*, abridged ed. (Akron, OH: Ohio University Press, 1970), 204.

THE CULTURE HERO QUETZALCOATL

1. Torquemada, quoted in Hubert Howe Bancroft's, *The Native Races: Myths and Languages, The Works of Hubert Howe Bancroft*, vol. 3 (San Francisco: The History Company, 1886), 258, Footnote 23.

2. Hubert Howe Bancroft, *The Native Races: Myths and Languages, The Works of Hubert Howe Bancroft*, vol. 3 (San Francisco: The History Company, 1886), 260.

3. Hunter and Ferguson, *Ancient America and the Book of Mormon*, (Oakland CA: Kolob Book 1964), 164.

4. Hubert Howe Bancroft, *The Native Races: Myths and Languages, The Works of Hubert Howe Bancroft*, vol. 3 (San Francisco: The History Company, 1886), 253.

5. Ibid., 465, note 13.

THE POST-CHRISTIAN DECLINE

1. William A. Ritchie, *The Archaeology of New York State,* revised ed. (Garden City, NY: Natural History Press, 1965), 216.

THE FALL OF THE HOPEWELL CIVILIZATION

1. A. J. Conant, *Footprints of a Vanished Races in the Mississippi Valley* (St. Louis: C. R. Barns, 1879), 118, 119.

2. John Thomas Short, quoted in Stephen Denison Peet's, *The Mound*

Builders: their Works and Relics, Prehistoric America, vol. 1 (Chicago: Office of the American Antiquarian, 1892), 178.

3. John Thomas Short, *The North Americans of Antiquity: Their Origin, Migrations, and Type of Civilization Considered,* (NY: Harper and Brothers, 1880), 253.

4. Mariano Veytia, *Ancient America Rediscovered*, (Springfield, UT: Cedar Fort, 2000), 189.

5. Brasseur de Bourbourg, quoted in John D. Baldwin's, *Ancient America in Notes on American Archaeology* (New York: Harper and Bothers, 1872), 201.

6. Hubert Howe Bancroft, "The Native Races: Primitive Races," *The Works of Hubert Howe Bancroft*, vol. 5 (San Francisco: A.L. Bancroft and Co., 1883), 220.

7. Ibid., 210, 211.

8. John D. Baldwin, *Ancient America in Notes on American Archaeology* (Montana: Kessinger, 1872), 202.

9. Ibid., 201.

10. Milton R. Hunter and Thomas Stuart Ferguson, "Founding of Tula (Teotihuacan) and its Kings" *Ancient America and the Book of Mormon*, ch. 29 (Oakland, CA: Kolob Book Company, 1964), 375.

11. Salvatore Michael Trento, *The Search for Lost America: The Mysteries of the Stone Ruins*, first ed. (Chicago: Contemporary Books, 1978), 93.

12. Joseph Smith, *History of the Church*, vol. 2 (Salt Lake City: Deseret News), 80.

13. Robert Silverberg, *The Mound Builders*, abridged ed. (Akron, OH: Ohio University Press, 1970), 62.

14. Henry Clyde Shetrone, *The Mound Builders*, reprint (D. Appleton and Co., 1930; Tuscaloosa, AL: The University of Alabama Press, 2004).

15. Walter Pidgeon, quoted in Robert Silverberg's, *The Mound Builders*, abridged ed. (Akron, OH: Ohio University Press, 1970), 100.

THE FALL OF THE NEPHITE CIVILIZATION

1. Orson F. Whitney, *Life of Heber C. Kimball: An Apostle:The Father Founder of the British Mission* (Salt Lake City: Stevens and Wallis Press, 1945), 25, 26.

2. Letter from Oliver Cowdery, Dean C. Jessee, *Joseph Smith Papers*, vol. 1 (Salt Lake City: Deseret Book), 79, 81.

3. Joseph Fielding Smith, *Doctrines of Salvation*, vol. 3 (Salt Lake City: Bookcraft), 240, 241.

4. John Heinerman, *Hidden Treasures of Ancient American Cultures* (Springville, UT: Cedar Fort, 2001), 46, 47.

5. E. E. Squire, *Aboriginal Monuments.*

6. Cecil B. McGavin and Willard Bean, *Geography of the Book of Mormon*, (Salt Lake City: Bookcraft, 1949), 87–88.

AFTER CUMORAH

1. Joseph Fielding Smith, *Doctrines of Salvation*, vol. 3 (Salt Lake City: Bookcraft), 325.

2. Harold B. Lee, “Ye Are the Light of the World” (Salt Lake City: Deseret Book, 1974), 350, 51.

FINAL THOUGHTS AND A VOICE OF WARNING

1. Ezra Taft Benson, *The Teachings of Ezra Taft Benson,* 8th Printing (Salt Lake City: Bookcraft, 1994), 53.

2. Ibid., 587, 588.

3. Ezra Taft Benson, “Our Divine Constitution,” *Ensign*, November 1987, 4.

4. Ibid.

5. B. H. Roberts, *New Witness for God,* vol. 2 (Salt Lake City: The Deseret News, 1951), 321, 322.

6. Ezra Taft Benson, *An Enemy Hath Done This* (Salt Lake City: Parliment Publishers, 1969), 117.

Partial Bibliography

Baldwin, John D. *Ancient America*. Franklin Square, NY: Harper and Brothers, 1872, 202.

Bancroft, Hubert Howe. *Native Races-The Works,* vol. 1-5. San Francisco, CA: The History Company, 1886.

Cunningham, Wilbur M. *A Study of the Glacial Kame Culture in Michigan, Ohio, and Indiana*. Ann Arbor, MI: University of Michigan Press, 1978, 15.

Collins, Andrew. *Gateway to Atlantis*. NY: Carroll and Graf Publishers, 2000.

Conant, A. J. *Foot-prints of vanished races in the Mississippi valley*. Edited by Chauncey R. Barnes. St. Louis, Missouri: C. R. Barns, 1879.

Dragoo, Don. "The Development of Adena Culture and its Role in the Formation of Ohio Hopewell," *Hopewellian Studies*, vol. 12. Edited by Caldwell, Joseph R. and Hall, Robert L. Springfield, IL: Illinois State Museum, 1964, 16.

Dragoo, Don. Mounds for the Dead: An Analysis of the Adena Culture, *Annals of Carnegie Museum*, vol. 37. Pittsburgh, PA: Carnegie Museum, 1964-1971.

Fairchild, Herman LeRoy. *Geologic Story of the Genesee Valley and Western New York* 1st ed. Herman Leroy Fairchild, 1928.

Fell, Barry, *America B. C.*. Muskogee, OK: Artisan Publishers, 1976.

Foster, J. W. *Prehistoric Races of the United States*, Chicago, S. C. Griggs and co., 1874.

Gordon, Cyrus, H. *Before Columbus*. New York, NY: Crown Publishers, 1971.

Gordon, E. O. *Prehistoric London: Its Mounds and Circles*. Muskogee, OK: Artisan Publishers (1985).

Hansen, L. Taylor, *He Walked the Americas*. Kempton, IL: Adventures Unlimited Press, 2014.

Hansen, Vaughn E. *Whence Came They*. Springville, UT: Cedar Fort, 1993.

Heinerman, John. *Hidden Treasures*. Springville, UT: Cedar Fort, 2000.

Hunter, Milton R. *Archaeology and the Book of Mormon*. Salt Lake City: Deseret Book, 1956.

Jowett, George F. *The Drama of The Lost Disciples*. Covenant Publishing Co Ltd: Bishop Auckland, London, 1970.

Judd, Robert B. *Atlantis, Mother of Empires*. Adventures Unlimited Press, Kempton, Illinois, 2015.

Kennedy, Roger G. *Hidden Cities*. New York: Free Press, 1994.

MacLean, J. P. *The Mound Builders*. Cincinnati, OH Robert Clarke and Co. 1893.

May, Wayne, *Ancient American*. Colfax, WI.

McGavin and Bean, W. *The Geography of the Book of Mormon*. Whitefish, MT: Literary Licensing, 2012.

McNeil, *Visitors to Ancient America*. McFarland and Co., 2004.

De Nadaillac, Marquis. *Pre-Historic America*. Arlington, VA: Anthropological Publications, 1969.

O'Brien, T. J. *Fair Gods and Feathered Serpents*. Bountiful, UT: Horizon Publishers, 1997.

Price, Joan Elliott. *Ancient Sauk, Ojibway and Winnebago Cosmology, Myths, Mounds and Artifacts*. Colfax, WI: Ancient American, 2000.

Peet, Stephen D., *The Mound Builders*. La Jolla, CA: University of California Libraries, 1892.

Peterson, Frederick. *Ancient Mexico*. Oakland, CA: University of California Press, 1962.

Priest, Josiah. *American Antiquities and Discoveries in the West*. Colfax, WI: Hayriver Press, 2005.

Roberts, Brigham Henry. *New Witness for God* 1-3 vols. Salt Lake City: The Deseret News, 1909.

Ritchie, William A. *The Archaeology of New York State*. Garden City, NY: The Natural History Press, 1965.

Shaffer, Lynda Norene, *Native Americans Before 1492*. London: Routledge, 1944.

Shetrone, Henry Clyde, *The Mound Builders*. NY: D. Appleton and Co., 1930.

Silverberg, Robert, *The Mound Builders*. Athens, OH: Ohio University Press, 1986.

Smith, Joseph Fielding. *Doctrines of Salvation* 1-3 vols. Salt Lake City: Bookcraft, 1954.

Jessee, Dean Cornell, ed. and comp. T*he Personal Writings of Joseph Smith*. Salt Lake City: Deseret Book, 1702.

Stephens, John Lloyd Esq. *Incidents of Travel in Central America, Chiapas and Yucatan* vol. 1 and 11. New Brunswick, NJ: Rutgers University Press, 1949.

Squier, Ephraim George. *Antiquities of the State of New York*. Charleston, South CA: Nabu Press, 1851.

Squier, Ephraim George, and Davis, Edwin Hamilton. *Ancient Monuments of the Mississippi Valley*. Washington, D.C.: Smithsonian Books, 1998.

Trento, Salvatore Michael, *The Search For Lost America*. Chicago, Illinois: Contemporary Books, 1978.

Thompson, Edgar Herbert, *The People of the Serpent*. Boston, MA: Houghton Mifflin Harcourt, 1932.

ABOUT *the* AUTHOR

Phyllis Carol Olive is the author of the bestselling book *The Lost Lands of the Book of Mormon* and its sequel, *The Lost Tribes of the Book of Mormon.* She lives in Las Vegas, Nevada, with her husband, Ron Olive. As her research on the New York setting for the Book of Mormon continued, another book followed, called *The Lost Empires and Vanished Races of the Book of Mormon*. The last and final book of the series, *The Lost Sheep of Ancient America*, is the culmination of the past eighteen years of research and is the most comprehensive and thought-provoking book of them all. Her website, bookofmormonlands.com, contains twelve linked pages dedicated to Book of Mormon geography and its place near New York's Hill Cumorah, with a related YouTube video on each page. Phyllis's other books include *The Millennium*; *Baptism: The Key to Heaven*; *The Gift of the Holy Ghost*; the historical novel, *The Lost Years of Moroni*; and a book on the last days, *America's Coming Storm*, which is on the horizon.

SCAN TO VISIT

0 26575 16614 9

WWW.BOOKOFMORMONLANDS.COM